OUR FAMILY, OUR TOWN

ESSAYS ON
FAMILY AND LOCAL HISTORY SOURCES
IN THE NATIONAL ARCHIVES

COMPILED BY
TIMOTHY WALCH

INTRODUCTION BY
THOMAS J. SCHLERETH

NATIONAL ARCHIVES AND RECORDS ADMINISTRATION
WASHINGTON, DC

PUBLISHED FOR THE
NATIONAL ARCHIVES AND RECORDS ADMINISTRATION
BY THE
NATIONAL ARCHIVES TRUST FUND BOARD
1987

Library of Congress Cataloging-in-Publication Data

Our family, our town.

  Includes bibliographical references.
  Supt. of Docs. no.: AE1.102:F21
  1. United States—History, Local—Sources—Bibliog-
raphy—Catalogs. 2. United States—Genealogy—Bibliog-
raphy—Catalogs. 3. United States. National Archives—
Catalogs. I. Walch, Timothy, 1947–   II. United
States. National Archives.
Z1250.095 1987 [E180]   016.973   86-600230
ISBN 0-911333-50-9

Preface

Our Family, Our Town is a collaborative effort that includes contributions from many archivists and researchers at the National Archives. The origins of the volume go back to the late 1970s, when the Education Branch of the Office of Public Programs began an effort to encourage wider use of the substantial family and local history materials in the National Archives. This innovative program included workshops, seminars, and other activities as well as publications aimed at genealogists and local historians. The work was conducted by Lorraine Branning and Sarah Larson under the direction of Elsie Freeman.

As part of this initiative, Branning and Larson prepared essays on selected series of records with particularly high research value. Each essay discussed records in the context of their historical background—why they were created, what information was in them, and how they could be used. Each essay also included selected examples of the records and a description of related records. The essays were published quarterly in *Prologue: Journal of the National Archives* under the masthead, "Sources in the National Archives for Genealogical and Local History Research."

Since it was first introduced in 1980, "Sources" has been the most popular feature in the journal. Over the years, other archivists and researchers joined Branning and Larson in writing "Sources" essays. Thousands of genealogists and local historians have learned of new research opportunities in dozens of series of records in the National Archives. Just as important, each "Sources" essay has reminded researchers that the National Archives holds millions of items that document the lives of ordinary citizens in local communities. Implicit in each essay is the emphasis that the National Archives is a research institution *of* and *for* the American people.

Our Family, Our Town is an effort to make these valuable "Sources" essays more widely available. Over the past 6 years more than 15 such essays have appeared in *Prologue*, and the best of these essays are included in this volume. In addition, *Our Family, Our Town* includes three essays—those by James D. Walker, Richard Maxwell, and Elaine Everly—that were first presented at a popular National Archives conference on family and local history. All of the essays have been reviewed by the authors and revised and updated as necessary.

In addition to Branning, Larson and Freeman, many other individuals have contributed to the value of *Our Family, Our Town*. Certainly, the major credit must go to the many authors who shared their substantial knowledge about particular records series with their fellow researchers. Credit also must go to the many archivists in the Office of the National Archives who reviewed the essays

to insure an accurate description of the records in their custody. Coordinating
this effort was Virginia C. Purdy, director of archival publications within that
Office. The editorial skills of Karen Levenbach and Shelby Bale are evident in
every essay, and their collaboration has made the volume more useful and more
readable. Finally, the capable team of Ann Mohan, Mary Ryan, and Dennis
Means guided the manuscript through the production process from edited manuscript to printed volume. It is the hope of all these contributors that this collection of essays will assist researchers in learning more about their families and
their hometowns by using the holdings of the National Archives.

Timothy Walch

Contents

PART VI
DISCOVERING AMERICAN MINORITIES

PART VII
REDRESSING GRIEVANCES

THOMAS J. SCHLERETH

Introduction

Many Americans, even if they have visited the National Archives in Washington, tend to think of it as remote from their private lives and home towns. While they sometimes affectionately call the National Archives "our national attic," they do not immediately think of it as a place where they can find family and friends.

Several reasons account for this. First, there is the sheer monumentality of the building itself—a massive stone edifice designed in John Russell Pope's federal classicism. Nothing about it has the human scale of a county courthouse, parish rectory, or public library back home. Second, the permanent exhibition in the domed Rotunda of this nation's Charters of Freedom—the Declaration of Independence, the Constitution, and the Bill of Rights—reinforces the stereotype of the Archives as primarily a custodian of precious documents that recall the epic moments of the nation's past. The atmosphere evokes feelings of public allegiance rather than private memory, of thoughts about the famous and the fateful rather than the familial and the familiar. Third, the erroneous assumption that the records preserved in the National Archives are only of national import overshadows the fact that a large part of the records of the executive, legislative, and judicial branches of the federal government are also, as the title of this book suggests, rich in information about "Our Family, Our Town."

The fact is that hundreds of thousands of documents preserved in the National Archives Building, its Washington-area annexes, and its 11 archives field branches around the country are of utmost importance for the study of family and local history. This anthology illustrates, for instance, that in the files of the War Department there are hand-written letters by black children describing their daily schooling in the post-Civil War South; that in the records of the Department of the Treasury there is information about 19th-century Louisiana's Red River steamboat trade, right down to minute details as to how some vessels were furnished with special stemware and gold-fringed tablecloths; that records of the Veterans Administration contain information ranging from the religious training and social mobility to the physical appearance of past military personnel. The authors of the essays that make up this anthology trace the impact of the federal government on American families and communities and indicate how this impact is reflected in the holdings of the Archives. The essays, however, do much more than that; they offer many practical suggestions of how private citizens and professional historians can mine this memory bank of national life for personal recollection and community history.

People and places are the anthology's major themes. Several essays (particularly the first three) survey the topics of family and community history. Others (especially essays 1, 4, 5, and 13) pay special attention to Archives' records useful in writing individual biographies or tracing family genealogies. Still others (such as essays 8, 9, and 10) demonstrate the value of federal records as diverse as pension applications, land warrants, and court cases in researching county histories and community studies.

Recommendations for how to use the federal decennial census, mandated by the Constitution and taken every 10 years since 1790, appear in almost every essay. The census, a resource frequently employed by genealogists to chronicle lines of descent and ancestry and to reconstruct a family's structure over time, proves to have many other applications beyond establishing a chronological spine for research. Census records can be employed to monitor demographic, ethnic, occupational, and economic shifts in a family's status. The same topics can be pursued for a collective biography of a neighborhood or a town. Jane Smith, in essay 8, for example, shows how this was done for both an individual, Paschal Bequette, and a community, Linden Township in Wisconsin.

Federal Records and Historical Research

In addition to being a basic tool for all kinds of family and community research, the census shares a characteristic with many of the other federal records discussed here: it is used for numerous purposes other than its original one. The census, for example, was first established not as a national inventory of vital statistics but rather as a means to determine a state's congressional delegation in the U.S. House of Representatives. While the administrative value of all but the most recent census records is limited, its historical content is still very valuable. So, too, with most federal records. They were created, not with the family or local historian in mind, but simply to assist officials in the three branches of the federal government do their various jobs. Hence, when seeking to use federal records, the researcher must first establish what might be called "the federal connection." As James Walker says in his essay, "prerequisite to the successful use of federal records is a knowledge of what relationship the person or persons we are studying had with the federal government."

Most federal records surveyed here have other traits in common. As a group, they include reactive, fragmentary, and cumulative types of information, and generally they are objective. In the first case, they are records of a government (particularly in the 19th century) usually reacting to change rather than initiating it. As such, the records usually were created because of some specific crisis, problem, or conflict, which, in turn, led to a legislative act, an executive order, or a court case—all of which required the collection of a certain amount of information. This is true, for instance, of the Philadelphia seamen's protection certificates (essay 6), the data generated by the Freedmen's Bureau (essay 14), and the files of the federal commissions on Southern claims (essay 16) and interstate commerce (essay 18).

The episodic origins of many 19th-century federal records (the census excepted) account for their being fragmentary and yielding only discrete pieces of a story. Frequently, thorough research means the examination of numerous records series. No single collection of records ever tells us all we wish to know. Research is not a matter of looking up the answer but of tracking down bits of information, and, usually painstakingly, of connecting diverse data into a plausible explanation.

The federal records of one governmental unit can often be augmented by information gleaned from the records of another federal agency, of state and local governments, of private institutions, and of individual people. Thus federal records can play a supplementary or supporting role in the family or local historian's research. Case studies by John Resch on Peterborough, NH (essay 5) and by Keith Schlesinger on Chicago (essay 11) suggest how this can be done.

Over time, the informational content of some types of federal records has greatly expanded. For example, passenger arrival lists, naturalization records, and, of course, the census, have become more comprehensive and informative each time the government went about collecting such data from its constituents. Military records, which are given much attention in this volume, are more extensive for Americans who served in the Spanish-American War than for those who fought with the Continental Army in the Revolution. Similarly, before 1883, the only information required of each immigrant arriving in the United States was name, age, sex, occupation, and nationality. After that year, immigrants had to provide this basic information as well as answer an increasing number of questions, including the names of employers or persons with whom they would live upon reaching their destination in America and the names of the nearest relative in the country of last permanent residence.

A final hallmark of some, but not all, federal records is a degree of neutrality or objectivity not always found in local sources. This is especially the case when the individual recording the information about a particular community scene was not a local resident. Anthropologists sometimes refer to this perspective as "critical distance," arguing that outsiders can sometimes see cultural patterns and assumptions that insiders often miss or find so basic to their ways of life that they do not document them. Government land surveyors, Bureau of Indian Affairs agents, and federal social workers on assignment from Washington, for instance, sometimes see a town quite differently than its inhabitants. Their reports, statistics, and/or photographs can be invaluable to a local historian wishing different vantage points from which to assess a community's development, as can be seen in the manuscript reports of local agents in the Freedmen's Bureau studied by Barry Crouch and Larry Madaras (essay 14).

Federal Records and Family History

Most of the sources in this anthology, however, are locally generated, "homemade" as it were, and thus are highly personal accounts of the past. A group that I find particularly fascinating for use in family history is the pension application records. Pension laws have generally required the veteran applicant or his dependents to prove entitlement by presenting evidence of military service, disability (if applicable), and poverty. The application that initiated a veteran's claim sometimes chronicled occupations and places of residence between discharge and date of application. A veteran's dependents also had to prove their relation to the veteran and to document his death and, in some cases, the death of his spouse. As Elaine Everly (essay 3) and Constance Schulz (essay 4) aptly demonstrate, this process often created a rich and varied file of documents. For example, pension files may include pages from family Bibles; certificates of birth, marriage, death, and baptism; discharge papers; commissions; and other personal or family records. Affidavits, depositions, and transcriptions of oral testimony were frequently provided by relatives, neighbors, friends, clergymen, officers, and comrades. Pension files average 40 documents each, representing either a single or multiple claim.

Pension files, like other federal records in which claimants had to prove something about themselves (such as alien registration papers or the records of the Southern Claims Commission), often turn out to be mini-archives for the family historian. They are also examples of serendipity in archival research. One starts out looking for one thing, only to come upon many other things. Take, for example, the case of Benjamin F. Chase, 5th Volunteer Infantry in the Civil War. A researcher seeking only to document Chase as a recipient of a military pension discovered much more about him and his family. In Chase's pension file were 10 original letters written home to his family. These letters graphically reveal the army life of a young teenager from New England who enlisted not because of the issues of abolition or the Union cause, but in order to make money for his family. Twenty years later, Ben's mother applied for a government pension and included the letters with her application in an attempt to prove how much the boy's financial support had meant to the family. Additional testimony came from a sister who described the emotional impact of her brother's death on their mother. "Before the war she was cheerful and singing about the house, but afterwards was sad and dejected and has never been heard to sing a word since."

Poignant, personal, and unique details of family life such as these often turn up for the patient researcher of federal records. For instance, in the homestead entry papers (1863–1908) of the Bureau of Land Management, one can learn about the kinds of houses people built and the types of crops they raised (or tried to raise) in their first years of settlement. Both the inventive genius and the impractical dreams of many a family eccentric or town "tinkerer" survive among the drawings and descriptions of the Patent Office. There is evidence of family troubles—child abuse, desertion, quarrelling over children's custody and support, separation, divorce—in various federal sources. Finally, the "otherness" felt by various American families can be traced in sources dealing with immigrants, blacks, and American Indians, as demonstrated in the essays in part VI of this anthology.

Federal Records and Local History

For enriching and expanding local histories, Richard Maxwell (essay 2) makes clear the usefulness of numerous federal land records—particularly those in the General Land Office (now the Interior Department's Bureau of Land Management), the State Department (when it administered a large part of the continental United States as territorial possessions, 1789–1873), the U.S. Geological Survey, and the Bureau of Reclamation. Thomas Wiltsey (essay 17) demonstrates the usefulness of the judicial records of the New Mexico territorial courts in the 19th and early 20th centuries by reviewing bankruptcy, naturalization, and public domain court cases and offering information about the region's economic cycles, marketing networks, consumer preferences, immigration patterns, ethnic composition, and real estate history. Leonard Rapport (essay 18), samples the 16,000 formal case dockets of the Interstate Commerce Commission and illustrates how the ICC case files can further an understanding of local history by extracting information about such places as St. Thomas, ND, Danville, VA, and Muskogee, OK.

Military agencies have also touched American communities in significant and substantive ways. Because the military has always been engaged in activities other than warfare, military records contain a wealth of data about its role in exploring, mapping, and charting our western frontiers and inland and coastal waterways; planning and constructing internal improvements, such as roads, bridges, and dams; and quelling civil disorders, pursuing criminals, and assisting local areas in times of natural disasters. In the Adjutant General's consolidated files, for instance, the local historian can locate source material on the Pullman Strike of 1894, raids by outlaws on border communities in Texas, the grasshopper plague in Nebraska in 1874–75, and the San Francisco earthquake of 1906.

Of all governmental agencies—ranging from the Army Corps of Engineers to the Works Progress Administration, from the Department of the Interior to the Department of Transportation—that have had an influence on local life, the former Post Office Department may be the most frequently overlooked. The records of the department, 1789–1971, provide the names of postmasters as well as the dates and locations of their appointments. They also contain site location reports filed by postmasters showing the geographical location of the post office and its distance from significant streams, rivers, railroads, public buildings, landmarks, and other post offices. Moreover, as any good typonymist well knows, many localities were officially named (sometimes renamed because federal postal workers wished a certain wording) with the establishment of their post offices. Some, for instance Scrange, AL, were named by or for postal clerks (in this instance, T. Martin Scrange) who worked not in the particular community but in Washington, DC.

For some American towns, the federal government not only provided their name, but also their reason for being. Throughout its history, the national government has been founding, shaping, or maintaining all sorts of American communities. Some of these have been transitory features on the landscape, for example, the 600 local Civilian Conservation Corps camps of the 1930s, or various prisoner-of-war compounds during different periods of national conflict, or the 10 relocation centers in the western states at which 110,000 persons of Japanese ancestry were interned during World War II.

Records of U.S. military garrisons and naval bases in western territories often offer the best evidence of the arrival of early settlers of pioneer settlements established before local civil governments were able to make and preserve adequate records of their own. Such installations (recall how many American place-names begin with "Fort") have often been the nuclei around which civilian communities grew, providing employment, among other things, for people in nearby towns and the rural hinterland.

Indian reservations are, in large measure, government towns. Established by treaty and by Congress, their local records—land allotments, census schedules, annuity payment rolls, school records—are all under federal jurisdiction and therefore in federal custody. No history of the first Americans or their collective life after the 1880s can be written without consulting this data.

A similar situation exists regarding the District of Columbia, the history of which is closely tied to the federal government. The Scientific, Economic, and Natural Resources Branch of the National Archives, for instance, has tax and assessment records showing District real estate and some personal property evaluations, deedbooks to real property in the District, and some daily precinct returns of the DC Police Department. Historians studying ethnic groups and age or sexual orientation of urban criminals frequently use the latter data. Moreover, these records are enhanced by other federal records relating to the District, such as those of the National Capital Planning Commission, the Commission of Fine Arts, and the Office of Public Buildings and Public Parks of the National Capital.

In addition to District of Columbia material, there is other evidence of the national government in the community-building business. Three greenbelt towns—Greendale, WI, Greenhills, OH, and Greenbelt, MD—were built before the onset of World War II by the Franklin D. Roosevelt administration and owe a large part of their local history to FDR's New Deal. The records that tell the story of these innovative planned communities—the files of the Resettlement Administration (which built them) and the records of the Public Housing Administration (which sold them)—are appropriately preserved in the National Archives.

Using This Anthology

What do the essays in this anthology have in common? What characterizes them as an anthology about archival research? To begin with, they exhibit an enormous geographical range in their subject matter. As a quick glance at the book's index will suggest, practically every region of the continental United States receives some attention. Although the National Archives and its archivists/researchers may be Washington-based, their scholarly foci range from Virginia City, NV, to Northhampton, MA; from Galveston, TX, to Fort Egbert, AL.

Methodology is a particular forte of the essays' authors. As professionals who have spent their careers working with particular record groups—either as a "visitor" exploring their contents or as a "custodian" arranging and overseeing their physical preservation, creating finding aids to their contents, and disseminating information about their contents in response to numerous public inquiries—they have given much thought to the techniques and theory of historical research. They are, therefore, apt at giving directions as to how to solve problems caused by either a paucity of data or a voluminous amount of evidence. Frank Serene (essay 13), for example, offers possible solutions to the problem of no index to the immigrant passenger lists of the port of New York from 1847 to 1896. To overcome this obstacle, Serene describes not one but three alternative methods for retrieving the information from this source. Perceptive questions posed by Sarah Larson (essay 16) when examining the Southern Claims Commission records are a fine demonstration of the mind of the historian at work. In the endnotes to these and other essays, we also find valuable citations to work of other scholars who have already used these records.

While the authors champion the expanded use of federal records for family and local history, they are mindful of the data's research limitations. Every essay has one caveat or another about the evidential problems of the sources it analyzes. Researchers are continually instructed to maintain a "constructive skepticism" about what these resources can and cannot reveal about the past.

In this regard, the anthology does labor under some limitations. One is the time period involved, most of the records described pertaining to the 19th century. This is due in part to federal restrictions on public use of more contemporary data (for example, population schedules of the U.S. census records are only open to 1910) and in part to the tendency to regard the modern era as not yet appropriately historical.

Many of the authors follow a case-study approach to their topics. Each essay includes background information and a description of the records, techniques for using the records, and information on related records. Case studies were chosen to illustrate types of information and research techniques that might be of value to potential researchers. The methodology formulated for documenting the pattern of settlement and pioneer history in a single Wisconsin township, for example, has applicability in any or all of the 30 public-land states of the nation.

To test the applicability of the anthology's insights and information, I reviewed how federal records in the National Archives add to what I know about my present home place: the University of Notre Dame in Notre Dame, IN. I was surprised, indeed, by how frequently the history of a private, church-related institution intersected with (and was documented in) the workings of the federal government.

To begin with, the land on which the university was founded resulted from several federal land grants issued to individuals in 1830–32. Its first president secured its designation as a U.S. post office in 1851 and served as its postmaster until his death in 1893. In the Civil War, he dispatched 8 priests to serve as chaplains and 80 nuns to work as nurses with the Union army. In addition to the institution's involvement in 19th-century military events, Notre Dame University has been a training base for all branches of the armed forces (army, navy, air force, and marines) throughout the 20th century.

Even Notre Dame's physical landscape has federal connections, which can be partially documented in federal records. U.S. Treasury architect Willoughby J. Edbrooke (1843–96) designed several of its 19th-century buildings, including the academy of music (which the university named Washington Hall). The U.S. Navy erected the present Aerospace Laboratory and ROTC buildings, and the U.S. Atomic Energy Commission built the Radiation Research Building. In 1946 the university and the Federal Housing Authority moved 39 prisoner-of-war barracks from a military camp in Weingarten, MO to the Notre Dame campus, creating "Vetville," a community where married students returning to college under the G.I. Bill were housed until 1961.

To me, these fragments of the history of Notre Dame—in a sense, something of its family and its town—validate the claims of this volume. Federal records expand and enrich the historical study of local lives. Such records portray, sometimes tediously, sometimes graphically, American people and places in the full panoply of their pluralism.

Conclusion

As sources of family history, federal records reveal an amazing amount about private lives. Since they are public, however, each of us can use them in the spirit of Carl Becker's famous essay "Everyman His Own Historian," to know ourselves by knowing our kinfolk.

As sources of local history, federal records provide an incredible storehouse of community experience. Since they are federal, however, each of us can use them as benchmarks by which to compare our local history with that of other American places across space and time.

Finally, these federal records and the ways suggested for probing them are particularly rewarding historical resources because they pay special attention to people and places who never imagined themselves to be historical. Consulting them allows us to compile family history that is much more than lists of names and dates, and local history that is much more than a recital of the famous and the flamboyant. In both histories, the personal and the collective, federal records help provide a denser, more complex account of individual behavior and a more representative presentation of community life.

PART *I*

FAMILY AND LOCAL HISTORY AT THE NATIONAL ARCHIVES

Typical American household scene, circa 1950.

Using family and local history sources in the National Archives often combines equal parts fascination and frustration. A researcher who finds a federal document that provides vital information about an ancestor or hometown can experience wonder and satisfaction. However, the researcher may also experience boredom and frustration after unsuccessfully scrolling through roll after roll of microfilm or paging through box after box of records looking for a particular document.

The substantial volume of family and local history sources in the Archives may leave the researcher feeling either the thrill of victory or the agony of defeat. The Archives has hundreds of thousands of cubic feet of records that relate to individuals and local communities. And, even though there are indexes to a few of these series of records, most family and local history sources in the Archives are described only in general terms. Usually, the only way to know for sure if a particular document is in the Archives is for researchers to roll up their sleeves and work their way through the rolls of microfilm and boxes of records.

As a prelude to their work, most family and local history researchers consult with the archivists at the National Archives to gain a better understanding of the types of records they will be using. Through years of experience in working with the records, archivists have come to know the easiest, most efficient way of conducting family and local history research in the National Archives.

The three essays that follow are a testament to the knowledge and experience of veteran archivists. Until his retirement in 1979, James D. Walker was a genealogical and local history specialist at the National Archives. A renowned genealogy lecturer and consultant, he is also the author of *Black Genealogy: How to Begin* and other works. Richard S. Maxwell worked with state and local history materials in the Civil Archives Division for more than 30 years before his retirement in 1980. Elaine C. Everly is currently the chief of the Modern Military Field Branch at the National Archives and has worked with military records for nearly 25 years. Together, these archivists provide an overview to the range of family and local history sources in the National Archives.

JAMES D. WALKER

The National Archives and Genealogical Research

Any good local history will include information about various social, economic, religious, and ethnic groups of a community. In the past, however, most such histories devoted little attention to the study of the background of individuals or specific families. Usually the only persons included in traditional local histories were individuals prominent in the community at the time of publication. (They were invited to supply their own biographies for the work and were expected to ensure the financial success of the undertaking by subscribing for copies.) The texts usually dwelt heavily on the political history rather than on the cultural history of a community.

Today, of course, the historian has realized that the study of individuals and families—their origins; their religious, philosophical, and political views; their ethnic backgrounds; their participation in civic affairs—can result in a different interpretation of the history of a town or county. Often the interests and values of the average citizen can determine the character of the place where he or she dwelt.

Although the lives of such less-than-prominent persons and their families can best be explored by using the methods developed by genealogists, the success of any study depends on finding appropriate resource materials. As in any other discipline, genealogy requires a thorough grounding in research methodology and a good understanding of the basic and important genealogical source materials.

Federal records are an important genealogical resource. They either supplement local vital statistics (birth, marriage, and death of an individual) and family, church, county, and state records, or they serve as a source when such records are nonexistent. Federal records were not created with the genealogist or local historian in mind. They are the evidence of the activities of the three branches of the federal government in the execution of their prescribed functions. Nevertheless, many of these records are useful in genealogical research.

In 1964, the National Archives published the *Guide to Genealogical Records in the National Archives*, which identified many of the more important genealogical sources among federal records. Since its publication, the importance of other records for genealogical research has been recognized and additional records have been accessioned. Also since 1964, many records have been inventoried or microfilmed and some few have been relocated in other National Archives repositories or transferred to nonfederal repositories. To account for all of this, the National Archives published a revised edition of the genealogical guide in 1982.[1]

More detailed descriptions of the vast resources of the National Archives appear in the basic National Archives finding aids: the *Guide to the National Archives of the United States*,[2] inventories of the records of particular agencies or bureaus (record groups), special lists, and descriptive pamphlets accompanying microfilm publications. Also available are several guides to records related to special subjects that should be of great value to genealogists and local historians.[3] A specific guide to local history sources is not presently planned.

Researchers who visit the National Archives can also receive advice and guidance from the research consultant staff of its Central Information Division and from reference archivists who have extensive knowledge of particular groups of records.[4] But a thorough study of the published finding aids is likely to yield more clues to the information sought than can be brought out in a short interview.[5]

Almost every National Archives record group contains records of genealogical or local history value. These records may be indigenous to one town; to a whole or a part of a county, state or territory; or to a family or several families. They may detail events taking place in a few days or spanning a number of years. And while records such as census schedules and military records involve many people and places and span centuries, sometimes a single series of claims made to Congress for relief of the victims of a flood describes a few days' plight of the people of one town or county.

Before the National Archives was established, federal records were often destroyed, mutilated, or lost. As a result, some records are incomplete or parts of them have been damaged. When the records lack indexes or other detailed research finding aids, they can be considered less-than-useful. But many series are complete, and even those that lack indexes have some logical arrangement that permits access to researchers. Fragmentary records about a person, a subject, or a place in the records of one federal agency can sometimes be augmented by information from the records of another federal agency. Thus, when all of the appropriate records are studied, an accurate composite picture of an individual or a family often can be drawn. Federal records are also a valuable aid in identifying records in local repositories—if the federal records contain information about local records. Thus, some federal records should probably be consulted at one time or another in the preparation of most genealogies or local histories.

Federal records in the National Archives that are significant for genealogical research and that are constantly used by genealogists include census, military, pension and bounty land, and federal court records, as well as records about American Indians, immigration, and other topics. Genealogists can consult birth, death, and marriage records reported on military posts and to U.S. consuls overseas.

The only federal records relating to particular individuals or groups are those generated by a federal agency whose activities affected those individuals or groups. To make the records more easily available for public use, the National Archives has microfilmed many of the ones used most frequently by genealogists. Microfilm publications are listed in *Genealogical and Biographical Research: A Select Catalog of National Archives Microfilm Publications* (1983), which may be obtained for a small fee from the Publications Division of the National Archives, Washington, DC 20408.

CENSUS RECORDS

Many genealogists first seek vital statistics about their ancestors in an attempt to reconstruct the family by learning the dates and places of births and deaths. But few states required registration of either births or deaths until the 20th century, and local communities have often lost such records if they were maintained. Prepared every 10 years beginning in 1790, the manuscript federal population census schedules are primary sources for such information. The schedules through the census of 1910 are open for research.

Descriptions of the data gathered in each census are presented in publications prepared by the National Archives and by the Census Bureau.[6] In general, however, the information sought by the census taker increased with each new census.

From 1790 through 1840, only the head of each household was identified by name; slaves were counted but Indians on reservations were ignored. While every resident of each free household is named in the 1850 and 1860 schedules (with occupations and birthplaces given in most cases), the relationship of each member to the head of the household is first shown in the census of 1880. The most useful censuses currently available are for 1900 and 1910, which provide, in addition to information in the earlier censuses, immigration and naturalization information for the foreign born, actual street address, and marriage and family size information, as well as data about the family's dwelling.

Besides the population schedules, post-1850 censuses include nonpopulation schedules that give information about products, labor, costs, and profits of agriculture, business, manufacturing, and industry. These records, arranged geographically, are invaluable to researchers in local history. Mortality schedules, another type of nonpopulation schedule, list names of persons who died in the year preceding the population census.[7] Only the nonpopulation schedules for 1850–80 are available on microfilm.

Still other schedules deal with certain social classes or handicapped persons. While some of this information was provided in pre-1850 censuses, no separate schedules were prepared. In 1820 and 1830, enumerators were required to determine if persons were immigrants (aliens). In 1840 persons who were Revolutionary War veterans had to be identified. In 1850 and 1860, separate slave schedules listed the names of slave owners with the ages and sexes of their slaves; and in 1890 a separate enumeration was made of veterans of the Union Army or their widows, listing their names, the soldier's rank, company, and regiment, dates of service, the nature of any disability, and the post office address.

For many reasons, federal population schedules are incomplete. The 1790 schedules for the states of Delaware, Georgia, Kentucky, New Jersey, Tennessee, and Virginia have been lost, although substitutes have been compiled from other sources for some of these states.[8] In a 1921 Washington fire, all but one percent of the 1890 population schedules were lost, as were all nonpopulation schedules except about 50 percent of those relating to the Union Army veterans and their widows. In other cases, the schedules for some counties or parts of counties are missing from schedules that have not suffered physical damage; some schedules have been lost or destroyed; and some schedules simply cannot be identified because they are poorly labeled or are mixed in with the records of other counties in that state or another state.

Most of the original records of the censuses of 1800–70 are in the custody of the National Archives. The original 1880 schedules were distributed to the states, as were the agriculture, business, industry, manufacturing, and mortality schedules for 1850–80. A list of the repositories to which the records were sent is available from the National Archives or from any of the Archives field branches.[9] The National Archives has obtained microfilm copies of most of the schedules. With the approval of Congress, schedules for 1900 and later have been destroyed. Only the population schedules of 20th-century censuses were microfilmed before destruction.

Census schedules are arranged by state, thereunder by county, and thereunder by local political subdivision. Large cities are subdivided by wards or election districts. In the absence of name indexes, effective use of these records depends on a knowledge of the specific community in which a person lived at the time of the census. And let the user beware that the accuracy of name indexes varies greatly.

The federal government prepared an index to the 1790 schedules when they were transcribed and published in 1908.[10] The Works Progress Administration (WPA) prepared indexes to the 1880–1930 schedules, using Remington-Rand Corporation's Soundex system. The system has been described in several National Archives publications, including the catalogs of the microfilm of the federal census schedules.[11] The only names in the 1880 census that were indexed are those of heads of households that included a child 10 years old or younger. Names of all heads of families in the 1900 census were indexed, as were the names of persons in institutions or the military or on vessels.

Additional indexes have been prepared by private individuals, groups, and commercial

Collecting census data. Census enumerators display versatility in finding their subjects. (Record Group 306, Audiovisual Archives Division, National Archives.)

firms. They also vary greatly in quality and must be used with great care. In addition, some researchers have made transcripts of census information. In every instance the researcher should consult the original schedules even though a name may not appear in an index and should verify the information given in census transcripts by comparing the transcripts with the original schedules. It should be noted that many finding aids exist to assist the researcher in identifying the schedules for a given community or to aid in the determination of the ward or other political subdivision in which a particular residence was located.[12]

In spite of the many handicaps that affect their use, census schedules are among the most useful records for genealogical study. And they are equally useful for the local historian. Because the population schedules are arranged largely in the order that the census taker received and recorded the information—as he walked down a city street or drove from one house to the next in a rural county—the schedules are invaluable for the study of geographical areas down to the neighborhood. By tracing individuals by name through several censuses, one can make a study that spans several decades of the persons in a local community or even on a particular city block.

At the National Archives Building and at each of the Archives field branches there are complete sets of the population schedules on microfilm. Many state, municipal, and private archives, libraries, and historical societies have purchased complete or partial sets of the microfilmed census schedules.[13] Libraries holding copies may also be willing to lend them on interlibrary loan. Catalogs listing microfilm and roll numbers (see note 7) are available in repositories that own microfilm or may be ordered for a small fee from the Publications Services Branch, National Archives and Records Administration, Washington, DC 20408.

A number of histories of the federal census and analyses of aspects of this great decennial undertaking can be consulted as aids to research.[14] In addition, the tabulations and reports published by the director of the Bureau of the Census after each census often contain useful statistical information and other data, and many large libraries have accessioned these reports as a part of the U.S. Government Documents Serial Set.[15]

PASSENGER ARRIVAL AND NATURALIZATION RECORDS

Genealogists generally try to trace their ancestry at least back to the immigrant ancestor—the first member of the family to come to America—hoping in the process to learn the specific city, town, or village from which the ancestor came or of his or her last residence before emigration. Similarly, students of local history are often interested in learning the specific locales of origin of major ethnic groups in the community under study. Researchers in genealogy and in local history would follow similar routes to obtain this information. The general sources of information relating to the date and place of arrival of immigrants are the "passenger arrival records," which is the composite term used to describe passenger lists and ship manifests, the two common documents issued by ship masters. Depending on the date of arrival, a passenger list typically consists of the names of the passengers with their ages, sex, occupations, and other personal information under the name of the ship and the date of arrival. It also provides dates and places of departure and arrival of the vessel.

Manifests are lists of the cargo carried aboard a vessel entering or clearing a port. In some instances cargo vessels also carried passengers, and the master used the manifest to record the names of passengers on board. Most manifests contain little of the other information found on passenger lists, while others show all of the data required by law. Few manifests are indexed, but copies of the WPA-transcribed and indexed manifests for the Port of New Orleans for the period 1813–67 are available at both the National Archives and the New Orleans Public Library.

Passenger arrival records are serviced from various name indexes, some more complete than others.[16] The Port of Baltimore has two indexes covering the same period. Gaps occur in the index to passengers arriving at the Port of New York, 1847–96, the Port of Boston, 1820–47, and the Port of New Orleans, 1820–52. Some of the passengers who entered through these ports can be located through an index to "Miscellaneous Ports."

Extant passenger arrival records date primarily from 1820, with a few—such as those for the Port of Philadelphia, and for Beverly and Salem in Massachusetts—from as early as 1800. The first law requiring information about passengers, enacted in 1798, was enforced so laxly that few records were kept. An act of March 2, 1819 (3 Stat. 488), resulted in a larger body of records, as did later laws, agency regulations, and interpretations thereof. Most laws specified the kinds of information to be recorded and the manner in which they were to be collected and reported. The earlier passenger records, made when the young nation was eager to accept new settlers, contain scant information about each immigrant. The records created under later laws and regulations include more comprehensive descriptions of the newcomers, especially after members of nativist movements began to attribute social and economic problems to an excess of undesirable immigrants.

Between 1820 and 1883, the only information required of each immigrant was name, age, sex, occupation, and nationality. After that year immigrants had to answer an increasing number of questions, including the names of the employers or persons with whom they would live upon reaching their destination in America, the name of the nearest relative in the country of last permanent residence, and other facts about themselves.

Transcripts of passengers, prepared by State Department personnel from these Treasury Department abstracts, repeated all or most of the information contained in the abstract. The State Department, in turn, transmitted its transcript to the Congress. (Abstracts and transcripts are sometimes referred to as "copies" in descriptions of passenger records, and one or the other may have been microfilmed in lieu of a lost or mutilated passenger list.)

Passenger arrival records are available for east coast and Gulf and some Pacific ports. The earliest arrival records begin approximately in 1820, and the most recent date to the early 1850s. Not all ports have records covering this time span. Records created in the 20th century are subject to some restrictions on access. Passenger arrival records for west coast ports before 1940 or for Great Lakes ports before 1906 were destroyed in fires or other disasters, or were lost.

While passenger arrival records serve as the chief source of evidence of the arrival of an immigrant, information about immigration can be gleaned from other sources. Naturalization records, including declarations of intention to become citizens and petitions to be naturalized, are primary sources. National Archives records relating to naturalization before 1906 are limited to a few from the District of Columbia and some federal court records. Under an act of June 29, 1906 (34 Stat. 596–607), changes in the naturalization process brought about the establishment of a central record of aliens in the United States. Before that time, whichever court (state, federal, county, or municipal) received the petition for naturalization or the declaration of intention to become a citizen retained the record it received or created. Since that time, the Bureau of Immigration and Naturalization, now known as the Immigration and Naturalization Service, has maintained records both in Washington and in its field offices.

Other records relating to immigrants arriving in U.S. ports are found in baggage lists, passport applications, visas, and 20th-century alien registration records. It should be noted, however, that access to records relating to aliens who arrived in the United States in the past 50 years are restricted by law.

The local or family historian who uses many of the various types of records about passenger arrivals and naturalization in conjunction with census records can learn a good deal about the ethnic makeup of a community.

Crew lists, another type of record related to shipping, can throw light on the character of the seafaring population. Required of domestic vessels but seldom found for foreign ships, crew lists record each man by name, age, occupation, place of birth, physical description, and most recent permanent address. Shipping articles also detail the length of the man's contract.

LAND RECORDS

High on the list of National Archives records sought by genealogists are those relating to land transactions, which are also extensively used by local historians. Federal land records are voluminous.[18] Land acquired by the federal government by purchase or treaty became public land or public domain, to be used as the government saw fit. Beginning in 1776, land was offered as an inducement to military enlistment or continuation of military service, and since 1800 the government has sold land or given it away to encourage settlement and development. Before 1820, land sales were conducted on both cash and credit bases; after 1820, only cash sales were allowed. Land grants were made to persons or companies that would use the land for specific purposes, such as developing mineral resources, raising trees for timber, building railroads, and supporting education.

When the United States initially acquired land, it was subject to claims of prior ownership—called "private land claims"—if it was already settled. Residents had to prove prior title in order to retain the land, and proof of ownership necessitated information about how the land was originally acquired by the claimant under the previous government. In some instances, the record of a claim may reflect ownership by members of several preceding generations before noting the means of original acquisition. Private land claims for the period

1788–1837 are listed in *American State Papers*,[19] which has been indexed. Later claims are often recorded in the journals of Congress and in the few indexes to those journals; a few indexes are on file with the claims.

Federal land was generally disposed of through the many land offices established throughout the country in 30 present-day states. There were no public lands in the original 13 states or in Maine, Vermont, West Virginia, Tennessee, Kentucky, Texas, and Hawaii. The first land office was opened at Steubenville, Ohio, on July 2, 1800.

Records of cash or credit sales are useful to the local historian only insofar as they indicate whether bona fide settlers in a community were able to purchase land directly from the government at minimum price or had to turn to speculators to secure land. These records contain little information about buyers.

Bounty-land claims resulted from warrants issued to veterans and their heirs and assigns as a reward for wartime service, 1775–1855. Under most laws relating to bounty land, the original application was submitted to the War Department, which, on approval of the application, issued a warrant for the amount of land to which the applicant was entitled in a particular location in the public domain. Although the warrant holder could surrender the warrant to a land office for a patent (i.e., a deed), he was free to dispose of the warrant in any manner. As a result, most of the warrants were sold to speculators, who in turn surrendered them to a land office for patents. These records are useful to the local historian because they show land transfer and ownership patterns as well as patterns of migration. In addition, the original application files often contain personal information about many veterans who secured patents and settled.

Donation lands is the name given to land grants made by the pre-Civil War federal government to prospective settlers who could meet certain conditions. Under an act of 1842, for example, the condition in Florida was willingness to bear arms.

Most Americans are familiar with the provisions of the Homestead Act of 1862, which opened land to settlement by citizens, or those intending to become citizens, if they built a house and lived on the land and cultivated it for 5 years. Later acts modified the requirements for particular kinds of land. For example, under an act of 1877, patents were not issued for desert land unless it was irrigated within 3 years of settlement.

Donation land files and homestead application files contain similar information. In addition to details about the land, each file supplies the name, place of birth, family size, marital status, and proof of citizenship for each applicant. Because the application also contains evidence that the settler has completed the requirements or fulfilled the conditions of settlement, those records are a rich source for local history. The homestead records, in particular, contain much demographic information and details, such as the kinds of houses built and the types of crops raised in the first few years of settlement. Fortunately for the researcher using these records for local history rather than genealogy, they are arranged geographically by state or territory and thereunder by land office. It is important to note in this regard that there are no name indexes for most land records; in fact, a legal description of the land is needed to use the records.

PRIVATE CLAIMS

Private claims unrelated to land titles are still another source of information for genealogy and local history, including, as they do, successful and unsuccessful attempts to persuade Congress to make reparation for damage alleged to be the fault of the federal government. This kind of claim was often submitted repeatedly before it was successful—if it ever was. Private claims were frequently submitted directly to Congress, rather than to an executive agency, because the laws permitting payment of such claims were vague or nonexistent. Claims submitted to Congress are indexed in

the catalogs of government documents, and some separate lists of claims were published by Congress at various times. Examples of private claims are those for damage caused by American Indian depredations, for loss of property and civilian lives in war, and for restitution of land by American Indians. If such claims were remanded to a federal executive or judicial agency, the records are found among those of the agency or court. Among the larger series are the French spoliation claims for damage sustained by U.S. shipping during the Napoleonic wars, the Cherokee claims, and various claims relating to the Civil War and other wars.

Relief claims—another type of private claim—were submitted to Congress for assistance for property damage caused by natural disaster. Generally unsuccessful in the 19th and early 20th centuries, these claims remain a part of congressional records because they did not receive approval to be remanded to an executive agency for handling.[20]

FEDERAL EMPLOYMENT AND MILITARY RECORDS

Other records of genealogical value pertain to persons employed in or appointed to positions in federal service in a civilian capacity. Most of these records—which relate to regular and contractual service in all agencies—are now at the National Personnel Records Center in St. Louis, the later ones subject to restrictions outlined in the Freedom of Information Act. In addition, agency records in the National Archives often contain lists or other information about agency employees. Employee records in each agency may include application papers, payrolls, and other administrative records. Lists of employees containing their names, titles or positions, salaries, and places of employment were published semiannually. Other lists appear in the *American State Papers* and congressional documents or reports.

Genealogists place great store by records relating to military service primarily because they hope to find a hero among their ancestors, to add another dimension to their genealogy, or simply to complete the picture of an individual's life. While military records may not appear to be so valuable to the local historian, they can provide data concerning the participation of residents in a local, state, national, or international conflict and information on the background of persons who settled on military tracts or who obtained homesteads under laws favoring veterans. During wartime, recruiting was an especially important part of local history because volunteer units were raised from the community and remained intact as they went into active service. The records of military posts in new territories are often the best evidence of the arrival of the earliest white or black settlers. Military installations often have been the nucleus around which civilian communities grew, among other things providing employment for people in nearby towns and rural areas. And, of course, where battles were fought near a community under study, detailed military tactics also may interest the local historian.

Records of the military service of individuals or benefits derived therefrom include those of persons who served in the Revolutionary War before the federal government was established and in the armed forces of the United States as well as in the Confederate forces. Pre-Civil War military service records are usually devoid of personal or family information, but records relating to applications for pensions or other benefits derived from military service in many instances include a good deal of that kind of material. This is increasingly true of 20th-century military and benefit records, but these are subject to many regulations governing access for research.

Records of individuals who served in volunteer land forces in time of war or emergency during the period 1775–1902 are contained in a series of compiled military service records, which were created in a project undertaken by the War Department in the late 19th century.[21] Clerks were assigned to examine original records and abstract onto a card the information relating to each individual's service. The abstract was then placed in a jacket on which was written the soldier's name, rank, unit, and period of service. The cards were indexed[22] and arranged by series, for the Revolutionary War,[23] post-Revolutionary War (1784–1811),[24] the War of 1812, Indian wars (1816–60), the Patriot War (1838–39), the Mexican War, the Civil War (Union Army and Confederate States Army), the Spanish-American War, and the Philippine Insurrection. The average jacket contains one or more abstracts and, if available, personal papers. (Except for the Civil War, separate records were made for each enlistment, but such service is not necessarily cross-referenced.) Each series contains one or more miscellaneous subseries of abstracts or documents relating to persons for whom no complete record of service or other information was found.

Unfortunately, the military service records are not complete. Revolutionary War records were destroyed by fire on November 8, 1800, and the records of some units were lost during the hostilities of the war itself.[25] The Confederate records are also incomplete because not all records created were received for deposit in the National Archives.[26]

For persons who enlisted or were commissioned for service in the regular army, records are divided into two distinct series—one for enlisted personnel and one for officers. Researchers interested in using these records should first consult *Military Service Records in the National Archives of the United States*, General Information Leaflet No. 7, available free from the Publication Services Branch. The principal document in the records of an enlisted man who served in the period 1789–1912 was an enlistment paper—that is, a contract or agreement to serve for a specified period. The soldier's name, age, place of birth, physical description, occupation at time of enlistment, date and place of enlistment, and the name of the person or officer who enlisted the soldier appear on the document. Enlistment papers are arranged in three chronological series: pre-1818, 1818–94, and 1894–1912. Beginning in 1894, they contain the name and address of a person to be notified in case of an emergency. An additional series of physical examination papers, 1894–1912, includes the soldier's date of birth and information about the health history of the soldier's family—in a few instances even mentioning family names.

The enlistment register consists of a two-page entry: the left side duplicates information appearing on the enlistment paper, and the right side gives information about the service and termination thereof, the name of the company and regiment, date and place and reason for separation, rank at discharge, and an evaluation of the soldier for reenlistment purposes.[27]

Also included for enlisted personnel are some medical records, unit muster rolls and payrolls, and other records of the unit in which he served. And, occasionally, various correspondence series include information about enlisted men. Compiled histories of ordnance sergeants, quartermaster sergeants, medical stewards, and other enlisted men who served on special duty are available in separate series or as a part of a correspondence series.

Army officers' records, 1789–1917, are not always maintained separately, usually being part of a routine correspondence series. Therefore, correspondence, reports, and other documents reflecting officers' service are filed as if they were routine communications received by or sent from the War Department or its offices and bureaus. After 1863, some attempt was made to segregate into a single file all information relating to all or a part of each officer's service. In some instances, records of service before 1863 have been included in the consolidated file.[28] Since 1863 there have been separate files for almost all officers.[29]

An officer's file may consist of a few documents or several hundred, but ordinarily it contains a letter of appointment and usually some information about the termination of the officers' service. Returns, muster rolls, pay records, orders, reports, and an odd assortment of communications received by or about him also may be sources of information about an officer's career. Histories of medical, ordnance, quartermaster, signal, and paymaster officers have been compiled for all or parts of their service, and for some other arms of the services. In a few cases, compiled military histories have been prepared for officers who served in line units (headquarters, infantry, artillery, and cavalry). Other records worth seeking concern appointments to and service at the U.S. Military Academy[30] or service in volunteer units.

To search for information about an enlisted person one must know the name, date and place of birth, date of enlistment and probably residence at the time of enlistment. Searching for records about an officer requires more extensive preparation, as many published biographical and historical registers reference dates of commissions, names of units, and, sometimes, particulars about officers' service.[31] A few such publications also indicate post-service careers.

National Archives records of U.S. naval officers and enlisted men, 1789–1885, include not only records of service in the U.S. Navy but also records of service in the Revolutionary War, the Confederate States Navy, and the U.S. Marine Corps.

Naval enlisted men's records are found in several National Archives record groups.[32] These records consist of enlistment registers, size rolls, enlistment rendezvous reports, enlistment papers, continuous service certificates for the 1865–99 period, muster rolls, payrolls, correspondence, and other miscellaneous records. Also included are records of persons who served as apprentices, as cabin boys (aged 8 to 16 years), and as volunteers during wartime; those who served on privateers; and those who occupied the U.S. Naval Home at Philadelphia.

For each enlisted naval person there are records of the date, place, term, and other conditions of enlistment, and a description of the actual service rendered.[33] This information may be augmented by referring to muster rolls and ships' logs. Many of the series mentioned are indexed, and a few summaries of sailors' service are in correspondence or appear on continuous service certificates. Researchers may also need to consult the records of the Naval Auxiliary Service (1913–17) and a series of abstracts of World War I naval service records.

The records of naval officers were maintained in different places for different periods, but the records are usually found in correspondence files. Those in the National Archives Building are dated 1798–1902. A searcher must examine numerous series of records in order to obtain a complete account of an officer's service.

Generally, each series is arranged by officers' ranks or duties and by ships or stations, but there are also series that summarize officers' duties or entire service for all or parts of their careers. The use of published biographies of naval officers is recommended.[34] Although many series cover Marine Corps officers as well as naval officers, there are also separate records for marines. Among the navy records, there is documentation of naval and Marine Corps officers' appointments and their service as volunteers in auxiliary service. A few series contain personal details about each officer's age, service as a midshipman or cadet, or complete service biography.

The separate records of the U.S. Marine Corps provide information about officers, enlisted personnel, and civilians serving with the corps between 1789 and 1895.[35] Marine Corps enlisted personnel records generally are located through a card file, arranged alphabetically by the initial letter of surnames. The index furnishes the date of enlistment or last reenlistment, and sometimes refers to a correspondence file, relating to a marine's career. The service records are arranged by year of enlistment or last reenlistment. The size rolls and descriptive lists contain information on physical descriptions of marines, registers of discharge or desertion, and muster rolls. Lists were kept of enlisted men (1921–23), of retired enlisted personnel (1885–1906), and of deaths (1838–1942). One series deals with indentured personnel (1814–56). Marine officers' records include rosters, applications and registers of commissions, monthly reports, military service records for two periods (1869–73 and 1899–

1904), military histories for 1904–11, and case files. Biographies of Marine Corps officers were published with those of naval officers.

Records about military service in the U.S. Coast Guard and its predecessor services—the Revenue-Cutter and Life-Saving Services—are on file for officers, enlisted men, and civilian personnel in the holdings of the National Archives. They are similar in many respects to those of the other services and include information about naval and other military personnel who may have been assigned to duty with the Coast Guard or with its predecessor organizations.

Most of the records of military service in the U.S. Army (officers after June 30, 1917 and enlisted men after October 31, 1912), in the U.S. Navy (officers after 1903 and enlisted men after 1886), in the U.S. Marine Corps (officers after 1896 and enlisted men after 1905), and in the U.S. Air Force have been sent to the National Personnel Records Center in St. Louis. Some personnel records of the U.S. Coast Guard are also there, but without a specific date block. Access to records of service that terminated within the last 75 years is restricted by law as outlined in the *Guide to the National Archives*. Inquiries should be made directly to the center.

Another principal genealogical resource that should interest local historians is the records connected with benefits derived from federal military service. They contain rich personal and family data not available in pre-20th-century military records. Over the years Congress has legislated many different kinds of benefits for veterans that include pensions, land, hospitalization and domiciliary care, markers for veterans' graves, and burial in federal cemeteries or plots in private cemeteries. Eligibility could be based on as few as 14 days' service or on participation in a single battle but is usually derived from a lengthier service or from disability.

Although pensions were first granted to disabled servicemen of the Revolutionary War and to the widows and orphans of those killed in action, legislation passed during the Civil

War provided that other dependents of a deceased veteran could apply for compensation. And although the earliest pension laws permitted judges and legislators in the 13 original states to determine eligibility for federal pensions, federal authorities have made that determination since 1789. Pension laws have generally required the veteran applicant to prove entitlement by presenting evidence of military service, disability (if applicable), and poverty. In order to qualify, dependents needed to prove that they were related to the veteran as spouse, parent, or other dependent. They also had to document the death of the veteran and in some cases the death of the spouse. Often, valuable personal and family history can be found in the filed documents, including the testimony of persons having knowledge of the veterans, their families, or their service. Pension files may include pages from family Bibles; certificates of birth, marriage, death, and baptism; discharge certificates; commissions; and other personal and family documents. Affidavits or depositions were frequently provided by relatives by blood and by marriage as well as by neighbors, friends, ministers, officers, and comrades. The application that initiated a veteran's claim sometimes summarizes occupations and places of residence between discharge and date of application. Pension files average 40 documents each, representing either a single claim or multiple claims.

Pension application files are arranged by war or by period of service. The earliest claims relate to service in the Revolutionary War but do not include many applications or claims filed before 1818.[36] The earlier records were lost in the fire that destroyed the War Department archives in 1800, and others were casualties of the British invasion of Washington in 1814. The Revolutionary War pension claims files often include bounty-land claims papers or references to such claims made in the 1790s for which all other papers were destroyed in the fires mentioned above. An index to the 80,000 claims in the Revolutionary War pension series was prepared by the National Genealogical Society.[37]

The Old Wars pension claims series contains claims based on death or disability suffered during military service performed between 1784 and 1861, generally (but not necessarily) including the two major wars of that period—the War of 1812 and the Mexican War.[38] These claims were made primarily by veterans of the regular army, the navy, and the Marine Corps or by their heirs. In addition, a few claims were approved by special acts of Congress or allowed under specific laws enacted to benefit persons who served as volunteers.[39]

War of 1812 pension claims, which relate to service performed between 1812–15, include service in the Creek War of 1814. In this series are numerous claims that had been filed initially as disability claims and were thus in the Old Wars pension series. For some veterans, bounty-land claims approved under the Bounty Land Act of 1855 have been consolidated with War of 1812 pension claims.[40]

The Mexican War pension series[41] is limited to claims of service in the war of 1846–48. Claims based on disability or death that occurred during or immediately following that war, and before passage of the general Mexican War pension act, are in the Old Wars pension series. However, many veterans of Mexican War service were also veterans of service in the Indian wars, which preceded or followed the Mexican War, or later served in the Civil War. Such veterans were, therefore, entitled to—and frequently did—file pension claims on both services. As a result, many claims based on Mexican War service are combined with, and filed with, the same veteran's claims for pensions on his other service and are, thus, filed with pension claims in the Civil War and Later pension series or with the Indian Wars pension series. The correct file number can be obtained from index or cross-reference cards. Unlike pension claims for the Revolutionary War and the War of 1812, no bounty-land claims papers for the same veteran are included with his Mexican War claims, but his pension file usually includes a reference to his bounty-land claim number.

Claims made for service in the numerous Indian disturbances of the 19th century are in the Indian wars pension claims series, with the exception of those based on service in the Creek War of 1814 and the Indian engagements that occurred during the Civil War.[42] As with Mexican War claims, many claims for benefits from service in Indian wars are consolidated with claims based on service in a major war.

The Civil War and Later pension claims series contains claims arising out of federal military service performed largely between 1860 and 1917, although some are dated as late as 1934.[43] Unlike records in the other series, claims in this series are divided into two classes—one for the army and one for the navy. Most of the claims relate to service in the Civil War, the Spanish-American War, and the Philippine Insurrection. Of these, only those claims that terminated before 1934 are on file in the National Archives. Those that continued beyond that date are still in the custody of the Veterans Administration. A researcher wishing to examine a claim that terminated after 1934 can usually do so by contacting the Veterans Administration regional office that serves the state in which the veteran resided when the claim was terminated.

An index to military units active in the Civil War, the Spanish-American War, the Philippine Insurrection, as well as units of the regular army and some units for World War ᵀ permits identification of all claims made ι members of a given military unit before 1934. Although an index to post-1934 claims is maintained by the Veterans Administration, it is not available for public examination.

Aids in identifying pensioners include various published lists of pensioners,[45] the 1840 Census of Pensioners of the Revolutionary War, and various lists of pensions approved by the House of Representatives that appear in congressional reports.

Additional records concerning veterans' benefits are on file, but except for those relating to a veterans' facility or a federally owned or maintained cemetery in a given area, they would have little or no local history value. However, all records concerning veterans' benefits are described in finding aids that are available for examination in the National Archives Building.

Not mentioned in the foregoing discussion of records of genealogical and local history value are numerous other large and small series of federal records. Although this paper has highlighted only those records having a broad interest, one or more series of records relating to a specific community, its people, or an event could be invaluable tools in a local history study. It is hoped that this brief discussion will shed some light on federal records and will help illustrate the fact that federal records can be a rich genealogical and local history resource. The researcher must find the key to unlock the vault that holds them. One fact bears repeating: prerequisite to the successful use of the resources is a knowledge of the relationship that the person or persons under study had to the federal government.

NOTES

1. Meredith B. Colket, Jr., and Frank E. Bridgers, *Guide to Genealogical Records in the National Archives* (Washington, DC: National Archives and Records Service (hereafter cited as NARS), 1964); U.S., National Archives and Records Service (hereafter cited as U.S., NARS), *Guide to Genealogical Research in the National Archives*, rev. ed. (1982).

2. U.S., NARS *Guide to the National Archives of the United States* (1974).

3. Henry Putney Beers, *Guide to the Archives of the Government of the Confederate States of America* (Washington, DC: NARS, 1968); Kenneth W. Munden and Henry Put-

ney Beers, *Guide to Federal Archives Relating to the Civil War* (Washington, DC: NARS, 1962); George S. Ulibarri and John P. Harrison, *Guide to Materials on Latin America in the National Archives of the United States* (Washington, DC: NARS, 1974); U.S., NARS, *Guide to Cartographic Records in the National Archives* (1971); Edward E. Hill, comp., *Guide to Records in the National Archives of the United States Relating to American Indians* (Washington, DC: NARS, 1981); Debra L. Newman, comp., *Black History: A Guide to Civilian Records in the National Archives* (Washington, DC: NARS, 1984).

4. U.S., NARS, *Using Records in the National Archives for Genealogical Research* General Information Leaflet Number 5 (hereafter cited as GIL 5) (revised edition, 1986).

5. U.S., National Archives and Records Administration (hereafter cited as U.S., NARA), *Select List of Publications of the National Archives and Records Administration*, GIL 3 (1986).

6. U.S., Bureau of the Census, Form 70-82-1, *Population and Housing Census Questions 1790–1970*; U.S., NARS, Form GSA-WASH DC-65-224, *Census Data 1790–1890*.

7. Katherine H. Davidson and Charlotte M. Ashby, *Preliminary Inventory of the Records of the Bureau of the Census*, Preliminary Inventory 161 (hereafter cited as PI 161) (Washington, DC: NARS, 1964), pp. 110–11.

8. Leon De Valinger, Jr., "Reconstructed 1790 Census of Delaware" (published serially), *National Genealogical Society Quarterly* 36–41 (September 1948–June 1953); *Substitutes for Georgia's Lost 1790 Census* (Albany, GA: Delwyn Associates, n.d.); Charles Brunk Heinemann and Gaius Marcus Brumbaugh, *First Census of Kentucky, 1790* (Washington, DC: 1940). For Virginia's lost 1790 census, the Census Bureau used state tax lists, 1782–85, as a substitute. The lists were published as the 1790 Census of Virginia when the other censuses were published in 1908.

9. "Census Information File," typescript available for staff use in the National Archives Building and in the 11 Archives field branches. The file also appears in U.S., NARS, *Guide to Genealogical Research in the National Archives*, rev. ed. (1982), pp. 28–38.

10. U.S., Bureau of the Census, *Heads of Families at the First Census Taken in the Year 1790* (1908); reprint editions, Baltimore: Genealogical Publishing Co., n.d., and Spartanburg, SC: The Reprint Company Publishers, n.d. See also *First Census of the United States, 1790*, National Archives Microfilm Publication T498, 3 rolls.

11. U.S., NARS, *Federal Population Censuses, 1790–1890: A Catalog of Microfilm Copies of the Schedules* (1979); U.S., NARS, *1900 Federal Population Census: A Catalog of Microfilm Copies of the Schedules* (1978); U.S., NARS, *1910 Federal Population Census: A Catalog of Microfilm Copies of the Schedules* (1982); Carmen R. Delle Donne, *Federal Census Schedules, 1850–80: Primary Source for Historical Research*, Reference Information Paper 67 (Washington, DC: NARS, 1973).

12. Davidson and Ashby, PI 161; *Census Enumeration District Descriptions, 1900*, National Archives Microfilm Publication T1210; Michael H. Shelly, comp., *Ward Maps of United States Cities: A Selective Checklist of Pre-1900 Maps in the Library of Congress* (Washington, DC: Library of Congress, 1975).

13. *Federal Population and Mortality Census Schedules, 1790–1890, in the National Archives and the States: Outlines of a Lecture on Their Availability, Content, and Use*, Special List 24 (Washington, DC: NARA, 1986).

14. Carroll D. Wright and William C. Hunt, *The History and Growth of the United States Census* (Washington, DC: Bureau of the Census, 1900); S. N. D. North, *A Century of Population Growth* (Washington, DC: Bureau of the Census, 1909).

15. *Publications of the Bureau of the Census, 1790–1916*, National Archives Microfilm Publication T825. Publications both included and not included in this microfilm publication are listed in various catalogs to U.S. government documents. See also U.S., Bureau of the Census, *Catalog of Publications, 1790–1972* (1974).

16. U.S., NARA, *Microfilm Resources for Research: A Comprehensive Catalog* (1986), pp. 30, 49–50; U.S., NARS, *Immigrant and Passenger Arrivals: A Select Catalog of National Archives Microfilm Publications* (1983), passim.

17. *Immigrant and Passenger Arrivals*, pp. 19–43.

18. Harry P. Yoshpe and Philip P. Brower, *Preliminary Inventory of the Land-Entry Papers of the General Land Office*, PI 22 (Washington, DC: NARS, 1949). Land records available on microfilm are listed in U.S., NARS, *Genealogical and Biographical Research: A Select Catalog of National Archives Microfilm Publications* (1983).

19. U.S., Congress, *American State Papers, Class 8, Public Lands*; Phillip W. Mc-Mullin, *Grassroots of America: An Index to the American State Papers, Class 8, Public Lands, and Class 9, Claims* (Salt Lake City, 1972); U.S., Congress, Senate, *Reports of the Committees on Private Land Claims of the Senate and House of Representatives*, S. Misc. Doc. 81, 45th Cong., 3d sess., Serial 1836, 2 vols. The index in the 2 volumes of Serial 1836 is incomplete.

20. U.S., Congress, Senate, *Private Claims, 14th–30th Congresses, Alphabetical List*, S. Doc. 67, 30th Cong., 1st sess., Serial 534; *List of Private Claims, 14th–46th Congresses*, S. Misc. Doc. 14, 46th Cong., 3d sess., Serials 1945–1946, 2 vols.

U.S., Congress, House, *Alphabetical List of Private Claims, 1st–31st Congresses*, H. Misc. Doc. (unnumbered), 32d Cong., 1st sess., Serials 635–655; *Index of Private Claims, 32d–41st Congresses*, H. Doc. 109, 42d Cong., 2d sess., Serial 1574; *Alphabetical List of Private Claims, 32d–41st Congresses*, H. Misc. Doc. 53, 47th Cong., 1st sess., Serial 2036; *List of Private Claims, Senate, 47th–51st Congresses*, H. Misc. Doc. 213, 53d Cong., 2d sess., Serial 3175.

21. U.S., NARA, *Military Service Records in the National Archives of the United States*, GIL 7 (1985). Military service records available on microfilm from the National Archives are listed in U.S., NARA, *Military Service Records: A Select Catalog of National Archives Microfilm Publications* (1985).

22. *General Index to Compiled Military Service Records of Revolutionary War Soldiers*, National Archives Microfilm Publication M860; *Index to Compiled Military Service Records of Revolutionary War Naval Personnel*, National Archives Microfilm Publication T516; *Index to Compiled Service Records of Volunteer Soldiers Who Served from 1784–1811*, National Archives Microfilm Publication M694; *Index to Compiled Service Records of Volunteer Soldiers Who Served During the War of 1812*, National Archives Microfilm Publication M602; *Index to Compiled Military Service Records of Volunteer Soldiers Who Served During Indian Wars and Disturbances, 1815–58*, National Archives Microfilm Publication M629; *Index to Compiled Service Records of Volunteer Soldiers Who Served During the Mexican War*, National Archives Microfilm Publication M616; *General Index to Compiled Service Records of Volunteer Soldiers Who Served During the War With Spain*, National Archives Microfilm Publication M871; *Index to Compiled Service Records of Volunteers Who Served During the Phil-

ippine Insurrection, National Archives Microfilm Publication M872; *Consolidated Index to Compiled Service Records of Confederate Soldiers*, National Archives Microfilm Publication M253. *Note:* All of the indexes cited above are consolidated name indexes to persons whose names appear in compiled service records for the war or period concerned. No similar consolidated index to the records of Union Army soldiers is available. There are separate indexes for each state or territory that furnished troops to the Union Army. Nearly all of the 40 indexes have been microfilmed. Microfilm numbers for these indexes can be found in U.S., NARA, *Microfilm Resources for Research: A Comprehensive Catalog* (1986) and in U.S., NARA, *Military Service Records: A Select Catalog of National Archives Microfilm Publications* (1985). Price information about the catalogs and the film can be obtained by writing the Publications Services Branch, National Archives and Records Administration, Washington, DC 20408.

23. *Compiled Service Records of Soldiers Who Served in the American Army During the Revolutionary War*, National Archives Microfilm Publication M881.

24. *Compiled Service Records of Volunteer Soldiers Who Served From 1784 to 1811*, National Archives Microfilm Publication M905.

25. Lucille H. Pendell and Elizabeth Bethel, *Preliminary Inventory of the Records of the Adjutant General's Office*, PI 17 (Washington, DC: NARS, 1949).

26. Elizabeth Bethel, *Preliminary Inventory of the War Department Collection of Confederate Records*, PI 101 (Washington, DC: NARS, 1957).

27. *Register of Enlistments in the United States Army, 1798–1914*, National Archives Microfilm Publication M233.

28. Pendell and Bethel, PI 17.

29. Ibid.

30. *United States Military Academy Cadet Application Papers, 1805–66*, National Archives Microfilm Publication M688.

31. Francis B. Heitman, *Historical Register and Dictionary of Officers of the United States Army from Its Organization, 29 September 1789, to 2 March 1903*, 2 vols. (Washington, DC: Government Printing Office, 1903; reprint ed., Urbana: University of Illinois Press, 1965); George W. Cullum, *Biographical Register of the Officers and Graduates of the United States Military Academy* (various publishers, 1803–90, with supplements through 1950); U.S., Adjutant General's Office, *United States Army Register* (1798).

32. Records of the Bureau of Naval Personnel, RG 24; General Records of the Department of the Navy, 1798–1947, RG 80; Naval Records Collections of the Office of Naval Records and Library, RG 45.

33. *Index to Rendezvous Reports, Before and After the Civil War (1846–61, 1865–84)*, National Archives Microfilm Publication T1098; *Index to Rendezvous Reports, Civil War, 1861–65*, National Archives Microfilm Publication T1099; *Index to Rendezvous Reports, Armed Guard Personnel, 1846–84*, National Archives Microfilm Publication T1101; *Index to Rendezvous Reports, Naval Auxiliary Service, 1846–84*, National Archives Microfilm Publication T1100.

34. *Official Register of the United States, 1816–1957*. Originally a list of "officers and agents, civil, military, and naval in the service of the United States," the *Register* continued to list all military officers and every civilian federal employee through 1916. After 1916, military officers were omitted, and in 1925 lower ranking civilian employees were

dropped, making the *Register* thereafter a "List of persons occupying administrative and supervisory positions in each executive and judicial department of the government." Published biennially 1816–1921 and annually thereafter, its preparation was the responsibility of the Department of State, 1816–59; the Department of the Interior, 1861–1905; the Bureau of the Census, 1907–32; and the Civil Service Commission, 1933–59. See also, U.S., Navy Department, *Register of the Commissioned and Warrant Officers of the United States Navy and Marine Corps* (1814–); Edward W. Callahan, ed., *List of Officers of the Navy of the U.S. and of the Marine Corps from 1775 to 1900* (New York: L. R. Hamersley & Co., 1901).

35. Maizie Johnson, *Inventory of the Records of the United States Marine Corps*, Inv. 2 (Washington, DC: NARS, 1970).

36. *Revolutionary War Pension and Bounty-Land-Warrant Application Files, 1800–1900,* National Archives Microfilm Publication M804; *Selected Records From Revolutionary War Pension and Bounty-Land-Warrant Application Files, 1800–1900,* National Archives Microfilm Publication M805.

37. Max Ellsworth Hoyt, *Index of Revolutionary War Pension Applications*, Special Publication No. 32, revised by Sadye Giller, William H. Durant, and Louis M. Durant (Washington, DC: National Genealogical Society, 1966).

38. *Old War Index to Pension Files, 1815–1926,* National Archives Microfilm Publication T316.

39. U.S., NARA, *Military Service Records in the National Archives of the United States,* GIL 7 (1985).

40. *Index to War of 1812 Pension Application Files,* National Archives Microfilm Publication M313.

41. *Index to Mexican War Pension Files, 1887–1926,* National Archives Microfilm Publication T317.

42. *Index to Indian Wars Pension Files, 1892–1926,* National Archives Microfilm Publication T318.

43. *General Index to Pension Files, 1861–1934,* National Archives Microfilm Publication T288.

44. *Organizational Index to Pension Files of Veterans Who Served Between 1861 and 1900,* National Archives Microfilm Publication T289.

45. *Secretary of War Communicating Pension List, 1 June 1813,* reprinted as *A Transcript of the Pension List of the United States for 1813* (Baltimore: Southern Book Co., 1959); *Secretary of War Report, January 20, 1820,* H. Ex. Doc. 55, 16th Cong., 1st sess., Serial 34, reprinted as *The Pension List of 1820* (Baltimore: Southern Book Co., 1959); *Report from the Secretary of War . . . in Relationship to the Pension Establishment of the United States, 1835,* S. Doc. 514, 23d Cong., 1st sess., Serials 249–251; *Names of Pensioners on Roll, 1 January 1883,* S. Ex. Doc. 84, 47th Cong., 2d sess., Serials 2078–2082, 5 vols.

RICHARD S. MAXWELL

State and Local History Sources in the Civil Archives Division

The records of civilian agencies and establishments of the federal government in the National Archives Building contain a wealth of information useful in the study of local and state history. Although most of these records were created in the furtherance of federal programs, the data collected and compiled refer to places, people, and events highly significant for the study of state and local history.

Records about places in the United States abound, as can be seen, for example, in those of the General Land Office (now the Bureau of Land Management in the Department of the Interior). In those records, researchers can find material from federal townsites on the public domain that were established throughout the American West, in Alaska, and in Indian Territory (now Oklahoma). Townsite records are available for hundreds of present-day cities and long-forgotten towns (now ghost towns), some with unforgettable names, such as Moose Pass, Last Chance, and Alice. Townsite records for 1855–1925, for example, include correspondence from prospective settlers and land office officials, legal papers, maps, plats, press clippings, photographs, minutes of meetings of townsite boards, and other materials. Local and state historians will find documentation on many western towns among these records.

Other General Land Office (GLO) records about places include those of abandoned military reservations, 1822–1927, documenting the role of the GLO in creating military reserva-tions on the public lands and in disposing of reservations abandoned by the Departments of War and the Navy. These records include executive orders creating reservations and correspondence, title papers, plats, maps, blueprints, and plans showing the location and size of buildings and other structures on the reservations. A local area that has an abandoned military reservation or fort will find part of its history included in these files. For example, the Alaska Historical Society has microfilmed the file for Fort Egbert, and a local history group in Florida has examined the files for Fort Brooks, Amelia Island, and Fort Marion, Florida. Moreover, data on military engagements, military personnel, and events at the forts can be found among various War Department and Navy Department records and can be used in conjunction with civilian records to create a good history of a specific fort or military reservation. Plans showing location and size of buildings on military reservations are especially useful in restoration projects that have been undertaken for certain of the more famous forts.

Information important to local and state historians can also be found in records of the Post Office Department concerning the establishment of post offices and the appointment of postmasters. Registers, 1789–1971, provide the names of postmasters, the dates of their appointments, and the names of the post offices to which they were appointed. The records also

Anadarko Townsite, Oklahoma Territory, 8 August 1901. (Record Group 48, Office of the Secretary of the Interior, 48-RST-7B-28.)

provide information about changes in classifications of post offices and the dates of their discontinuance or of transfer of service to another office. There are also site location reports filed by postmasters showing the geographical location of each office and its distance to significant streams, rivers, railroads, and other post offices. The records also show that many localities were officially named with the establishment of their post offices.

The records of the U.S. Geological Survey contain seldom-used but significant documentation about local and state areas. For example, geologists' field notebooks, 1867–1939, are a fine source of data. The notebooks are usually in the form of diaries and contain rough sketches, maps, and diagrams of geologic investigations of specific areas and individual mines. One of these notebooks describes in de-

tail the investigation of the "diamond hoax." This field notebook, number 1113, consists of pencil notes made by S. F. Emmons in 1872 about a hoax set up by a group of speculators who salted a hillside in California with imported diamonds in an effort to sell shares in a diamond mine. Emmons investigated the so-called diamond fields and reported that some of the diamonds he recovered bore diamond toolcutters' marks from being faceted and worked. Field notebooks also available for W. H. Holmes's studies of the Colorado River include a book of sketches of Yellowstone Park. Other interesting notebooks describe Cape Cod and Martha's Vineyard in Massachusetts and the Oatman District of Arizona.

Documentation of places also appears in the records of the U.S. Coast Guard, a civilian agency of the Department of Transportation (except in time of war). The 1789–1939 site files of the Bureau of Lighthouses and its predecessors include records on lighthouses throughout the United States, including legal case files on the acquisition and disposal of sites, deeds, contracts for construction, drawings of lighthouses and lifesaving stations, and other related records. A good project for a local historian would be to develop the history of a lighthouse site and illustrate it with incidents that happened there. Collateral information about marine wrecks and disasters can be found in the records of the Coast Guard relating to the Life-Saving Service, 1874–1915.

Local and state historians will find a wealth of information about their local buildings among records of the Public Buildings Service of the General Services Administration. These records include drawings, plans, and specifications for post offices, courthouses, customhouses, defense housing, mints, and other structures built from 1835 to 1945. Historians in San Francisco recently used the records relating to their old mint during a major construction project at the mint. Collateral records relating to public buildings are contained in a series of 1838–1968 title papers that include warranty deeds, abstracts and certificates of title, site proposals, and related title papers for public buildings sold or otherwise disposed of by the United States. Used in conjunction with locally maintained deeds and land records, these records could provide a good history of many local buildings.

Other documentation of interest to local historians on places in the United States appears in records of the Department of State that involve U.S. territories from 1789 to 1873. There are 70 volumes of "territorial papers," including correspondence, reports, journals of proceedings of legislative assemblies, and other records relating to the territories from Alabama through Wyoming, including Old Northwest Territory, Orleans Territory, West Florida, and Puerto Rico. Much of the local administrative history of each territory is contained in this series, and the records are an apt starting place for students of the history of various states. The complete collection for each territory is available as a microfilm publication.

The records of the Coast and Geodetic Survey, 1806–1957, provide interesting information about many state and local areas in the United States. There are records about ship canals, harbors, bays, and anchorages; monthly reports and journals of field parties; and a narrative report of a survey of the North Carolina coast made in 1806. There are records of survey parties in the Florida Keys, the Gulf coast, New England, and the Mississippi Valley. Local historical information appears throughout a massive collection of scientific records, 1816–1948, which contains notebooks, portfolios, and reports on azimuth and time observations, sunspots, eclipses, benchmarks, leveling surveys, and an 1869 manuscript on Indian place-names in Maine. Although much of this material is purely scientific in nature, it could be utilized in local history studies by persons knowledgeable about scientific activities that took place locally or by those in pursuit of obscure happenings in their areas.

Local historical information also appears in records of the Bureau of Reclamation relating to its projects, chiefly in the western United States, 1902–60. These records include the project history library of the bureau's Washington office, which consists of detailed historical reports on projects as submitted by the engineers and managers working on each project. A great deal of local and national controversy developed over the issue of private or public power development in some of these projects—for example, the Hells Canyon Dam. Students of local history could use these project history files (available as microfilm publication M96, 144 rolls), along with the correspondence of the bureau and the Army Corps of Engineers, as background for local histories of reclamation projects.

The Scientific, Economic, and Natural Resources Branch of the Archives contains perhaps the finest collection of records in federal custody about a specific place—the District of Columbia. Holdings of records of the District include 1824–98 tax and assessment records showing real estate and some personal property owned, names of taxpayers, and amounts of taxes paid or owed; deed books to real property in the District; and some daily precinct returns of the District of Columbia Police Department. (Precinct returns have been frequently used by scholars in studies of ethnic groups and age or sex orientation in urban crime.) These records are enhanced by the presence of certain other federal records relating to the District of Columbia, such as those of the National Capital Planning Commission, the Fine Arts Commission, St. Elizabeths Hospital, and the Commissioners of Public Buildings and Grounds of the National Capital. The history of the District of Columbia appears throughout this extensive documentation.

Thus far this essay has been primarily concerned with places; however, the National Archives contains many significant records, beyond those standardly used for genealogical research, about people. For instance, the Department of the Interior was the employer of hundreds of persons who worked in a variety of positions throughout the American West and the Southeast. Those local communities that had land offices (such as Florence, AZ) or Indian agencies (such as Fort Peck, MT) or those territories after 1873 that had governors (such as Utah, where Brigham Young served as governor, or New Mexico, where Lew Wallace served) are represented in these records. The Appointments Division records of the Interior Department, 1849–1907, include applications and recommendations for appointments to all of the offices under departmental control. Scholars and students of local and state history can use these records to determine which local citizens held offices and what biographical or political information about them appears in the files. In addition, these appointment papers can be used in preparing broader studies of state political history.

Other significant information about persons appears in land-entry papers of the General Land Office, 1785–1951. Not only do these records have vast genealogical importance, but they can be used also for other historical purposes. The southeastern states of Alabama and Florida and all of the western states except Texas were once parts of the public domain. Students of local history in those great geographical areas can determine the names of the first *legal* settlers in their areas by examining the tractbooks to see who first located land in their communities. Land-entry papers show the names of the entrymen or women, date of the entry, description of the land, price paid, and other administrative information. Examples of the use of land-entry papers for state and local history are numerous. Dr. Paul Wallace Gates of Cornell University, for one, has written extensively on land settlement in numerous articles and books, such as "The Disposal of the Public Domain in Illinois, 1848–1856," in the *Journal of Economic and Business History* 3 (1931) and "Land Policy and Tenancy in the Prairie States," in the *Journal of Economic History* 1 (1941). Another example of land-entry papers as utilized in local history can be found in Berlin B. Chapman's article "The Land Run of 1893, as Seen at Kiowa," in the *Kansas Historical Quarterly* 31 (1965).

An untapped research area involves land-entry papers that have gone almost unnoticed in black history studies. Although these papers make no reference to race or national origin (except where naturalization papers appear), it is possible to use decennial census schedules to determine the race of individuals living in public land areas in order to determine ethnic patterns of settlement where blacks were known to have settled on public land.

In 1933, during the Great Depression, the Civilian Conservation Corps (CCC) was formed to create jobs for certain of the nation's unemployed who were to perform works of a public nature in reforestation of lands and prevention of forest fires, floods, and soil erosion. The records of the CCC, 1933–42, document this work in hundreds of local communities. Included are records of the organization and work of the corps; monthly progress reports of all camps in operation, showing the nature of the work done; and statistics on the workers and material involved. There are also inspection reports relating to camp administration, morale, health, education, and other internal matters. The records of the CCC include a great deal of information that would be useful in compiling histories of local camps. In addition, other civilian records in the National Archives Building contain documentation of CCC activities. The records of the National Park Service, for example, include material on the supervision of more than six hundred CCC camps by the Park Service; narrative reports of the superintendents of camps in national, state, and local parks, 1933–37, containing general descriptions of the work done; stories of interesting events; analyses of local reaction to the camps; and a pictorial presentation of camp life made possible by thousands of photographs. These largely unexploited records could serve as the basis for many state and local histories of the CCC and its activities during the Great Depression.

In the 1930s, the government also established programs to employ artists, writers, playwrights, and other cultural artisans in their own fields. A great many artworks and written manuscripts were done locally, and hundreds of post offices, schools, courthouses, prisons, and other local buildings were decorated with artworks produced by the Federal Art Project, the Treasury Relief Art Project, and the Fine Arts Section of the Public Buildings Administration. Local and state historians can make good use of these records in documentation of artworks in their own areas, as well as in writing about controversies that developed in art projects, such as the dispute in California over the Anton Refregier murals in the Rincon Branch of the Post Office at San Francisco. Considered too modern in the 1930s, these paintings of symbols of social progress in the state have since been much praised.

Among the many other civilian agency records in the Civil Archives Division relating to relief efforts in the Depression are those of the Work Projects Administration (WPA) and its predecessors, the Federal Emergency Relief and Civil Works Administrations. The WPA was established in 1935 as the agency respon-

sible for the execution of the work relief program as a whole. The records of the WPA, 1933–42, include state files where most of the important administrative correspondence and reports concerning the operations of state programs can be found under such subject headings as drought, education, medical care, women's projects, vocational training, art, drama, music, and hundreds of other subjects. The WPA and its predecessors reached into almost every U.S. community with their programs. Local and state historians can make extensive use of these records as they document local history.

Many events in U.S. history have local and state significance and are well documented in civil records. There is, for example, a continuing controversy over who was the first homesteader. National Park Service records include files for Homestead National Monument in Nebraska, erected on land homesteaded by Daniel Freeman, popularly believed to be the first homesteader. General Land Office records include Freeman's Homestead Entry Number 1 at Brownsville, NE, dated January 1, 1863, and his final certificate (also number 1) completed in 1868. The controversy arises over how one defines "first"—a tedious and complex endeavor. It is important to note, however, that many areas on the public domain had a first homestead entryman, and many other persons made cash purchases, tree claims, and desert-land entries that are documented in the records and await search and publicity by local or regional historians and genealogists.

Few events in U.S. history have had the impact on national development and migration of population as the discovery of gold in California. In 1848, John A. Sutter's partner in a sawmill venture on the American River discovered gold at Sutter's Mill. Edward Fitzgerald Beale and many others spread the word of the discovery of a gold strike so rich that nuggets could be picked up in bushel baskets, and in 1849 the gold rush was on in earnest. General Land Office records include the claim of John Sutter to land at Sutter's Mill. Local historians could use the land records and census schedules to determine names of local citizens who went to the goldfields. Passenger lists and cargo manifests of ships in the Records of the U.S. Customs Service provide data on people and supplies moving around the Horn to California. And reports from consular offices and officials in Central America and Mexico provide accounts of the movement of people across this area on the way to California.

An event that greatly stirred the population of the United States was the assassination in 1865 of President Lincoln. The civilian records relating to that tragic event include documentation among the records of the government of the District of Columbia of the arrest of the assassins. Records of the General Accounting Office include records of expenses for attending physicians as well as for expenses of the funeral. Records of the Office of the Commissioners of Public Buildings and Grounds refer to the plans for the state funeral and the transportation of the body to Illinois. Records of the Office of the Secretary of the Interior document the funeral and the transportation expenses of the train that carried Lincoln's body to Springfield. Although this event has been described in the context of national history, the same records could be used, with local newspaper and magazine accounts of the funeral and the passage of the train through local areas, to provide background data for interesting articles on local impressions and feelings toward the event.

This has been an attempt to provide a few examples of civilian records of the government that furnish information useful in writing state and local history. There are thousands of other examples of records about places, people, and events in the United States—records that are the basic sources for undertaking studies of our nation's history.

ELAINE C. EVERLY

State and Local History Sources in the Military Archives Division

Since the founding of our nation, the military has played a significant role in state and local history, though this may not be as apparent as that of other departments of the federal government. Although the military today is greatly involved with foreign affairs, this was not always the case.

Until the Spanish-American War in 1898, almost all engagements involving U.S. military forces took place inside or near our own borders, and all installations were in the United States. Despite the fact that this circumstance changed dramatically after World War II, the United States remains the base for the recruitment, supply, and training of U.S. military forces, greatly affecting the areas in which these activities take place. Because the military has always been engaged in activities that have little to do with warfare, there is a wealth of information in the records about such nonmilitary functions of the army and the navy as exploring, mapping, and charting our western frontiers and inland and coastal waterways; planning and constructing internal improvements such as roads, bridges, and dams; and conducting scientific experiments. This paper will explain some of the types of information on state and local history that are available in military records; the paper is not, however, more than a general survey of the records and the data contained in them.

From the colonial period to the present, there have been a large number and variety of military installations in the United States. In the 19th century, army posts were almost synonymous with the development and expansion of the western frontier. They were often located in sparsely settled areas where confrontations with the Indians were likely to occur. But there were other kinds of posts, too. As early as the 1790s, the War Department began to plan for a system of artillery fortifications along the Atlantic seacoast; these were extended to the Gulf of Mexico and the Pacific coast as our nation grew. Since the early 1800s, the Navy Department has maintained yards and shore establishments for the construction and repair of vessels and equipment, and the War Department has operated arsenals and armories where weapons and powder were manufactured, tested, and stored. Since the involvement of the United States in foreign wars in the 20th century, large facilities have been established for the training of recruits and the assemblage of equipment, the number and size of which increased greatly in times of war.

Records relating to military installations document far more than the obvious activities that took place there; they also tell us much about the economic and social conditions of the area. Although western posts have been greatly romanticized by Hollywood, their records have valuable information about the relationships of the white settlers to the Indians; a post was the War Department's observatory for possible outbreaks of violence and often the

Band of Apache Indian prisoners at rest stop beside Southern Pacific Railway, near Nueces River, Texas, 10 September 1886. Among those on their way to exile in Florida are Natchez (center front) and, to the right, Geronimo and his son in matching shirts. (Record Group 106, Smithsonian Institution, 106-BAE-2517A.)

place where Indian allotments or rations were dispensed. (At the conclusion of hostilities, Indian chieftains and warriors were often incarcerated there—perhaps the most famous detainees being Geronimo and his Apaches who were imprisoned in Florida and later Fort Sill, OK, from the 1880s to the 1900s.) From a western outpost, officers reported about an area before it was fully settled. For example, beginning in 1868 the post surgeon was required to keep a medical history that included data about the establishment of the post, the flora and fauna of the region, and weather conditions. These are among the records of the Adjutant General's Office. From the early 19th century to the present, navy yards and arsenals have employed large numbers of civilians, and payrolls and other employment records for many of these installations are among the records of the Bureau of Yards and Docks and the Office of the Chief of Ordnance.

During the 20th century, military installations have become even more closely integrated with the economic and social life of the region than in earlier days, and the records reflect this. For example, during the period beginning with World War I there are files relating to posts, camps, and airfields among the records of the Adjutant General's Office that include correspondence with members of Congress, local government officials, and chambers of commerce regarding such subjects as proposed construction of facilities, the closing of installations, conflicts of military personnel with civilians, and reports on the local labor supply, housing, water supply, and availability of land for lease or purchase. Among the War Department's General and Special Staffs records are files of the commission on training camp activities established by the Secretary of War in 1917 to determine the recreational and social conditions in many areas. Also of great interest are the files relating to prisoner-of-war camps in the United States during World War II, which are among the records of the Provost Marshal General. They include camp reports, diaries, rosters, and correspondence regarding the construction of and conditions in the camps in addition to studies concerning local opinion or attitudes toward the camps.

Army posts were parts of larger geographic commands into which the U.S. Army had been divided. The number, size, and area encompassed by these commands changed with great frequency during the 19th century, but the concept of geographic army commands remained virtually the same from the early 19th century to 1942. At times during the last century, the army was divided solely into geographic departments, such as the Department of Florida, Department of the Missouri, and so forth; at other times the departments were further subdivided into districts; and at still other

times there were divisions to which the departments were subordinate. In 1920, the military departments were abolished and the United States was divided into nine geographic corps areas, which existed until 1942 when the commands were reorganized along both functional and geographic lines.

Regardless of the structure, the army command was responsible for military activities in a given area, and the voluminous command records in the National Archives are great sources of information about local areas. In addition to correspondence with and reports from post commanders, the records include documentation relating to expeditions, such as Custer's famous Black Hills Expedition in 1874, the building of military roads, and railroad surveys. Records of the western commands from 1866 to 1890 are excellent sources for the study of the Great Plains and the Rocky Mountain areas, but other command records are also rich in local history. For example, there are the records of the army and the Department of Florida that cover the period of the second Seminole War, and the records of the Tenth Military Department that document the U.S. occupation and establishment of government in California during and after the Mexican War and include correspondence with Mexican officials and leaders in the area of present-day California. In the 20th century, the command records have files on the evacuation of Japanese-Americans from the west coast to relocation camps during World War II. Although the War Relocation Authority, under civilian control, set up and managed the camps, the army was responsible for the physical evacuation of Japanese-Americans from areas considered sensitive for the defense of the west coast.

Perhaps at no time during the 19th century did the army become more involved with local affairs than during the Civil War. The Civil War and Reconstruction Era command records are very good sources for data about the political, economic, and social conditions in the South during this period. As the Union armies advanced, civil government in the South ceased to exist and the U.S. Army became the sole source of law and order in the occupied areas. Most of these policing duties were extended to the departmental and district provost marshals, whose records include such items as registers of disloyal persons and persons taking the oath of allegiance, licenses, passes, and trade permits issued. In towns and cities of occupied areas, provost courts were established with jurisdiction over both criminal and civil cases, and documentation relating to these courts is included in the command records. However, the closely related proceedings of the military commissions that tried civilians during this period are among the records of the Office of the Judge Advocate General.

During and after the war, offices of civil affairs were established within the military commands, and the records of these offices are replete with correspondence with state and local political leaders. The records also include such items as voter registration lists, applications for appointments to civil positions, and correspondence relating to the election of delegates to the state constitutional conventions.

The War Department's collection of Confederate records includes material relating to the conscription and supply of the Confederate Army and the operations of the government in Richmond and two large files that were artificially assembled by the War Department after the Civil War. One consists of papers relating to citizens who had business transactions with the Confederate government, the other consists of records relating to citizens who were either suspected of disloyalty or were arrested by the U.S. military authorities.

In the summer of 1865 the Bureau of Refugees, Freedmen, and Abandoned Lands was established in the War Department to supervise all government programs dealing with freedmen and to administer all confiscated or abandoned lands. The voluminous field office records of the Freedmen's Bureau contain many reports about conditions in the South and the relationship between whites and blacks in the postwar era. They also have many letters and reports from teachers in the newly established schools for black children, which were being funded by the bureau.

Last but not least are the draft records for the Civil War. State and district offices were established under the Provost Marshal General's Bureau in Washington, DC, to enroll and draft men for military service and to detect and arrest deserters. The voluminous records of these state and district offices include registers of persons enrolled for the draft as well as correspondence dealing with local reaction to the draft.

Throughout the 19th century, the regular army was actually a very small force that was augmented by the state militia or volunteer forces mustered into federal service in times or threats of war. Although there is no easy way to determine the county in which a specific unit was organized, there are many records relating to these units in the National Archives. There are muster rolls and payrolls of state organizations brought into federal service from the Revolution to the Philippine Insurrection. Beginning with the Mexican War, there are often regimental papers, which include correspondence, orders, and recruiting returns. For the Civil War, the Spanish-American War, and the Philippine Insurrection there are also regimental books consisting of letters sent, orders issued, and descriptions of enlisted men. Correspondence and orders relating to National Guard units during the World War I period and other nonconsolidated materials are also found in these records.

Since most 19th century military engagements took place in the United States, Canada, or Mexico, reports of these actions are an important part of local history. Unfortunately, the War Department's collection of Revolutionary War records contains virtually no reports of engagements that took place during the U.S. War for Independence. However, the letters received by the Secretary of War, the Adjutant General, the army commands, and the Secretary of the Navy include reports of battles and engagements of the War of 1812, the Seminole wars, the Black Hawk War, the Mexican War, the Civil War, and the numerous wars with the Indians that occurred from the close of the Civil War to about 1890. For the post-Civil War period, there are many consolidated files among the letters received by the Adjutant

General that contain most of the important reports relating to specific campaigns against the Indians, such as the Modoc War in northern California. But for the pre-Civil War period, most reports are interfiled with other communications, and in most instances it is necessary to know the name of the reporting officer and the approximate date of his report. Although many reports have been published in the *American State Papers,* the Congressional Serial Set, and the *Official Records of the War of the Rebellion,* there are still many unpublished accounts that would be of interest to local historians.

As noted earlier, military forces have been used for purposes other than to repel an enemy during times of war. Throughout the 19th and 20th centuries, troops have been used to quell civil disorders, pursue outlaws, and assist local areas in times of natural disasters. For example, there are large consolidated files among the letters received by the Adjutant General relating to the use of troops during the railroad strikes of 1877, the Pullman strike of 1894, raids by outlaws along the Mexican border, the Chicago fire of 1871, the grasshopper plague in Nebraska in 1874–75, and the San Francisco earthquake of 1906, to name only a few. There are files relating to similar subjects for the period after World War I, including the use of troops during race riots.

Both the army and the navy have mapped and explored our country, but the Army Corps of Engineers is most closely associated with this work. Although many reports of expeditions undertaken by the engineers have been printed in the Congressional Serial Set, the records also include maps and the survey notes that accompanied the reports, not all of which were published.

There are letter books, fieldbooks, field reports, topographic atlas sheets, and other records of the Office of the U.S. Geographical Surveys West of the 100th Meridian, 1869–83, often known as the Wheeler Surveys after Captain George M. Wheeler, who was in charge of the surveys.

While the Navy Department always had more global concerns than the War Department, that department has explored and charted parts of the United States. One of the most famous of the 19th-century scientific expeditions, the Wilkes Expedition, was a naval undertaking that explored California and the Pacific Northwest. Records of this famous expedition, including logs and journals, have been microfilmed by the National Archives. Other navy records that may be of interest to local historians are the correspondence and reports of surveys made by the Hydrographic Office and of magnetic and telescopic observations made at various points in the United States under the auspices of the Naval Observatory.

In the 20th century, the U.S. military posture has changed considerably, and so too has modern warfare, involving the civilian population in ways that were unknown in earlier times. On the whole, modern records contain much more data about the mobilization and preparation of the nation's material and manpower resources for war, although they are not entirely lacking from earlier records. Both army and navy records include many files relating to such topics as civil defense, war production, wage compensation, and the seizure of plants. Of special interest are the records of the War Production Board, which exercised general direction over war procurement and production during World War II. These records include detailed files about industrial firms in various areas and about wartime industries. In our present energy crisis it is also pertinent to point to the files relating to oil shale reserves that are among the Navy Department records.

In conclusion, I would like to reiterate that military records are good sources for the study of state and local history. To quote from Dr. Philip C. Brooks, former head of the Truman Library and a luminary in the archival profession: "The riches that lie in countless repositories can be mined productively only if the seeker knows what he is looking for, where he may expect to find it, and how to recognize it." The staff of the Military Archives Division in the National Archives is available to assist researchers with these endeavors.

PART II

THE CITIZEN SOLDIER AND HIS FAMILY

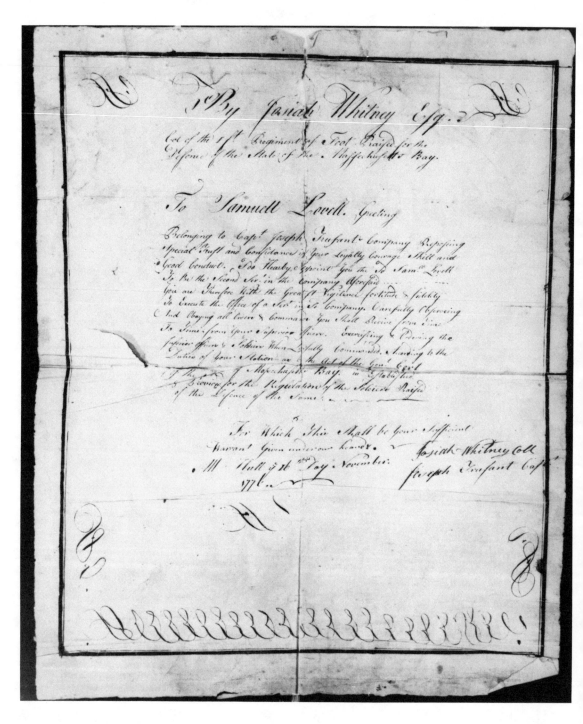

Commission of Samuel Lovel as second sergeant of Captain Joseph Trufant's company, Hull, MA November 16, 1776.

The years from 1774 to 1789 constitute one of the most important and exciting periods in U.S. history. During these 15 years, the colonies proclaimed their independence, waged and won a protracted war with the most powerful nation in the world, established alliances and signed treaties with the major nations of Europe, developed a plan for the settlement of the land that now comprises many of the Midwestern states, and created a governmental system that has lasted almost two centuries, one of the most extraordinary achievements in world history.

The impact of these events on ordinary citizens and local communities was monumental. Evidence of the aftereffect of the Revolution can be found in the series of records described in the following essays. The Revolutionary War pension and bounty-land warrant application files, a part of the Records of the Veterans Administration (Record Group 15), document the military service and postwar lives of tens of thousands of men who served in the War for Independence. The files were created as one result of congressional action to award pensions to the veterans of the Revolutionary War or their descendents. The documents in these 80,000 files provide vivid portraits of individual families before, during, and after the war.

Constance B. Schulz and John P. Resch provide fresh perspectives on these important files. Schulz, an assistant professor of history at the University of South Carolina, provides an overview of the pension files—how they were created and how the pension application process was administered. Resch, an associate professor of history at Merrimack Valley College in New Hampshire, provides a case study of how the pension files can be used to document the history of local communities in the early years of the 19th century.

CONSTANCE B. SCHULZ

Revolutionary War Pension Applications: An Overview

Thousands of documents illustrative of the lives of ordinary Americans are buried in the files of one of the most useful but least used sources for the study of family and social history of the 19th century: the Revolutionary War pension and bounty-land warrant application files. Part of Records of the Veterans Administration, Record Group 15, in the custody of the National Archives and Records Administration (NARA), the estimated 80,000 separate files range in size from a single bounty-land warrant card to hundreds of documents. They were filmed by NARA between 1969 and 1974 and issued in two microfilm publications. In filming the files, the NARA staff selected the most significant genealogical documents and placed them in the front of each file. These "selected records," plus the entire contents of any file containing 10 or fewer documents, constitute the 790 rolls of Microfilm Publication M805, *Selected Records From Revolutionary War Pension and Bounty-Land Warrant Application Files, 1800–1900.* The complete files, an estimated 1.25 million items, make up the 2,670 rolls of Microfilm Publication M804.[1]

Access to information in this formidable body of material is largely through a name index to the veterans for whose service pension or bounty-land warrants were claimed. The index, prepared manually by genealogists from the original files, first appeared in installments in the *National Genealogical Society Quarterly* between 1943 and 1962 and was subsequently

republished by the National Genealogical Society in bound volumes in 1966 and 1976.

This rather brief description scarcely does justice to the wide variety of materials within the files, the usefulness of which genealogists have been aware for years. Until the files were sent to the National Archives, letters of inquiry to the Veterans Administration and predecessor agencies from applicants for membership in the Daughters of the American Revolution, or other similar hereditary societies, were routinely included in the files, along with handwritten or typed summaries of the files prepared in reply by Pension Office clerks. Recently, a number of historians have begun to appreciate the richness of this material for reconstructing the lives of a broad spectrum of people who lived in the first half of the 19th century. This essay will describe in some detail the particular kinds of documentary evidence preserved in the pension records for the vast majority of individuals who left no diaries, few wills, few literary records, indeed few records of any kind. First, it is necessary to describe the history of the legislation responsible for creating this vast body of records, because the changing restrictions in the laws delineating who was eligible to receive payments, and how that eligibility might be proved, determined the kinds of historical evidence in the records.

Pensions for military service, whether awarded to a veteran or to his dependents, fall into two broad general categories: "invalid pensions," based on disability of a soldier caused by his service in the armed forces, and "service pensions," based on some degree of service. To encourage enlistments and discourage desertions, pensions have been part of this country's heritage from the very beginning of its military experience. Colonial governments promised to care for the disabled and for the widows and orphans of wartime casualties, and pension provisions "were commonly included in acts organizing the militia or levying soldiers for some particular military enterprise."[2] To encourage officers to remain in service until the end of the Revolutionary War, in spite of the prevailing fear of the danger of a standing army, a May 15, 1778, resolution of the Continental Congress followed the long-standing example of the British and promised officers who served for the duration of the war half-pay for 7 years after the conclusion of the war. The resolution of October 21, 1780, extended this for life. After the resolution of May 22, 1783, this obligation could be redeemed as a "commutation" payment of 5 years of full pay, either in money or in securities with an annual interest rate of 6 percent. When the war ended, the paymaster general estimated that 2,480 officers were eligible for half-pay or commutation.[3]

Invalid pensions for officers and enlisted men were also enacted by the Continental Congress as early as August 26, 1776. The pension, half-pay for the duration of the disability, promised a small income to veterans of land and sea service incapable of supporting themselves as a result of injuries.[4] In 1782, this was reduced to $5 per month for enlisted men. When the first federal Congress confirmed its obligation to pay invalid pensions and assumed payments for this purpose formerly made by the states, the pensions were fixed at $5 per month for enlisted men and no more than half-pay for officers.[5] The Continental Congress was less generous to dependents. A resolution of August 24, 1780, gave widows and orphans of officers (but not enlisted men) half-pay for 7 years if the officer had enlisted for the remainder of the war.[6]

Until 1818, 35 years after the conclusion

of the war and the disbanding of all but a small "peace-time establishment" army, these arrangements formed the basis for Revolutionary War pensions. Federal acts in 1793, 1803, 1806, and 1808 increased coverage for invalid pensions until the national government was making payments not only to former Continental troops but also to volunteers, militia, and state troops who had "served against the common enemy" before 1783, and to officers and men of the regular army disabled after the war. In 1816, 185 officers and 1,572 enlisted men received $120,000 in invalid pensions for revolutionary service.[7] In that year, Congress raised the monthly payment for enlisted men from $5 to $8, and added $2 or $3 to officer stipends. Widows and orphans, whose time limit for making claim to the 1780 benefit expired in 1794 and was not renewed, received only that part of a benefit left unclaimed at the time of their veteran's death, except in some cases in which Congress passed special legislation to relieve their distress.[8]

The end of the War of 1812 and the accompanying burst of nationalism, an unexpected surplus in the treasury from customs revenues collected on the flood of imports after the establishment of peace, and the growing burden of local relief costs for the aging Revolutionary War veterans and their families led in 1818 to a radical departure from the established pension provisions.[9] In a burst of patriotic rhetoric, trumpeting "Let us show the world that Republics are not ungrateful,"[10] Congress approved, on March 18, 1818, "an act to provide for certain persons engaged in the land and naval service of the United States in the revolutionary war." The act entitled "every commissioned officer, non-commissioned officer, musician, and private soldier, and all officers in the hospital department and medical staff, who served in the war of the revolution until the end thereof, or for the term of nine months, or longer, at any period of the war, on the continental establishment," and each veteran who had served similar terms in the Continental naval establishment "who is, or hereafter, by reason of his reduced circumstances in life, shall be in need of assistance from his country for support," to a pension— $20 per month for officers, $8 monthly for all others. To receive this payment, each applicant had to swear, before a court of record near his residence, to what unit he belonged while in service and when he had entered and left the service. He also had to relinquish his claim to any other federal pension to which he might be entitled.[11]

The documents in the pension file resulting from this law consist of court depositions of veterans and their friends and families swearing to their service, an occasional official paper submitted as proof of honorable discharge at the conclusion of the war, letters from officers attesting to the service claimed, and the obligatory oath that the veteran had served "against the common enemy" and was in need of the assistance of his country. Most of the testimony was oral, recorded in the scrawling script of court stenographers, much of it signed only by the applicant's mark.

Supporters of the 1818 act had assured its opponents that only a few needy veterans of the revolution still survived and that no more than a few thousand would apply for the law's benefits. The flood of applicants, however, totally overwhelmed the ability of the War Department to investigate the eligibility of claims, and in February 1823, Secretary of War John C. Calhoun reported to the Senate that 18,800 claimants were admitted to the pension rolls under the 1818 act. Pension payments in 1818, primarily to invalids eligible under older laws, totaled $105,000; in 1819 payments were $1,811,000. Congress appropriated $2,766,000 for fiscal 1820, but in the face of declining revenues during the Panic of 1819, decided to reevaluate its policies, and on May 1, 1820, adopted a substantial revision of the 1818 act. Veterans would now be required to prove their need for a pension; all payments under the 1818 act were to be suspended until each applicant reappeared in court with a schedule "containing his whole estate and income (his necessary clothing and bedding excepted)," whereupon he was required to take an oath

that that constituted his entire estate or that he had not sold or given away any property in order to qualify for a pension. A copy of these oaths, which were filed in the local court clerk's office, was forwarded to the Secretary of War to determine whether the veteran was "in his opinion, in such indigent circumstances as to be unable to support himself without the assistance of his country." All others were striken from the rolls, with the exception that former invalid pensioners thus removed from the general pension list could be reinstated on the basis of their disability.[12] By September 4, 1822, the pension rolls had been reduced to 12,331 veterans, and Secretary of War Calhoun steadfastly interpreted the law to mean that any individual thus removed from the rolls could not subsequently be reinstated. With a fuller treasury restoring their compassion, Congress passed an act on March 1, 1823, allowing the Secretary of War to restore the benefits of veterans who, subsequent to removal from the list, had fallen below the War Department's poverty level, established by regulation in 1826 at $300 worth of property.

Nevertheless, for the next decade, proof of poverty remained the basis of eligibility for a service pension, with one interesting category of exceptions. The communication certificates for officers had formed the basis for much of the fierce argument over the adoption of Alexander Hamilton's proposal in 1789 to fund the full amount of the federal debt at its face value to the current holders of the certificates. At the time, James Madison had objected that most of those certificates had been sold for ready cash at a loss by the officers who had earned them and had passed into the clutches of speculators. Congress rectified the injustice against the officers resulting from passage of Hamilton's plan by the provisions of a May 15, 1828, law granting full pay for life to surviving officers and enlisted men of the Revolutionary War who had been eligible for benefits under the Continental Congress Resolution of May 15, 1778.[13]

The effect of this series of laws was to increase greatly the number of documents in the

War Department.

REVOLUTIONARY CLAIM.

I CERTIFY that, in conformity with the Law of the United States, of the 18th of March, 1818, *John Bacon* late a *Captain* in the Army of the Revolution, is inscribed on the Pension List, Roll of the *Vermont* Agency, at the rate of *Twenty* dollars per month, to commence on the *Twenty eight* day of *March* one thousand eight hundred and *Eighteen*

GIVEN at the War Office of the United States, this *Fifteenth* day of *July* one thousand eight hundred and *Nineteen*

J. C. Calhoun

Secretary of War.

As Secretary of War, John C. Calhoun had to certify who was eligible for a pension under the 1818 act. This certificate is for Captain John Bacon.

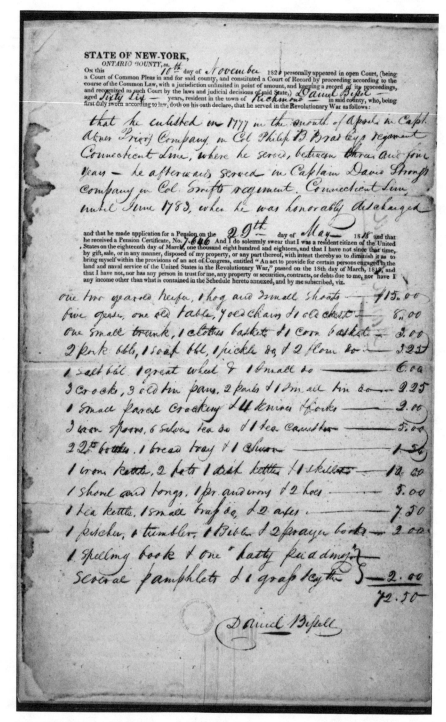

STATE OF NEW-YORK,
ONTARIO COUNTY, ss.

On this *10th* day of *November* 1820 personally appeared in open Court, (being a Court of Common Pleas in and for said county, and constituted a Court of Record by proceeding according to the course of the Common Law, with a jurisdiction unlimited in point of amount, and keeping a record of its proceedings, and recognized as such Court by the laws and judicial decisions of said State,) *Daniel Bissel* aged *sixty six* years, resident in the town of *Richmond* in said county, who, being first duly sworn according to law, doth on his oath declare, that he served in the Revolutionary War as follows:

that he enlisted in 1777 in the month of April in Capt. Abner Priors Company, in Col. Philip B. Bradleys regiment Connecticut Line, where he served, between three and four years — he afterwards served in Captain David Strongs Company in Col. Smiths regiment, Connecticut Line, until June 1783, when he was honorably discharged

and that he made application for a Pension on the *29th* day of *May* 1818 and that he received a Pension Certificate, No. *7.646* And I do solemnly swear that I was a resident citizen of the United States on the eighteenth day of March, one thousand eight hundred and eighteen, and that I have not since that time, by gift, sale, or in any manner, disposed of my property, or any part thereof, with intent thereby so to diminish it as to bring myself within the provisions of an act of Congress, entitled "An act to provide for certain persons engaged in the land and naval service of the United States in the Revolutionary War," passed on the 18th day of March, 1818, and that I have not, nor has any person in trust for me, any property or securities, contracts, or debts due to me, nor have I any income other than what is contained in the Schedule hereto annexed, and by me subscribed, viz.

one two yeared heifa, 1 hog and small shoats	$15.00
five geese, one old table, 7 old chairs & 1 old chest	8.00
one small trunk, 1 clothes basket & 1 corn basket	2.00
2 pork bbls, 1 soap bbl, 1 pickle do & 2 flour do	3.25
1 salt bbl 1 great wheel & 1 small do	6.00
3 crocks, 3 old tin pans, 2 pails & 1 small tin do	2.25
1 small parcel crockery & 4 knives & forks	2.00
3 iron spoons, 6 silver tea do & 1 tea cannister	5.00
2 2£ bottles, 1 bread tray & 1 churn	1.50
1 iron kettle, 2 pots 1 dish kettle & 1 skillet	12.00
1 shovel and tongs, 1 pr. andirons & 2 hoes	5.00
1 tea kettle, 1 small brass do, & 2 axes	7.50
1 pitcher, & tumbler, 1 Bible & 2 prayer books	2.00
1 spelling book & one "hasty pudding"	
several pamphlets & 1 grass scythe }	2.00
	72.50

Daniel Bissell

Daniel Bissell submitted this property schedule listing everything he owned, worth only $72.50. An 1820 law required that pensioners under an 1818 act prove their need of assistance.

pension files. In addition to the newly required property schedules, there were also added substantial depositions detailing the length and type of military service, as a diligent War Department more rigorously examined eligibility on the basis of that service. Letters, copies of deeds of gift, bills of sale, and court decisions relating to indebtedness were submitted to prove that transfer of property had not been intended to defraud the government by making the veteran eligible for a pension. Officers eligible for the full-pay provision of the 1778 resolution and the 1828 act swelled the rolls and expanded the files with their documents. Medical records were added to files, as former invalid pensioners no longer eligible for service pensions because of their wealth were returned to the invalid rolls and were required to submit to biannual medical examination by two surgeons or physicians. Pensioners removed from the rolls often discovered that many of the increasing disabilities of old age had their roots in the hardships or hazardous experiences of Revolutionary War service and applied for disability benefits.

The continued expansion of the federal revenues during the early Jacksonian period stimulated a renewal of efforts in 1829 and 1830 to make service alone, rather than need, the basis for Revolutionary War pensions. The next major revision in pension legislation was enacted on June 7, 1832. It was opposed by southern members of the Senate, who objected to the resulting increase in taxes, while it was supported by senators from impoverished New England states, where lived a substantial number of indigent veterans. This act gave full pay for life to all citizens (foreign officers excluded) who had served for at least 2 years in any military unit. Those who had served less than 2 years, but more than 6 months, were entitled to receive proportionately smaller pensions.[14] During the first months after enactment of the 1832 law, veterans already receiving invalid pensions were required to relinquish them in order to qualify for the new benefits. In 1833, however, Congress passed a supplemental act

(14 Stat. 612) allowing invalids to collect both invalid and service pensions.[15]

No further fundamental changes occurred in pension laws for the veterans themselves. Under this expanded eligibility, an additional 24,000 claims for pensions had been presented to the Pension Bureau by February 1833. In the fall of 1834, 51 years after the conclusion of the Revolutionary War, approximately 40,000 pensioners were on the rolls, or nearly 22 percent of those who had enlisted for Continental, state, and militia service.[16] Twelve pensioners were still alive in April 1864, when Congress granted an additional $100 annual payment to all Revolutionary War pensioners. A February 1865 special bill increased this to $300 annually for the five named individuals then still alive, the last of whom died on June 30, 1867. A special act of Congress thereupon put on the pension rolls at $500 a year the last two survivors of the war, who previously had received no pension. The last pensioned Revolutionary War veteran, Daniel F. Bakeman, died on April 5, 1869, more than 86 years after the Treaty of Paris ended the war.[17]

In 1833, to administer the burgeoning decisionmaking and paperwork that the expanded pension rolls created, Congress authorized the creation of the Office of the Commissioner of Pensions under the supervision of the Secretary of War.[18] The local courts charged with the initial screening and receipt of applications for the new benefits were eventually supplied with a printed form to be filled in for each veteran. This form required each applicant to spell out in detail all of his enlistments, his military units, the names of the officers under which he served, and the engagements in which he had fought. In addition, perhaps to simplify the complicated recordkeeping for local pension office payments in a more mobile society, each applicant was required to state where he had enlisted and to list his dates and places of residence since his discharge. All of these statements had to be sworn to in a court of law and "supported by the statements of two or more character witnesses, including a clergyman if possible."[19] Once again, the pension files ballooned with the addition of new successful applicants for pensions and their various depositions, battle narratives, letters attesting to service, and discharge or other official military papers.

The final series of legislative acts that brought a substantial number of new pension recipients onto the rolls dealt at last with the question of the obligation of the nation to the widows of veterans. The 1832 act had allowed widows and orphans to collect the portion of a pension unpaid at the time of a veteran's death. In 1836, perhaps because of the growing burden on local relief rolls of elderly women whose households had been supported by pension checks until the deaths of their husbands, Congress allowed widows to claim their husband's 1832 act pension as long as they were married before the expiration of his last period of service. Two years later, widows married before January 1, 1794, were granted a 5-year pension; in 1843, 1844, and 1848, these benefits were extended for additional time periods. In a later 1848 act, Congress made the widows' pensions available for life and extended eligibility to those married as late as January 2, 1800. Subsequent congressional acts in 1853 and 1855 made all widows, whenever married, eligible for pensions if their husband would have been eligible under the 1832 act. Finally, in 1878, more than a century after the beginning of the Revolutionary War, widows of soldiers who had served for at least 14 days in any engagement became eligible for lifetime pensions.[20]

This legislation added 22,600 widows' pensions to the rolls because many veterans who did not live to file claims themselves were survived by newly eligible widows. Nearly 5,000 widows received pensions under the strict limitations of the 1836 act, and more were admitted to the pension rolls with each liberalization of eligibility requirements. During the Civil War, widows in seceding states were cut off from pensions, and after the war, in order to be reinstated, they were required to swear that neither they nor their sons had supported the Confederacy. In 1870, there were still 727 Revolutionary War widows on the rolls, 13 of whom were under 60 years of age. The last pensioned Revolutionary War widow, Esther S. Damon, who at the age of 21 in 1835 had married 75-year-old Noah Damon, died on November 11, 1906, at the advanced age of 92. The Pension Bureau estimated in 1915 that total costs for Revolutionary War pensions amounted to approximately $70 million, of which an estimated $20 million was paid to surviving widows.[21]

The widow pension applications added new and even more voluminous documentation to the pension files because these women not only had to prove their husband's service but also (until 1853) had to establish the dates of their marriages. New categories of evidence included sworn testimony from the minister who performed the ceremony, county or parish marriage register records, and reminiscences (duly attested in court) of friends or relatives present at the wedding. Pages torn from family Bibles, sometimes the entire Bible itself, bearing entries either of marriage or of the births of children, were submitted as evidence that a marriage had taken place before the cutoff date for eligibility.

The final category of documentation in the Pension Bureau files related not to pensions but to bounty-land warrants. The Continental Congress, perennially short of currency, had used promises of land from the public domain to encourage men to enlist and remain in Continental service. The basic legislation defining eligibility and benefits was passed in 1776 and 1855. The first act granted the right to free land, in graduated amounts ranging from 100 acres to 1,100 acres dependent upon rank in service, to those who continued to serve until the end of the war. The later act "authorized the issuance of bounty-land warrants for 160 acres to soldiers, irrespective of rank, who had served for as few as 14 days in the Revolution or had taken part in any battle."[22] On November 8, 1800, a disastrous fire in the War Department destroyed all records accumulated in pension and bounty-land warrant files before that date; but early land warrant claims are represented in the present files by single information cards describing the soldier's rank, his state or the organization in which he served, the date his warrant was originally issued, and the name of any other individual to whom the warrant may have been assigned. Other papers of veterans, their dependents, or heirs related to land warrant claims are similar to those for pension applicants, submitted to prove length and type of service.[23]

The opportunities for research in these files—particularly social and family history research—are limitless. The records are rich in detail, providing substantive information on population mobility, occupational patterns, poverty, and health. "In the process of proving pension eligibility," notes John Dann "veterans and their widows trace their individual family histories over time and place as periodic censuses cannot do."[24] Just as important are the anecdotal materials that recount, sometimes vividly, the details of the extraordinary and everyday events of these families, including marriage, childbirth, the loss of a spouse, and the tasks undertaken to keep a family together while a husband was away from home. "We hear," adds Howard H. Peckham, "indeed, we are privileged to overhear what their children and grandchildren must have heard."[25] The Revolutionary War pension files—available for research at the National Archives Building in Washington or on microfilm—provide researchers with insights into the Revolutionary generation unavailable in any other source.

NOTES

1. *Revolutionary War Pension and Bounty-Land Warrant Application Files, 1800–1900*, National Archives Microfilm Publication M804.

2. William Henry Glasson, *Federal Military Pensions in the United States* (1918), p. 18.

3. Ibid., pp. 19–22.

4. Howard Wehmann, *Revolutionary War Pension and Bounty-Land Warrant Application Files, 1800–1900* (1974), pamphlet describing M804, p. 1.

5. Gustavus Adolphus Weber, *The Bureau of Pensions: Its History, Activities, and Organization* (1923), p. 9.

6. Wehmann, *Pension Files*, p. 1.

7. These figures do not include invalid or widow and orphan pensions relating to service in the War of 1812, for which separate legislation existed. The total does include payments made to 443 officers and men injured between 1783 and 1812. Glasson, *Federal Military Pensions*, pp. 26–33.

8. Wehmann, *Pension Files*, p. 3.

9. Evidence of the importance of nationalistic sentiment in the decision to award pensions to the heroes of the Revolutionary War can be seen in the eulogies delivered on the floor of the House and Senate during the course of the debate on the new law; U.S., Congress, *Annals of Congress*, 15th Cong., 1st sess., 1817. The argument that treasury surpluses (and increasingly after 1820, the desire of northern manufacturing interests

to preserve the customs and tariff structure from which they were derived) provided the motivation first for passing and then for perpetuating some sort of service pension is found throughout Glasson, *Federal Military Pensions*, especially pp. 66–68, 69–70, 77–81, 96. The evidence of the burden of indigent veterans on local communities is scattered throughout the pension records and reflected in the considerable effort that local government officials expended in procuring pensions for illiterate and destitute survivors of the Revolution. It is not the purpose of this essay to reexamine the reasons for adoption of the first general pension laws; Glasson's study is marked throughout by the conviction that the passage of those laws was a mistake, the ultimate costly consequences of which were perceived from the outset by southern legislators who had legitimate financial reasons to object to their adoption. His conclusions, therefore, about the importance of the surplus and the tariff as causative factors should be reopened to investigation. One avenue of investigation might be to look more closely at the early versions of the bills, and various committee documents, contained in Records of the U.S. Senate, Record Group 46, and Records of the U.S. House of Representatives, Record Group 233, National Archives.

10. Quoted in Glasson, *Federal Military Pensions*, p. 66.

11. 3 Stat. 410. The laws relating to federal pensions are summarized by Wehmann, *Pension Files*, pp. 2–3; the complete texts are printed in Robert Mayo and Ferdinand Moulton, *Army and Navy Pension Laws and Bounty Land Laws of the United States . . . from 1776 to 1852* (1852), in which the 1818 statute appears on pp. 119–120.

12. Wehmann, *Pension Files*, p. 2; Glasson, *Federal Military Pensions*, pp. 68–72; and Mayo and Moulton, *Army and Navy Pension Laws*, pp. 128–129.

13. Glasson, *Federal Military Pensions*, pp. 76–77; Mayo and Moulton, *Army and Navy Pension Laws*, pp. 132–133; and Wehmann, *Pension Files*, pp. 2–3.

14. Wehmann, *Pension Files*, p. 3. The act is reprinted in Mayo and Moulton, *Army and Navy Pension Laws*, pp. 161–162.

15. Weber, *Bureau of Pensions*, p. 10.

16. Glasson, *Federal Military Pensions*, pp. 86, 89, 90. In a footnote, Glasson observes that this is comparable to a figure of 18 percent of those enlisted in the Civil War who were on the pension rolls in 1915, 50 years after the end of that conflict.

17. Ibid., p. 93.

18. Wehmann, *Pension Files*, p. 4. In March 1849, the Office of Pensions was transferred to the Department of the Interior, where it became known as the Bureau of Pensions.

19. John C. Dann, ed., *The Revolution Remembered: Eyewitness Accounts of the War for Independence* (1980), p. xvii.

20. Wehmann, *Pension Files*, p. 3. The widow pension acts described are those of July 4, 1836 (5 Stat. 128), July 7, 1838 (5 Stat. 303), Mar. 3, 1843 (5 Stat. 647), June 17, 1844 (5 Stat. 680), Feb. 2, 1848 (9 Stat. 210), July 29, 1848 (9 Stat. 265), Feb. 3, 1853 (10 Stat. 154), Feb. 28, 1855 (10 Stat. 616), Mar. 9, 1878 (20 Stat. 29). All are reprinted in Mayo and Moulton, *Army and Navy Pension Laws*.

21. Glasson, *Federal Military Pensions*, pp. 92, 94, 96. Esther S. Damon's file is on roll 733, M804. Her actual married life was brief; her elderly husband abandoned her

and returned to live with his sister in 1848, when he himself became a pensioner. Iron-ically, he died in July 1853, a few months after passage of the 1853 widow pension leg-islation that made his estranged wife eligible for lifetime payments.

22. Wehmann, *Pension Files*, pp. 4–5.

23. Ibid., pp. 8–9.

24. Dann, *Revolution Remembered*, p. xix.

25. Ibid., p. xi.

JOHN P. RESCH

Pension Records and Local History: A Case Study

The Revolutionary War continues to attract researchers and readers interested in the conduct of the opposing armies and the battles that determined the course of the war. Recent histories of the war, however, have focused on the citizen soldier enriching our understanding of the Revolutionary Era. Even though scholars have vividly portrayed the wartime experiences of ordinary citizens and what the Revolution meant to them in later years, they have not been able to agree on who fought the war and why they fought. Some scholars contend that the army was composed of citizen soldiers, while others believe that it was filled with society's dregs. Some scholars argue that patriotism motivated soldiers, others emphasize profit as a motive. The debate on these questions has invigorated military history research by stimulating further study of the ordinary soldier.

One new area of research deals with the lives of ordinary soldiers after they left the service. Some scholars have traced the lives of a few individuals, but little is known about the conditions of the veterans as a whole. The Revolutionary War pension and bounty-land warrant application files, a part of the Records

The author acknowledges the assistance of John Shy of the University of Michigan, David Hackett Fischer of Brandeis University, and the National Endowment for the Humanities.

of the Veterans Administration in the National Archives, provide an opportunity to broaden and deepen our understanding of the men who fought and to address thoroughly the question of what happened to the veterans and their families after the war. In particular, the 20,000 pension applications by veterans of the Continental Army, which compose about a quarter of the pension records, are a rich source of information. The applications were made under the 1818 Revolutionary War Pension Act and its amendments in 1820 and 1823, but they have not previously been studied systematically. These records produce a vivid mural of the veterans and their households about 40 years after the Revolution and provide a major checkpoint for reconstructing the lives of individual soldiers and groups of veterans.

This article combines some results of a collective biography of the 20,000 pension applicants, a study of veterans in a single community, and an illustrative history of one of the community's veterans to address two major issues. The first issue is concerned with the extent, conditions, causes, and consequences of poverty for individuals and their households in the early Republic. The second involves the impact of the pension, a form of federal relief, on the recipients and their households. The article begins with a summary of the 1818 pension act before moving to the collective biography, the community, and the case study to address these issues.

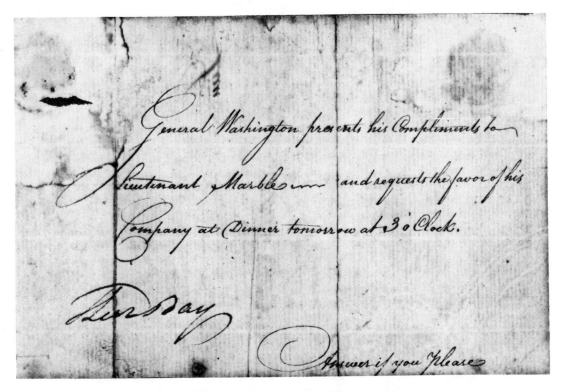

Henry Marble of Massachusetts was invited to dine with General Washington.
Years later the invitation was submitted to prove his military service.

THE 1818 PENSION ACT
AND APPLICANTS

In 1818, Congress combined features of a military pension and a poor-law to provide assistance to veterans of the Continental Army who were "in reduced circumstances."[1] The act created the first federal policy to grant direct relief to a group of poor people. In 1820 the poor-law aspect was stiffened by the addition of a means test. Furthermore, the War Department, which administered the program, applied a wealth line to help determine which applicants were in the "lowest grade of poverty." Nearly 20,000 veterans submitted to the means test; 18,000 were declared eligible for the lifetime pension. An analysis of accepted and rejected claimants reveals that, while no ab-solute poverty line emerged, the department did award pensions primarily to applicants who had less than $100 in personal and real property.

These military pension records provide a wealth of data on elderly, poor survivors of the Revolutionary Era and their households. The data in a typical application includes an inventory of real and personal property, valuation for each item, a court's assessment of the total value of the applicant's property, and the claimant's income, debts, occupation, age, and disabilities. In addition, each applicant had provided the names, ages, and disabilities of all persons in his household and disclosed sources of charity. These military pension applications have been sampled for statistical description and analysis.

Half of the applicants were 65 years of age or older, but only a small portion, about 3 percent, were in their 80s or 90s. Over two-thirds of the veterans reported that they had no occupation, worked as laborers, or were tenant farmers. The remainder were almost equally divided among tradesmen, yeomen, and business proprietors. Nearly 25 percent of all applicants swore that they had once received, were receiving, or would soon be forced to seek charity from their family, friends, or town.

Courts determined the official wealth figures by adding the values of the personal and real property cited on an applicant's estate inventory. Most inventoried estates consisted of household goods, a few farm implements, a couple of animals, some tools, and an occasional decorative piece. Real property was reported in 1 case out of 5, and only 1 veteran in 25 claimed income. Applicants averaged $129 in court-assessed wealth, but half had less an $37 in property. Applicants fell far below contemporary standards of wealth. In 1819, for example, New York state residents had an average of $205 in real and personal property compared with $30 per capita reported by New York state pension applicants.

The records indicate that veterans' household compositions varied greatly. Households averaged between 3 and 4 people, but a large number, 25 percent, had 5 or more members. Only 15 percent of the claimants lived alone. Conjugal households, those composed of only a husband and wife, were reported in more than a quarter of the applications, while nuclear households containing husband, wife, and children were found in nearly half of the claims. Less than 12 percent of the veterans lived in extended households, a figure that falls within the range expected for most Western societies.

A hierarchy of wealth separated the types of households. Solitary veterans were at the lowest level, with an average of $20 in court-assessed wealth, followed by applicants living with kin, who had an average wealth of $64. Conjugal households had an average of $141 in assets, while those at the highest levels were the extended households that functioned as refuges for the veteran's kin or housed non-relatives.

Important distinctions emerged between nuclear households reporting debts and those that did not. The data shows that debtor households contained more males and females 15 years old and older than nondebtor households. Sons and daughters may have remained at home to preserve their stake in their fathers' estates, or filial support of parents may have been more readily given when there was danger of slipping into pauperism than after such a state had been reached.

In nearly one case out of five, applicants claimed dependency. A scaling of need among household types corresponded to the hierarchy of wealth. The percentage claiming aid was highest for solitaries and applicants living with kin. It was lowest for the nuclear households and households where kin were living with the applicant.

The diverse origins and living conditions of the applicants are underscored by statistical data. The claimants were not members of a single impoverished class; they came from various levels of the social structure. The picture shows a mixture of laborers, farm owners, and businessmen; the geographically mobile and immobile; the literate and the illiterate; the very old and the middle-aged; debtors and nondebtors; and the destitute and those on their way to destitution. No one household type characterized these poor. Most households seem to have been in a process of decomposition, yet in a number of instances household recomposition had occurred, as evidenced among claimants living with kin and veterans taking in kin and nonrelatives. In a number of cases, assistance from kin and friends bolstered a weakened household economy. For others, especially the solitaries, who were also the poorest and oldest group of claimants, town relief had become their main support.

While the statistics offer an invaluable picture of the group as a whole, they do not adequately answer questions as to what were the causes and consequences of poverty among the veterans, and what was the impact of federal relief. This essay pursues these issues by studying every Continental soldier in a single community—Peterborough, NH.

Peterborough is a convenient focal point primarily because of an antiquarian's masterpiece.[2] Jonathan Smith reconstructed the military service and included available biographical information for every militiaman and Continental soldier credited to Peterborough. The military service and pension records in the National Archives provide informational check-points for the early and latter parts of the lives of the Peterborough Continentals. In addition, the excellent tax, genealogical, land, town meeting, and church records that exist for the town can help to fill in the gaps.

THE EARLY HISTORY OF PETERBOROUGH

Peterborough was settled in 1750 by Scotch-Irish immigrants who had lived for a time in Townsend and Lunenburg, MA, and in Londonderry, NH.[3] In 1760, the settlement changed from a proprietary to an incorporated town. Even though it was remote, Peterborough was not isolated; for example, in 1775 one out of every four males was out of town sometime during the year in military service. In all, 115 town residents, possibly half of the eligible men aged 15 to 50, were on active duty during the war between 1775 and 1777. A third of these men, 37 in all, were credited with Continental service.[4]

After the war, kin networks and trade increasingly linked the community to broader social economic developments. Between 1780 and 1815, marriages connected Peterborough families back to Townsend, Lunenburg, and Londonderry but also to new settlements like Dublin, Alstead, and Spofford, NH, and Cavendish, VT. During this period Peterborough's economy was more strongly tied to the region's market. In the mid 1790s, paper-making, woolen mills, and related craft shops appeared on a small scale, and in 1809 the town's first cotton mill was constructed. Textile production and paper-making expanded over the next 6 years because of a favorable combination of water power, a work force of farmer/mechanics and women, local investment capital, and an expanding market.

An occupational shift accompanied economic change. Slowly the agrarian population was complemented by mechanics, traders, shopkeepers, mill managers, and laborers; many of them were from Peterborough. The conclusion of the war with England in 1815 resulted in a temporary collapse of manufacturing, and nearly a decade of economic constriction followed. The hard times were exacerbated by a poor harvest in 1816—the year without a summer—and the 1819 panic. Major demographic changes accompanied economic constriction: the town stopped growing; migration from the community accelerated; and it appears that the average age of the population jumped faster than the natural rate because of the exodus of young men and women. The economic recovery, which began about 1822 or 1823, signaled substantial change in Peterborough's character. In particular, the nonfarm population gradually displaced the farm population, and farming sections shrank. For example, in 1819 one outlying farming district, school precinct #5, had 128 residents. In 1840 only 48 people lived in the same area—a drop of over 60 percent. In the same period Peterborough's population rose from 1,500 to 2,163—a 30 percent increase. Furthermore, the increase appeared to be due to new people; that is, families not related to the town's first two generations.

Between 1815 and 1830, major changes occurred in the community's social structure. When founded in the mid-18th century, Peterborough, probably like other New England towns, was built around two kin networks: intermarriage among clan within Peterborough and contiguous settlements and marriage along clan lines back to areas of origin and on to new settlements. By the 1820s, economic and demographic forces had eroded these networks. In the early 19th century, Peterborough's political and religious structures were substantially altered. Partisanship formally splintered the political structure. Disestablishment of churches in 1818 eliminated a principal support of the town's corporateness.

THE SOCIAL PATTERNS OF PETERBOROUGH

A preliminary analysis of Peterborough tax, genealogical, political, and military data reveals several patterns. Among them two demographic patterns stand out. First, town composition was ever changing at a rate historians consider characteristic of cities of the region. About one out of three taxpayers no longer appeared on tax lists within 5 year intervals from 1796 through 1823.

The second demographic pattern contrasts sharply with the first. On the one hand, as pointed out above, Peterborough's society experienced a rapid turnover of families. On the other hand, the social order was stabilized by a core of families who formed the bedrock of the community structure. A comparison of the tax lists for 1796 and 1823 shows that slightly more than half of the families on the 1796 tax list also appear on the 1823 list.[5]

These rough results underscore the presence of at least two social dynamics of nearly equal proportions: an enormous amount of transience and substantial continuity among a large number of families. Knowing this raises further questions for research. For example, what kinds of households and people were involved in each of these processes? Were women residents in 1796 subject to the same dynamics as the men? Were Revolutionary War veterans more or less geographically mobile than non-veterans? Among the veterans, who moved and who stayed? Military and local history sources, such as tax and genealogical records, can be used to answer these questions.

The records reveal distinct patterns of wealth, power, and status among Peterborough residents. The amount and distribution of wealth, as reflected in tax assessments, remained fairly steady from 1796 through 1823. The average tax ranged from about $4.50 to $5.50 and the median tax spread was approximately $3.50 to $4.50. As expected, wealth was tied to political office.[6] Generally, the tax reported by office holders was twice that of the rate payers as a whole. For the most part, office holders were drawn from the top 15 percent of the taxpayers. The amount of wealth was also directly related to the status of members within the town church. In 1799 the wealth of the 32 Coventers averaged over 60 percent more than that of the average church member.

THE CONTINENTALS OF PETERBOROUGH

Thirty-seven Peterborough residents served in the Continental Army, generally enlisting in 1776 or 1777. They were less likely to return to town after the war than were members of the militia. Nearly 55 percent of the Continentals moved away from the town after the war, compared to 45 percent of the militiamen. Furthermore, those who served long enlistments in the Continental Army were more likely to leave Peterborough than those with short enlistments. To be specific, the 20 Continentals who left Peterborough after the war averaged just over 4 years of service, compared to just under 3 years for the 17 who returned to Peterborough. These figures suggest that extended military service may have attracted the least-rooted Peterborough residents and/or acted like a solvent to dissolve weak social ties. Even though 20 residents with Continental service left Peterborough after the war, 7 of the town's new postwar residents had served in the Continental Army. One had served under Peterborough's John Scott, and two had served under Capt. John Parker at Lexington.

In 1818, 18 of the town's 25 Continentals were alive—72 percent. (One more had returned to town in 1816 after a 30 year absence.) Of the remaining 19 who had moved after the war, by 1818 nine were alive, six had died, and four were unaccounted for. If these figures represent survival rates for the whole Continental Army, possibly 63 percent to 73 percent of all veterans were alive in 1818.

In 1818, 12 of the 18 Peterborough Continentals received pensions. Two who did not apply did not meet the military eligibility criterion of at least 9 months service, and one had an invalid pension and died in May 1819. Eight pensioners were continued under the 1820 poor-law provision, two were suspended and later restored, and two more were removed from the rolls for not submitting to the means test. The 10 who fell under the federal government's poverty line collectively produced a profile, based on their application information, that nearly matched the statistical profile of the sample taken from the 20,000 pension applications. In other words, the Peterborough Continentals appear to be a microcosm of the Continental Army survivors previously sampled in pension files.[7]

How and where did the Peterborough Continentals fit in the town? To answer this question I linked the social, economic, political, and military records of 20 men to sketch their biographies. Ten were non-Continentals and the other 10 were Continentals. Five of the non-Continentals were the sons of town founders and the other five came to town during or shortly after the Revolution. The second group of 10 was composed of Continental Army veterans, most of whom fell under the federal government's 1820 poverty line. Many of them were also sons of founders.

The groups produced three distinct social strata that are easy to describe, but a discussion of their significance requires more study. From 1796 to 1823 the 5 sons of founders who did not serve in the Continental Army ranked in the top 10 to 30 percent of taxpayers. In contrast, the 10 Continental veterans never rose above the average amount paid by Peterborough's taxpayers. Those men who settled in Peterborough after the war fell between the two groups.

Other differences appeared in family size and in the number of elective offices. The Continental veterans, in contrast to their fellow townsmen, had substantially fewer children, an average of four and seven respectively. Finally, while some veterans held town offices, office holding was far more prevalent among the other two groups. For example, between 1800 and 1804 the 10 veterans could account for only 4 offices. The other 10 men counted 15 positions among them.[8]

WILLIAM DIAMOND, CONTINENTAL VETERAN

The life of William Diamond may help to illustrate the features of that strata occupied by Peterborough Continentals.[9] Diamond was born in 1755 in Boston, apprenticed as a wheelwright, and at age 19 moved to Lexington presumably to practice his trade. Diamond was a drummer boy under John Parker's command at Lexington, and his flight from the battle and the loss of his drum are part of popular history. Diamond returned to action at Bunker Hill, joined the Continental Army for the New York campaign, and was discharged in July 1777 after a year's service. The roster reports that he was a small man, 5 feet 5 inches tall, and "dark." Diamond's last enlistment was under Capt. Daniel Shays from July to December 1780.

After that enlistment Diamond returned to Lexington. In March 1783, he married Rebecca Simonds of Lexington—6 months later, the first of their six children was born. Diamond had married into a well-established family. Rebecca's great-grandfather had been a founder of Lexington and a large landowner, and her grandfather had held many town offices. The Simonds family had been actively involved in military resistance against the British. In 1795, the Diamond family moved, for unknown reasons, to Peterborough. However, he retained his ties to Lexington through his wife's family.

For 3 years Diamond worked as a "laborer" living as a tenant on Asa Carley's farm. His last child was born there. In 1798, Diamond purchased 60 acres of wild land for $200 put up by his brother-in-law. For the next 8 years Diamond appears to have worked as a farm laborer and at his wheelwright trade while converting those 60 acres of wild land into a farm. By 1806, Diamond had become a husbandman, aided by his two sons William and John. He had moved into a solid position among Peterborough's poorest third with a small farm (still mortgaged to his brother-in-law) and a trade. In 1811, at age 56, Diamond identified himself as a "yeoman," retired the mortgage on his farm, and sold a small portion of his holdings to a Peterborough resident, possibly for profit or to help pay off the mortgage.

In 1817, at age 62, Diamond secured continued support for himself and his wife by dividing his farm between William (age 33) and John (age 27)—both unmarried. Title, however, was not formally transferred to the sons for 4 and 11 years, respectively, possibly as a precaution to ensure filial support. The following year Diamond received his pension under the 1818 Revolutionary War Pension Act. He claimed to be "very destitute of property." While that was not the case, he was in the lowest third of taxpayers and his sons were even lower. The "ownership" of the property was shared by father and sons at this time.

The pension, as in other cases studied, bolstered the family's fortunes. That year Diamond's sons bought additional land next to their shares of the farm. These transactions underscored the continued mingling of family and financial ties back to Massachusetts. The seller was Abel Davis, a "gentleman" from Concord, MA. In 1819, Davis's daughter, Octavia, married John Diamond. These connections to Massachusetts through marriage and land purchases suggest that the Diamond household was more closely tied to friends and kin in Concord and Lexington than to its neighbors in Peterborough. The fact that between 1796 and 1823 none of the Diamonds held a town office, even though a few men of similar economic standing held minor town posts, also indicates that the Diamonds were not fully a part of the Peterborough community.

In 1820, Diamond reapplied for the pension. He claimed no real property, $42 in livestock, and a life lease on 32 acres at $6 per year. His household consisted of his wife and his daughter Lydia and her two children who had been abandoned by their father. Diamond said "he was unable to work" and owed "$50.00" in debts.

The report was obviously incomplete and not completely accurate. Only after Diamond was continued on the rolls did son William take legal title of his share of his father's farm (March 16, 1821). The lease Diamond referred to was not transacted with son John until October 1822. Diamond appeared to live with John and his family, paying John lease money and contributing what he could to the household.

While his oldest son had gained property and household independence—he married in 1822 at age 37—Diamond's younger son struggled. He appeared to have been hurt by Peterborough's economic contraction from 1816 to 1823. In 1820 and 1822, John sold and mortgaged some of his land, possibly to meet debts. The full impact of these difficulties seems to have been mitigated by the kin economy bolstered by Diamond's pension and lease. That economy was upset by the veteran's death in 1828. His estate of $163 was whittled down to $4 after debts were paid. Shortly thereafter, John's economic fortunes declined. He sold his share of Diamond's farm to his brother, turned to his Massachusetts in-laws for help to purchase land, and struggled to make a living as a wheelwright. Not until 1834, at age 44, had John recovered enough property to be taxed at his 1827 rate of $3.35. He remained at that level, in the lower third of rate payers, for the rest of his life. Brother William never suffered the bad luck that his brother did; William glided along at the same level his father had reached in 1816. Neither brother ever was able to exceed the economic status of their father.

Father and sons climbed and oscillated within a narrow band of Peterborough's society, working with each other and with kin in Massachusetts. They had achieved a measure of independence as small farmers and craftsmen. The crucial transition period in life when Diamond had to provide for his own and his sons' security and secure a stake for his sons was marked by general economic contraction and panic.

This story, multiplied by the thousands of pension applicants, reinforces the picture of the precarious grasp veterans had on their holdings and status at a time of economic contraction and transition in proprietory rights from father to son. The pension smoothed out the bumpy economic road somewhat and provided an opportunity for the family to strengthen its grip on the little it had worked so long to obtain. William succeeded in holding on. John slipped when the pension ended with his father's death, but slowly recovered to renew his hold on the third lowest rung of Peterborough's economic ladder.

In closing, Peterborough's preindustrial community offers a complex of structures and dynamic processes. Comparable European studies suggest that these structures and processes can be woven into a complete community fabric, but the research on Peterborough veterans and the Diamond household is beginning to indicate another approach to understanding local history. While the community as a whole continues to be interesting, it may not be the nexus of the varied patterns emerging from these early findings. Instead, economic strata may have discrete characteristics and may not be bound together by any interconnecting processes. Theories of vertical mobility within the community therefore seem less applicable to Peterborough than a notion of rhythmic change within the community's various strata. The most powerful social dynamics may occur within the strata, not among them. As a consequence, the meaning of local history—as this study of Continentals and the Diamond household suggests—may have to expand beyond reference to a small geographical area. In Peterborough's case, social dynamics may best be understood through the reconstruction of community strata and kin networks that extended beyond the community. The larger question that takes center stage is how these different Peterborough economic and kin networks were affected by the Revolution, military service, and change.

NOTES

1. The following account of the pension act and statistical study of the Revolutionary War pension files summarizes a more complete discussion of the pension legislation and application data that appeared in a previously published article. See John P. Resch, "Federal Welfare for Revolutionary War Veterans," *Social Service Review* 56 (June 1982): 171–195.

2. Jonathan Smith, *Peterborough, New Hampshire, in the American Revolution* (1913). John Shy referred to Smith's book as "an antiquarian work so carefully wrought that it invites systematic analysis." Shy used Smith's history as a basis for his article on Peterborough's "Long Bill" Scott. John Shy, "Hearts and Minds in the American Revolution: The Case of "Long Bill" Scott and Peterborough, New Hampshire," in John Shy, *A People Numerous and Armed* (1976), pp. 163–179.

3. This sketch of Peterborough's history synthesizes information from a number of different sources. For an account of Peterborough's settlement and institutions see Albert Smith, *History of the Town of Peterborough*, 2 parts (1876).

Also see accounts of the church and ecclesiastical history of Peterborough. These accounts, which were anonymously written, can be found in the manuscript collection of the Peterborough Historical Society. Other manuscript sources that contributed to the town history include the Unitarian Church Records and the Samuel Smith papers, all in the manuscript collection of the Peterborough Historical Society. Histories of individual Peterborough families added to the sketch of the town's history. See George Abbot Morison, *Nathaniel Morison and His Descendents* (1951); George W. Moore, *The Moore Family, 1848–1924* (1925); John Hopkins Morison, *A Memoir* (1897); and Jonathan Smith, *The Home of the Smith Family in Peterborough, New Hampshire* (1900). Also see *Historical Sketches of Peterborough, New Hampshire* (1938), pp. 1–8, 33–41, 149–177, 277–286.

The information about marriage patterns and kin networks is drawn largely from Albert Smith, "Genealogy and History of the Peterborough Families," found in Smith, *History of the Town of Peterborough*, part 2, pp. 1–365.

4. The estimate of the total number of eligible males of military age, 15 to 50, living in Peterborough from 1775 to 1777 was derived from the genealogical data found in Smith, *History of the Town of Peterborough*, part 2, pp. 1–365. Those data were quantified for statistical analysis.

5. Peterborough resident valuation lists exist for 1792, 1796, and onward. Earlier lists were reported lost in a fire. I have recorded tax information and the name of the rate payer for 1792 and for 1796 through 1823 in data files for quantitative analysis using the Statistical Package for the Social Sciences (SPSS). With this data it is possible to trace the amount of tax paid by each rate payer or group of taxpayers. See *Peterborough Tax Lists* on microfilm at the Peterborough Town Hall.

6. For a list of town office holders see *Peterborough Town Book*, volumes 1 and 2, 1760–1856, located in the Peterborough Town Hall, and a list of town officers in the manuscript collection of the Peterborough Historical Society.

7. Smith, *Peterborough, New Hampshire in the American Revolution* provided detailed information on the service records of each soldier, militia and Continental, who was credited to Peterborough. Additional information was obtained from the applications for pensions under the 1818 Revolutionary War Pension Act as amended in 1820. The following is a list of the 10 Peterborough residents who received a pension under the amended act: Benjamin Alld, Revolutionary War Pension File S45498 (hereafter cited as Pension File); William Blair, Pension File W21680; William Diamond, Pension File W22911; John Scott, Pension File W24918; David Smiley, Pension File S43164; Samuel Spear, Pension File S43171; Amos Spofford, Pension File W22292; John Swan, Pension File S43992; James Taggart, Pension File S43192; Christopher Thayer, Pension File S43994; Records of the Veterans Administration, Record Group 15, National Archives (hereafter cited as RG15, NA).

8. The 20 men were chosen from the genealogical information on Peterborough families. Their selection from a larger pool of eligible males was based on two criteria. The first was to limit the number of men chosen because of the large amount of information to be compiled by hand on each person. The second criterion was to select those men with fairly complete tax, office-holding, and genealogical information. The 10 Continentals, including men who did not receive a pension, were William Blair, William Diamond, Randall McAllister, John Scott, William Scott, Jr., David Smiley, Samuel Spear, Amos Spofford, John Swan, and Christopher Thayer. The five town founders or their children included James Cunningham, Nathaniel Holmes, Samuel Miller, Jr., David Steele,

and John Todd. The five men who moved to Peterborough during or shortly after the Revolution who were chosen for this study were Timothy Ames, Oliver Carter, Jr., John Field, Kelso Gray, and James Porter.

9. This discussion of William Diamond's life is a synthesis of material from a wide range of sources. Military and genealogical information appeared in Smith, *Peterborough, New Hampshire, in the American Revolution*, pp. 405–408; Smith, "Genealogy and History of the Peterborough Families," found in Smith, *History of the Town of Peterborough*, part 2, pp. 53–55. Tax information was found for every year from 1796 to Diamond's death in 1828 in the Peterborough Tax Lists, Peterborough Town Hall. William Diamond's land sales, leases, and mortgages and those of his sons are recorded in the Hillsborough County Deed Records (hereafter cited as HCDR) in Nashua, NH. See HCDR Book 47, p. 199; Book 47, p. 288; Book 48, p. 455; Book 90, p. 572; Book 92, p. 478; Book 133, p. 408; Book 138, p. 8; Book 154, pp. 485–486. For transactions involving Diamond's sons but not including the father, William Diamond, see HCDR Book 126, p. 292; Book 135, pp. 30–31; Book 140, p. 164; Book 150, pp. 92, 323, 447; Book 153, p. 403; Book 154, p. 486; Book 158, pp. 110–111; Book 215, p. 522; Book 222, p. 537. William Diamond died intestate but his estate was inventoried. See Hillsborough County Court, Probate Court Records, 02641. Diamond's wife's estate and his son William's will are also recorded: Hillsborough County Court House, Probate Court Records 02871 and 1756. For information on the Simonds or Symonds family in Lexington, MA, see Charles Hudson, *History of the Town of Lexington* (1868), pp. 214–219. Also see William Diamond, Pension File W22941, RG15, NA.

PART *III*

CITIZENSHIP
IN THE
EARLY AMERICAN
REPUBLIC

United States of America,

STATE OF MARYLAND—TO WIT:

WILLIAM WARNER, Print.

I, JOHN GILL, *Notary Public by Letters Patent under the Great Seal of the State of Maryland, Commissioned and duly Qualified, residing in the City of Baltimore, in the State aforesaid, do hereby* **Certify, Attest, and Make Known,** *That, on the day of the date hereof, before me personally appeared* John Guyer
an American ~~Seaman~~ Merchant
Aged twenty three *Years or thereabouts.*
Height five — *Feet,* eight & three quarters *Inches.*
Complexion dark
Eyes dark hazle
Hair very dark nearly black
both the little fingers a little crooked inwards. has a Mole on the left Side

Who being by me duly and solemnly Sworn did depose and say that he is a Native *Citizen of the United States of America, being* ~~born~~
—— *at* Annapolis —— *State of* Maryland and
~~At the same time appeared before me the said Notary~~

~~Who being by me duly and solemnly Sworn did depose and say that a has been acquainted with the above named and described~~

Which I Notary attests

In Testimony Whereof, *The said Deponent ha*th *hereunto subscribed* his *Name and I the said Notary, have hereunto set* my *Hand, and affixed my Notarial Seal, the* 17th *Day of* March —
in the Year of our Lord, One Thousand Eight Hundred and fourteen

John Guyer

Jno. Gill Not. Pub.

Citizenship paper for John Guyer, 1814.

58

In 1782, a Frenchman named Michel-Guillaume Jean De Crèvecoeur published a little book that posed a question that all of Europe was asking. "Who, then, is this new man, this American?" Crèvecoeur asked. In many ways this was also the most fundamental question to be answered by Americans during the last quarter of the 18th century and the first quarter of the 19th century. As Americans set out to establish themselves in the worlds of art, science, and literature, they wished to send a message to Europe and the world that declared the existence of a distinctly American culture. On a practical and administrative level, Americans also had to establish a mechanism for documenting who was an American citizen and who was not. It was not always enough for a man to proclaim himself an American; in certain circumstances, he also had to prove his citizenship.

The essays that follow provide insights into two problems faced by the federal government during the early years of the republic. To prove citizenship on the high seas and thereby avoid impressment into the British navy, for example, American merchant seamen carried "protection certificates" that attested to their citizenship and provided detailed descriptions of their physical appearance. The applications for these certificates are a wonderful source for family history. Moreover, the federal government kept detailed records on the movement of enemy aliens and prisoners of war who were in the United States during the War of 1812. Because many of these aliens became American citizens after the war, their descendents may find useful information in the "War of 1812 Papers."

The authors of these essays bring diverse backgrounds to the task of describing the two series of records. Ira Dye is a retired navy captain who has written extensively on merchant seamen of the early 19th century. He is currently a Senior Research Fellow in the School of Engineering at the University of Virginia. Sarah Larson is a private consultant on genealogy and local history who has worked extensively with the holdings of the National Archives.

The Philadelphia Seamen's Protection Certificate Applications

Are you looking for a forebear who was a sea captain or a jack tar in the early days of the republic? Or are you interested in the social history of the labor force of early America? Perhaps you would like to take a close, intimate look at the sailors who manned our frigates and privateers in the War of 1812.

For any or all of the above, there is a set of records in the National Archives that is unmatched in its detail and in the sense of immediacy that it conveys even at a distance of 175 years—the Philadelphia seamen's protection certificate applications.

These records—about 10,000 of them for sailors of the 1796–1820 period plus another 38,000 for 1820 until the Civil War—are an accidental survival, all that remains of perhaps ten times that many records originally issued in the various seaports of the east and gulf coasts in our early years.

Like many of the records in the Archives, they came into being as the result of a problem, which led to a law, which then required certain information to be collected.

The problem in this case was impressment—the forced recruitment—of American sailors into the British Navy. This practice was a major irritant to Americans from the start of the Napoleonic wars in 1793 until their final end in 1815.

Impressment was the Royal Navy's legal and time-honored means of recruitment in times of crisis. In times of peace there were usually enough volunteers and men sent in by the courts to man the ships. But when war impended or an expansion of the navy for other reasons was directed by the British government, the authority was given to press. All British citizens who were seafarers of any description—merchant sailors, fishermen, watermen of the rivers and harbors—were fair game to be forcibly recruited in British ports by Royal Navy "press gangs" or to be taken from British vessels at sea.[1]

Before independence, American seafarers—still British subjects—could legally be pressed, and often were. However, after the Treaty of Paris in 1783, the United States was recognized as a separate nation and her sailors were legally beyond the reach of the press—although not in fact beyond the reach of the ubiquitous Royal Navy.

The problem came to a head in the early 1790s. England went to war with revolutionary France and a rapid expansion of the Royal Navy began. There were always lots of American ships in British ports—England was our largest trading partner—and, given old habits, language similarities, and the fact that many British sailors served on American merchant ships, many sailors—both British and American—were impressed from American ships in British ports and, a little later, at sea.[2] The British did not assert the right to impress

American citizens. What they did say was that British subjects could not of themselves give up their British citizenship, even if they wanted to. Thus, they not only took bona fide British sailors, but also seized British-born sailors who declared themselves to have become naturalized American citizens. And frequently they went beyond this and took native-born Americans as well. This became wide-spread enough to enrage a lot of Americans, although, surprisingly, few shipowners cared much about it one way or the other.

Then, as now, noisy wheels usually resulted in Congress' applying some grease. In this case, the Fourth Congress in May 1796 passed, and President Washington signed into law, the Act for the Relief and Protection of American Seamen.

Then, as now, laws tended to produce paperwork, and this one generated quite a bit. The surviving fragments of this paperwork are the subject of this discussion.

The act provided a way for the seafarer to obtain an official document identifying him as an American citizen. The process was designed to be simple: The seaman was to bring some authenticated proof of his American citizenship to the collector of customs in any one of the 26 U.S. ports of the time, and the collector was to give him a document that would protect him from being impressed. The original thought was that the seaman would be able to get a birth record from his town or his parish, but it soon developed that many—if not most—sailors were too transient to have any town roots, were often operating far from their birthplaces, and, in any event, were from a social strata for which few records were kept. Therefore, the requirement was relaxed to allow a sailor to bring to the collector an affidavit, sworn to by the seaman and one witness, that he was a citizen. This obviously opened the way for some abuse of the system. A British sailor wishing to avoid impressment could, for example, find a friend to be his witness, swear he was born in Wiscasset, MA, or wherever, and, if the notary taking the affidavit was complaisant or not alert, the sailor

would receive a legal document—an affidavit—that he could take to the collector of customs and exchange for an official, U.S.-backed certificate in the form provided by the act. The British government was aware of this weakness in the system and asserted that none of the certificates issued by the collectors were any good. However, the certificates were normally accepted as proof of American citizenship if the description on a certificate matched the appearance of the bearer and if the bearer did not have a strong British accent.

The affidavit or proof of citizenship that was brought in by the sailor is called the "Seaman's Protection Certificate Application," which we will refer to as the SPCA. The certificate that the collector gave to the seaman is called the "Seaman's Protection Certificate," which we will call the SPC. In the common parlance of the day, this was the "Protection."

There were some other provisions of the act that are beyond the scope of this discussion.[3] I will briefly note two of these provisions in the course of this essay. Each collector was required to keep a book into which were entered the names of the seamen receiving protections. Some of these books apparently survive in personal and historical society collections, but I have never been able to locate the ones (there would be several) for Philadelphia. Also, the collectors were required to send to the State Department, each quarter, lists of seamen receiving protections. Many of these lists survive in the State Department records in the National Archives.[4]

Only fragmentary groups of SPCAs and SPCs survive, particularly for the early years.[5] Protections were issued in all 26 of the active ports of the pre-1820 period and in a broader group of ports as time went on. There were about 100,000 Americans active in the seafaring work force in 1810, which is roughly the time of the peak of the impressment problem, and nearly all of them obtained protections. This is a "steady-state" figure, meaning that between 1796 and 1820 probably twice that many passed into and out of the seafaring group, usually obtaining protections sometime in the process. In Philadelphia alone about 26,000 protections were issued before January 1819.

Very few of these records remain for any port other than Philadelphia, where 9,761 SPCAs survive from a total of 25,948 SPCs issued between the passage of the law in mid-1796 and the end of 1818. For most of the period from 1819 to 1861 (when the surviving records end), the records seem to be complete or nearly so. This essay is concerned primarily with the early records, those from 1796–1818; those from 1819 to 1861 will be dealt with only briefly. The table shows the year-dates and serial numbers for the surviving 1796–1818 SPCAs. You can see from the table that only scattered "clumps" of SPCAs are extant for the very early years, but that starting in 1804 there are sizable numbers of them extant for most years.

What information is available in the early records, and how can we most easily get access to it?

Although the Philadelphia SPCAs were prepared by a variety of aldermen, notaries, and other public officials, each of the printed forms (and the totally manuscript SPCAs) record nearly the same information, the required information having probably been specified by the collector:

- The name and age of the seaman, and, if he was nonwhite, one of the quasi-legal racial designators that were in common use at the time; e.g., "a free black man";
- His height, hair color, eye color, and complexion;
- Scars, other distinguishing marks, and tattoos;
- His stated place of birth, or place and date of naturalization, or a statement that he was a resident of the United States prior to September 3, 1783—the date of the Treaty of Paris, which established the international legal independence of the United States;

- His signature (or mark) swearing to the truth of the information;
- The name and signature (or mark) of a witness, swearing that the facts about the seaman were true "to the best of his knowledge and belief";
- The name and title of the official giving the oath;[6] and
- The date the oath was taken.

When the SPCA was brought to the collector he put a serial number on it, the same serial number that was put on the protection certificate then issued to the seaman. If at some later date the seaman lost the protection and wanted a duplicate issued to him, he went again before an oath-taking official, swore that he had lost it, and received *another* piece of paper—an affidavit describing the loss and requesting a new one. The collector then issued a duplicate protection (with the original number), noted this fact on the back of the SPCA in his files, and filed the new paper with the SPCA.[7]

The later SPCA records, for the period after 1820 and preceding the Civil War, are less informative. Even before the end of the Napoleonic wars in 1815, the British Navy was demobilizing, and by the 1820s most seafarers were convinced that any real danger of impressment was behind them. However, the protection certificate continued to be of practical use to the seafarer as an identification document and continued to be issued under the 1796 law. However, in Philadelphia the method for obtaining them changed, the sailor coming directly to the collector of customs, where a clerk filled out a minimum set of information on an application form—less than the usually full description of earlier times and without the signature of a witness.

Now, returning to the pre-1819 SPCAs, there are very few sources that have this range of information about specific nonprominent Americans of that period. Here we can see what an individual sailor looked like, get a pretty good idea of how literate he was, and in

List of Surviving Philadelphia Seamen's Protection Certificate Applications 1796–1818

Year	Number SPCAs surviving (approx.)	Number SPCs originally issued (approx.)	Inclusive Nos. originally issued (approx.)
1796	13	800	1– 800
1797	13	1,200	800– 2,000
1798	358	1,000	2,000– 3,000
1799	9	1,450	3,000– 4,450
1800	3	1,950	4,450– 6,400
1801	191	1,650	6,400– 8,050
1802	1	800	8,050– 8,850
1803	258	1,250	8,850–10,100
1804	780	1,800	10,100–11,900
1805	710	1,620	11,900–13,520
1806	660	1,620	13,520–15,140
1807	680	1,480	15,140–16,620
1808	180	530	16,620–17,150
1809	990	1,280	17,150–18,430
1810	1,040	1,070	18,430–19,500
1811	835	850	19,500–20,350
1812	250	540	20,350–20,890
1813	210	260	20,890–21,150*
1814	165	1,225	21,150–22,375*
1815	1,105	1,125	22,375–23,500
1816	310	520	23,500–24,020
1817	470	1,400	24,020–25,420*
1818	500	530	25,420–25,950

*It is uncertain whether some of these numbers were originally issued.

his witness see the name and signature of a friend or, quite often, a relative. Or, if we wish, we can look at these early seafarers as a group.

Let us look at the use of this information from three perspectives. First, we are looking for a specific individual by name; second, we wish to examine individuals, but are not searching for anyone specific; and third, we want to look at seafarers as a group, or at a subgroup of them.

Searching for an individual among these chronologically (not alphabetically) organized records appears at first sight to be a close to overwhelming task. However, take heart. About one-quarter of the roughly 10,000 pre-1818 records have been alphabetized, and the rest of them can be checked in about 6 hours of steady work—not counting the time needed

to get the records down from the stacks. The records are filed in order of the certificate (SPC) number, which places them in roughly chronological order. Each SPCA is folded "in-three" like a standard modern business letter and has the name of the seafarer and the number written on the back, where it can be easily seen without opening the certificate. The certificates are tied in bundles of 100 numbers with genuine government red tape, now faded to a pinkish white. If one is searching for a name, the certificates can be riffled through without untying the bundles.

As noted above, some of the records are alphabetized. The 785 records surviving from the period from March 1812 to May 1815 are available in the Microfilm Research Room, organized not only alphabetically but also by state of birth.[8] All surviving records from the start of the SPC program in 1796 through the end of 1803—a total of 853 records—are also alphabetized, and queries as to individual names may be directed to the author. Also alphabetized are the records of 970 men between 1796 and 1818 whose records show tattooing. Queries related to these can also be directed to the author.

Looking through these records in search of anecdotal material about early seafarers, or perhaps simply trying to get a feel for what these men were like, is very rewarding. Would you like to see what kinds of pictures they were tattooed with? Look at the SPCA of William Gaines, No. 12279, who had 30 tattoos; Samuel Anderson, No. 11314, who had nine; or, more typical, Joseph Martien, No. 20410, with four. Do you like footnotes to history? Look up the record of Marcus Marsh, whose application is dated March 2, 1798, and folded inside you will find a manuscript note from the widow of Richard Stockton, prominent Revolution Era patriot and signer of the Declaration of Independence, giving Marcus, born a slave in the Stockton family, his freedom. For black history, the SPCAs are particularly rich—see the record of Israel Clark, No. 19016, or many, many others.

Using these records as a lens through which to look at our early seafarers as a group can be a very rewarding experience, although some serious work is required. Some work has been done in this area, but there is a lot of scope for more. A paper by the author, published in 1976, could serve as a starting point.[9] A very useful project would be to computerize the records for the periods 1804 to March 1812 and June 1815 to December 1818. A more thorough analysis of the SPCAs of black seafarers would also be useful. The author would be very interested in being contacted by anyone planning serious work in these records.

So, these are the Philadelphia seamen's protection certificate records. Go to the National Archives and look at some of them. You will be transported back 175 years as you unfold them and some of the sand cast on the wet ink by a long-dead Philadelphia notary sifts onto your desk in the Archives reading room.

NOTES

1. The net did not always stop there—landsmen of all descriptions were frequently caught up by the press.

2. International law of the day did not recognize merchant ships as extensions of the territory of a sovereign nation.

3. For greater depth, see J. F. Zimmerman, *Impressment of American Seamen* (1925; reprint ed., Kennikat Press, 1966).

4. Quarterly abstracts have survived from 48 ports, usually in small quantities and usually from the period after 1815. These abstracts give the name of each seaman and very brief descriptive material.

5. Beyond the Philadelphia records, which are the subject of this article, some individual protection application forms survive from the ports of Alexandria, Bath, Middletown, New Haven, New London, New Orleans, Newport, and Nantucket Island. From New York, some affidavit-applications plus a few actual protection certificates survive. This material is in Records of the Bureau of Customs, Record Group 36, National Archives.

6. There were roughly 100 officials in Philadelphia of the kind authorized to take these oaths: the mayor, aldermen, justices of the peace, and notaries. Not surprisingly, the ones near the waterfront got most of the business.

7. The loss of a protection is frequently described in terms such as, "It was taken from me and torn up before my eyes by the boarding officer from HMS_____." There is always the possibility, of course, that it was sold or given to some Britisher who wanted one.

8. *Computer Processed Tabulations of Data From Seamen's Protective Certificate Applications to the Collector of Customs for the Port of Philadelphia, 1812–1815,* National Archives Microfilm Publication M972.

9. Ira Dye, "Early American Merchant Seafarers," *Proceedings of the American Philosophical Society* 120 (Oct. 1976): 331–360.

The War of 1812 Papers
of the State Department

Caught in the backwash of the War of 1812, Dr. George K. Jackson, church organist, teacher of music, and British citizen, was wrenched from his family in Boston by administrative fiat in March 1813 and dispatched to Northampton, MA, as an enemy alien.

This enemy alien had come from England in 1795 with his wife and three small children, determined to take up permanent residence and "prosecute my profession as an Organist and teacher of Music."[1] After some 10 years in New York City, he accepted a commission from the large Brattle Street Church of Boston in mid-1812.

Pursuant to a congressional directive ordering all British subjects to register their whereabouts and loyalties with their district marshal, Jackson had dutifully reported to the marshal in New York in July 1812. But he evidently did not believe that his departure for Boston in August would be of interest to anyone except his new congregation. It was only weeks after the February 1813 deadline had passed that Jackson learned he should have registered with the marshal of his new district.

By failing to report, Jackson automatically became a suspicious enemy alien ordered removed from the coast by the State Department to prevent contact with the British. Thus did Jackson find himself in Northampton, unable to support his wife and, by this time, five children.[2]

The case was immediately appealed to James Monroe, Secretary of State, and from the letters of influential friends there emerges a portrait of Jackson: gifted, trustworthy, and pleasantly peculiar. "Sir, you may be assured that the old gentleman is so incapable of hostile designs against our country or its government, [he] is so much absorbed in his musical engagements which he pursues with devoted enthusiasm, that I believe scarcely any political event would for a moment abstract him from these favorite pursuits," wrote one friend.[3] Another wrote, "His whole life has been engaged in promoting Concord in all the Senses either as moral, musical, or a political Good And his Exile to the Banks of the Connecticut has greatly interrupted the Harmony of our Circles both public and private."[4] The writer added that the church congregation was "sadly deranged" by Jackson's removal.

The Standing Committee of the Brattle Street Church urged Monroe to return their organist, pointing out that Jackson had showed no evidence of a "hostile disposition": "We regret the necessity which subjects him at an advanced period of life with an infirm habit of body, to leave the society of his family and to travel at this season to a distant place."[5] The committee stressed that Jackson was willing to take an oath of allegiance and would have become a citizen long since were it not "that his children have some little property in England, which he has been apprehensive might be affected thereby."[6]

Even the district marshal wrote Monroe to the effect that the musician was less an enemy alien than an inept alien, while the father of one of Jackson's students wrote that Jackson was:

Withal, a quiet, urbane harmless creature, disqualified by mind, body, and disposition to take any active part in anything beyond a concerto . . . I can imagine no shadow of blame that can be imputed to him, but his having been professionally engaged to perform an ode at the celebration of the Russian Victories (which he did *not* however perform), but the poor fellow would perform an ode anywhere and upon any occasion, so that the music were good.[7]

The case of "Dr. Jackson, Professor of Musick" continued into June of 1813, with Congressman Artemas Ward (Federalist, MA) providing the comment, "He is too full of music to have any room for treason."[8]

Ironically, this man who lived almost exclusively for music, who cared nothing for international affairs, achieved immortality of a sort because of the War of 1812. Had he not been removed to Northampton there would be no collection of testimonials and appeals on his behalf preserved as part of the national record. There would be no description of his immigration and settlement in America, no mention of the property still owned in England, no suggestion of whimsy to delight the researcher and inform the descendant.

WAR OF 1812 PAPERS

These fragments of the story of Dr. Jackson are among the "War of 1812 Papers" of the Department of State, 1789–1815. Part of the General Records of the Department of State, Record Group 59, the papers make up the seven rolls of National Archives Microfilm Publication M588. The "War of 1812 Papers" include intercepted correspondence as well as records relating to letters of marque, enemy aliens, passports, passenger lists, and prisoners of war.

Rarely do the microfilmed records present a complete story. There is no indication that Dr. Jackson was returned to his family and congregation in Boston before the end of the war. However, the problem of incompleteness is a familiar one to genealogists and local historians who rely primarily on government documents that were never intended to preserve the history of community or family.

But no single body of records is complete for any researcher, no matter what the field. Research is, after all, not a matter of looking up the answer but of tracking down the answer, of following leads, of piecing together a patchwork out of seemingly unrelated scraps of information. In the "War of 1812 Papers," the genealogist and local historian may find information that will add a new dimension to work in progress. But these are not records to approach without prior research. The genealogist must be sufficiently well-versed in his family's history to know whether a hunt through War of 1812 documents is even pertinent. Likewise, the local historian must be familiar with the community under study or the names and letters and lists encountered will have little significance.

As with the use of any federal records, it is essential to begin by considering what government body generated the documents and for what purpose. The "War of 1812 Papers" represent the expanded activities of a wartime State Department. Nearly all the letters and reports are addressed to Secretary of State James Monroe or President James Madison. This was no mere formality; there was virtually no bureaucracy to pass the letters on to. In 1801, the State Department consisted of one chief clerk, seven lesser clerks, and a messenger; 20 years later, the staff had grown by only two clerks, an assistant messenger, a laborer, and two watchmen.[9] The chief peacetime responsibilities were corresponding with foreign and American ministers of state and with governors, judicial officers, marshals, and U.S. attorneys; issuing passports; compiling passenger lists of those entering the United States and of registered seamen; preserving public papers; printing laws; and supervising the Patent Office and the census.[10]

Being small, the government was highly personal. Thus, it is not unusual to find among the "War of 1812 Papers" a letter from an enemy alien making pointed reference to a previous conversation with Monroe. Moreover, since Madison preceded Monroe as Secretary

STRICTLY *confidential* . The commanders of private armed vessels are to keep this paper connected with a piece of lead, or other weight, and to throw the whole overboard before they shall strike their flag—that they may be sunk, and not fall into the hands of the enemy. For this purpose a cover of sheet lead will be the most convenient. And such commanders are not to allow any person whatever, excepting *one confidential officer* , ever to *see, or to have a copy* of, this paper, or to be in any manner *apprized of its contents* , on pain of forfeiting their commissions, and incurring all the penalties of law.

That our *public* and our *private armed vessels* may be able to *know each other at sea* , the following *signals are established:*

On falling in with each other, the private armed vessel will hoist two flags, one above the other, and fire two guns to leeward, viz.

[red.] [blue.] The public ship of war will answer by hoisting any two of her flags, one above the other, and firing one gun to windward.

The private armed vessel will then haul down the two flags first displayed, and hoist one flag on the mainmast, viz:

[white.] The public ship of war will answer by hauling down her two flags first displayed, and hoisting one flag on the mainmast on hoisting this flag she will cease to give chace, and the private armed vessel will immediately join her, unless the public ship should then hoist a white flag; in which case the private vessel will be at liberty to pursue her course.

By command of the President.

Secretary of State.

of State and took a lively interest in the department, there is many a note from the President regarding some supplicant.[11]

This focus on the individual runs as a common theme throughout the "War of 1812 Papers" and is the key to their use. Though incomplete and largely unindexed, the papers contain a wealth of information about individuals and communities. The papers are also beguilingly interesting and it is no hardship to go through the microfilm frame-by-frame treasure hunting. In most cases, the researcher who wishes to learn whether the passport was actually issued or whether the enemy aliens in a community were allowed to remain in their homes must go beyond the "War of 1812 Papers" to state and local records. Yet the papers may well provide the unknown birthplace or an overlooked business relationship. Petitioners wrote in great detail to prove their loyalty to America and their need to have their requests granted.

A comparatively small collection of records of surprising diversity, the "War of 1812 Papers" indicate how the war affected the daily lives of people, disturbing the peace of their communities. The papers are yet another demonstration that the unlikeliest government forms and records yield details that breathe life into person, place, or period.

Roll 1: Letters Received Concerning Letters of Marque and Enemy Aliens, 1812-14

When America declared war on England in 1812, the U.S. Navy squared off against the greatest sea power in the world with only 5 frigates in commission and 5 laid up for repairs, 3 sloops, 7 brigs, and 62 coastal gunboats.[12] The Republican government had refused to prepare for war, fearful that increasing taxes, debt, military forces, and the executive branch would destroy republican principles.[13] Casually dismissive, the *London Times* described the U.S. Navy as a "few fir built frigates with strips of bunting, manned by sons of bitches and outlaws."[14]

The *Times* failed to take into consideration American privateers—in effect the navy's militia.[15] Privateers were privately owned armed ships authorized by law to prey upon any British vessel.

American-designed merchant ships proved admirably suited to commerce raiding; they were light and had both speed and "an uncanny ability to sail into the wind."[16] Able to outrun warships, these American trading vessels could out-maneuver and outfight British merchantmen. There were some 526 American privateers, many of whom made only one or two raids on British ships. According to Marshall Smelser, "The privateers of this war were the most successful of all time," taking between 1,300 and 1,400 prizes.[17] While not crippling, these losses proved highly annoying to British merchants who not only lost cargo but paid escalating insurance rates.[18] Just as important, these successful naval duels raised public spirits by causing the British to reassess "the Power whose maritime strength we have hitherto impolitically held in contempt."[19]

Letters of marque, of which there are only a few in the microfilm, were signed by both Madison and Monroe. The bearer was authorized to capture any British vessel and haul it into the nearest American or "friendly" foreign port. All prizes were divided between shipowners, officers, and crew, with 2 percent of the net paid over to the port collector of customs as a fund for widows and orphans of the war dead and for the support of those disabled while serving aboard a privateer.[20] Both the applications for letters of marque and lists of those to whom permits were issued are highly informative. Applicants described the vessel and crew; named all owners, the commander, and the first lieutenant; detailed number and kinds of arms; and posted bond, naming two disinterested individuals as sureties. Consider the possibilities. A genealogist could discover that a seafaring ancestor with no military record had gone off to do battle with the privateer militia or that a landlocked forebear had owned an interest in a merchant vessel. Interesting to both local historian and genealogist are the business relationships revealed by the listing of shipowners, commanders, and those who stood as sureties.

Roll 1 contains many lists summarizing the letters of marque issued. Drawn up by customs collectors in the various districts, these summaries include all the information required of applicants and neatly identify shipowners of like intentions. The lists are not arranged in any particular order on the microfilm.

There are also numerous letters pertaining to enemy aliens. Once all subjects of Great Britain in America were declared enemy aliens, proof of citizenship, already of concern to seamen in danger of British impressment, became a general preoccupation. There was no federal office that issued citizenship papers. Rather, citizenship was handled on the state level by the courts. For example, a Baltimore notary signed the citizenship paper of John Guyer, merchant, "Aged twenty-three Years or thereabouts. Height five Feet, eight & three quarter Inches. Complexion dark. Eyes hazle [sic]. Hair very dark nearly black, both little fingers a little crooked inwards has a Mole on left Side."[21]

Unindexed and unarranged, the letters regarding enemy aliens—usually from the alien or his witnesses—are valuable for the detailed personal information they contain. From these anxious petitions, the researcher may glean suggestions for further research. One such letter is that of John Harden, removed to the interior from Charleston, SC.

A "mechanic [artisan] by profession," Harden had worked many years in America as a tobacconist, for proof of which he directed attention to his Charleston tax returns. He had never engaged in trade, except for "now and then a small consignment of Bacon . . . sometimes a few shingles, the Commission amounted in the Year to a mere nothing."[22] Harden wished permission to invest his "small capital" in a brewing business with a friend in Alexandria, VA, or at least to be allowed to move to a place "where I might embrace my accustomed industry—being tired of this idle life."[23]

The researcher may now turn to Charleston tax returns, to records of the city of Alexandria, and possibly to the records of the Society of Friends. The petitioner addressed his letter, "Friend," used "thee" and "thy" throughout, and signed it "very Respectfully thy friend John Harden."[24]

Rolls 2 and 3: U.S. Marshal's Returns of Enemy Aliens and Prisoners of War, 1812–15

Including those from Ireland and Canada, there were thousands of British subjects in America at the outbreak of the war. Many of them had moved to the United States as permanent residents but had not yet been able to satisfy the terms of naturalization. As happens to immigrants in every war, when hostilities broke out these British subjects were suddenly suspect as spies.

The lists of enemy aliens drawn up by district marshals for submission to the State Department show name, age, time in the United States, family size, place of residence, occupation, date of application for naturalization, and remarks. Apparently, women were not considered to be a threat to American security. Marshals did not record the names of wives nor do there appear to be any single women listed in the microfilm. When enemy aliens were ordered to be removed from the coast inland, husbands left wives and children behind.

Fortunately there is an index to rolls 2 and 3: Kenneth Scott's *British Aliens in the United States During the War of 1812*.[25] Scott points out in his introduction that these reports are not just of interest to the genealogist in pursuit of a specific person.[26] Economic patterns can be picked out, revealing rapidly expanding areas that attracted skilled immigrant labor.

But these records do more than suggest the texture of American economic and social development. They show, with both poignancy and humor, how inconvenient it was to be an enemy alien. Consider the case of Thomas Higham, enemy alien from Charleston, SC. Higham was taken with seven other enemy aliens to a hotel in Columbia, SC, far from the coast and far from his wife and two children. Never robust, Higham found the move "Northward" disastrous to his health. "Since my return to the Northward, I have been severely afflicted by a Nervous and Rheumatic affection in the head, which Kept me in great agony for many days, and confined me to my room for several weeks."[27]

Higham explained that his doctor had determined that he should take the sea air just before the State Department ordered him inland. Pointing out that he engaged in no commerce except the collection of prewar debts, and that he was the author of several religious essays as well as secretary of the Charleston Society for the Advancement of Christianity, Higham asked to travel to mineral springs within the United States and to cruise with his family to any neutral port. Stressing that his wife was a loyal native of Charleston and that he had been an upstanding resident of South Carolina since his arrival from England in September 1805, Higham concluded with a physical description of himself—presumably to facilitate the making out of a passport.

It's hard not to be amused by Thomas Higham's intermingled protestations of loyalty to the United States and his descriptions of ill health. "I had scarcely recovered from a severe illness when the order of the Government appeared, in March, to remove Aliens from the Sea Coast. Unwilling to be the cause of an Exception, and in the hope of benefiting my health, I came hither [to Columbia] at a short notice."[28] It is hard to remain unmoved by an afterthought tacked onto a letter: "Please to . . . accept my best wishes for the health and happiness of yourself and family. I have two fine little boys who with their Mother were well by the last accounts from Charleston."[29] Thomas Higham was eventually allowed to travel to the hot springs in Virginia and New York.[30]

In another case, Adam Donaldson of Fredericksburg, VA, was surprised to find himself pronounced an enemy alien and carted off to the interior. Donaldson, being "extremely illiterate," didn't realize that he was a foreigner. "He failed to become a Citizen under the laws of our Country, from Ignorance & not Intention; believing as he declares that his intermarriage with a native Woman & the acquiring of Property gave him all the Privileges of an American Citizen."[31] Evidently, civil authorities had been somewhat casual about Donaldson's status also; he'd been serving on juries and civil patrols for years. On the strength of his marriage, government officials acceded to pleas that Donaldson "be permitted to return & pursue his *little Business* which is a very confined & limited Grocery, without any article of dry Goods whatever."[32]

Some letters regarding enemy aliens amount virtually to a family saga. The case of

Hall Neilson, of Richmond, VA, is one of the few in which the entire story is told by the records on microfilm, from the first testimonials submitted by friends to a scribbled note including his name on a list of aliens permitted to return home. Here is a case where research persistence pays off. Three hundred frames after the case is introduced, there are letters detailing the continuing efforts to secure Neilson's release. Forty frames on, in one brief note, is evidence of the success of those efforts.

The Neilson family included seven brothers and two sisters, all of whom came to America from Ireland over a 20-year period. In keeping with the times, the sisters weren't even identified by name in the records. But the efforts of the brothers to create a small mercantile empire are richly detailed. In the early 1790s, John, the eldest, and Samuel came to Augusta, GA, to establish the first mercantile firm. Thomas, in America since childhood, settled permanently in Petersburg, VA, in 1806. Robert landed in Richmond and by 1813 was a citizen and able to defend vigorously his three youngest brothers who had been transformed into enemy aliens. Hall arrived in Richmond in 1807, where he settled as a merchant, but William and James, arriving in 1811, traveled for some months before choosing Norfolk as a likely spot.[33]

These Irish immigrants did not use their large, competent family to insulate themselves from their new country. Hall Neilson's loyalty was vouched for by Richmond's elite, including the mayor. All attested to his sound character and good business sense, one adding in a back-page postscript, "I am just informed by an intimate friend of Mr. Neilson, in whom I place entire Confidence, that he is very much attached to our Republican Institutions."[34] Though Hall Neilson had never lived in the city, a testimonial was drawn up on his behalf by nine Philadelphia merchants.[35]

Reflecting the intimacy of government, Robert Neilson finally went to Washington to sort out the tangle, with another Philadelphian smoothing the way by mail.[36] Three months later, it was reported that the brothers had been allowed to return home.[37]

The "War of 1812 Papers" contain tantalizingly incomplete lists of prisoners of war from both sides. Roll 3 of M588 gives lists of prisoners in no particular order and with no index. But these handwritten rosters make good reading. There is the "List of [American] Prisoners sent from Halifax N.S. to England under various pretences."[38] And the "Exchange List of 73 Officers & Privates of the United States Militia Captured at Detroit," in which a major is worth eight British soldiers, a captain six, a lieutenant four, an ensign three, and a private one.[39]

Though information varies from list to list, most of the prisoner reports note name, rank, regiment or vessel, where and when captured, and date of exchange. Many also indicate age, place of birth, place of enlistment, physical description, and by whom captured. It gives a sense of the diversity of the army to find John Shaw, "blackman," and John Baptist, "dark Mulatto," among the fair and light-complexioned British prisoners.[40]

Roll 4: Requests for Permission to Sail From the United States, and Passenger Lists of Outgoing Vessels, 1812–14

Roll 4 must be approached with a magnifying glass; the microfilm is exceptionally light and difficult to read. But that which is legible gives an inkling of how the war disrupted the shipping industry.

How galling it must have been for men from the adamantly Federalist northeast to be forced to apply to a Republican President and Secretary of State for permission to sail. The war was unpopular enough in New England without its serving as an excuse for the pro-agrarian Republicans to supervise the shipping industry.

Applications for permission to sail are much like those requesting letters of marque. The ship is described, the crew enumerated, and the owners and commander usually named. There were three ways in which shipping was regulated: issuance of passports to individuals, issuance of passports to ships, and approval of the provisioning of ships preparing to depart.

Interspersed with the formal applications for passports are complaints. John Downey wrote fretfully to Monroe that he had been waiting weeks for his passport with his crew on board and on the payroll and his provisions rotting in the hold. Monroe, in turn, sent a brusque note to an American navy officer, requesting him to ascertain why the British ship *Bostock* hadn't left port, having long since been given all necessary passports and supplies.[41]

With the passport complaints and supplications are passenger lists, most of which show name and nationality, occupation, age, date of arrival in the United States, complexion, and color of hair and eyes. Most of the lists on roll 4 of M588 are for the port of Philadelphia and, with a few exceptions, are grouped together at the end of the reel. Many of the lists are virtually impossible to read, the faded ink trailing across the page in a cramped scrawl.

Roll 5: Correspondence Regarding Passports, 1812–14

The letters requesting passports illustrate how varied in background and occupation the population of America was in 1812. For instance, there was Joseph Pametti, an Italian who came to America in December 1792, settling permanently in New York City. Pametti was naturalized in 1802 and he owned $10,000 worth of property in Havana, Cuba, which required immediate personal attention.[42] Pametti hastened to add, however, that he had every intention of returning to America quickly.

J. Watts of New York applied for a passport in the name of art. Thrusting aside personal considerations, Watts argued:

> I have reasons for going to Europe which I trust will appear to you of importance. This is the advancement of an art (casting Stereotype plates for printing) which I have for some time practiced in this city with much success; but, for want of a few facilities only to be obtained

in Europe, the business cannot be carried on to such an advantage as to place us on a par with the English foundries.[43]

Lest this appeal to James Monroe's patriotism was insufficient, Watts added that he had been encouraged to write by Monroe's "well known love of the arts, the advancement of which, it is hoped, will not be impeded by the war."[44]

William Nugent's request for a passport reads like Horatio Alger in reverse. A native of Ireland, Nugent came to the United States in 1810 because he had heard that aliens with legal training would be admitted to the New York bar. "To his great Mortification," Nugent discovered that the rules of the court had been altered. "Being thus defeated in the great object of his coming here, and having nothing but his profession to look to for the support of himself and Wife, he was reduced nearly to want the necessities of life."[45] Nugent finally found work in an office as a writer at a salary his employer unabashedly described as "so small as not to afford a living to himself and family."[46] While that employer seemed disinclined to pay a living wage, he did write a stirring letter to Monroe, pointing out that Nugent had come to America in good faith and, should he be removed to the interior rather than given a passport to return to Ireland, "he and his family must either be Supported by the Parish, or Starve."[47]

Roll 6: Agreements for the Exchange of Prisoners of War, 1812, 1813; Miscellaneous Letters Received Concerning the Release of Prisoners, 1812–15; Reports of William Lambert, Secret Agent, 1813; Memorandum Regarding Proper Dress for a U.S. Minister

In an era when the rules of international law and diplomacy are suspended at will, it seems incredible that the belligerents in the War of 1812 could have at each other on the battlefield and simultaneously sit down to draw up an agreement on the expeditious exchange of prisoners. Yet, in November 1812, British and American lawyers, officers, and diplomats drew up an agreement for the exchange of prisoners of war.[48] Prisoners would be treated humanely and exchanged as quickly as possible, with officers of increasing rank being worth a greater number of men.

Each side would employ agents to handle prisoner exchanges and, should one party have no one to trade, the other party could release its prisoners on parole. Specific ports were identified in which prisoners would be held. Thus, the British agreed to hold all their captives at Halifax, Nova Scotia; Bridgetown, Barbados; Kingston, Jamaica; and Falmouth and Liverpool, England. The United States pledged to keep prisoners only at Salem, MA; Schenectady, NY; Providence, RI; Wilmington, DE; Annapolis, MD; Savannah, GA; and New Orleans, LA. What might seem humane and expeditious to warring nations, however, might seem less so to the prisoner. One American writing for help reported that he was one of 65 hostages on board a prison ship in Halifax and "God only knows when we shall be liberated."[49] Urging that someone intervene to arrange his exchange or parole, he added, "Six months is a very long time to be a prisoner."[50]

Each side accused the other of inhumanity; while the British were aghast at the barbarism of Americans who tried to perfect a submarine missile to blow up enemy vessels, the Americans pointed to men like impressed seaman Richards who, refusing to fire upon an American privateer, was beaten and thrown into a prison ship with broken ribs and a gashed head. "He replied that it was useless to beat him, they might kill him for he could never think of firing into any Vessel that bore his Country's flag."[51]

The lists of American prisoners sprinkled throughout roll 6 of M588 are detailed, most including name, rank, brief history of capture, and an abstract of each prisoner's personal history. Thus, there is George Jackson, belonging to the schooner *Madisonia*, bound from Brazil to the District of Columbia, taken on August 3, 1812, by the *Garland*. Jackson had sailed from New Orleans on February 9, 1808, in the ship *Experiment* of Philadelphia bound to Montevideo and remained in South America until he returned to America in the *Madisonia*.[52]

Best of all are the letters that appeal to one's risibilities. In 1813, a bottle washed on shore at Chatham, NY, with a message inside from John Banks, an impressed American seaman wishing to be rescued. Evidently Banks had been captured 5 or 6 years earlier, though his message had only been bobbing towards shore for 3 months.[53] The microfilm includes several letters from Banks's uncle and brother in Hampton, VA, but there is no indication that anyone learned, for purposes of liberation, which ship Banks was on.

Less dramatic is a missive from Nathaniel Miles to his nephew John Siters, prisoner aboard the H.M.S. *Leviathan*: "I set Down to write under impressions of both Joy & sorrow, that notwithstanding your afflicted state that you are still in the Land of the living."[54] Miles was doing his best to document his nephew's American citizenship and obtain his release. However, Miles did not want Siters to go haring off around the world again: "Think of your Aged, feeble & tender Mother, and your Disconsolate Wife & return to your Native happy Land where you may enjoy the blessings of this life in abundance, Lest a greater Judgment over take you."[55]

The remainder of roll 6 of the "War of 1812 Papers" is given over to reports from secret agent William Lambert, who spent a great deal of time fretting that the war was passing him by as he perched at the mouth of the Chesapeake.[56] However, his tenure was not without its moments. "The near approach of the enemy to this place, has occasioned considerable alarm; and every family on the shores have moved . . . this circumstance will prevent me from giving a particular statement of vessels passing up and down the Potomac, for some time to come, if it ever has been of any service to the community."[57]

Roll 6 closes with instructions for the dress of American foreign ministers, specifying em-

broidered cuffs, gold knee buckles, white silk stockings, a three-cornered chapeau bras with black cockade, and a sword.[58]

Roll 7: Miscellaneous Intercepted Correspondence, 1789–1814

Roll 7 offers an array of largely unrelated intercepted British correspondence, probably of little use to the genealogist but of some potential to the local historian. The letters discuss British policy in the Great Lakes region, ranging from mundane supply orders to strategy on dealing with the local population.

Most interesting is the section "British Military Correspondence Relating Principally to Indian Affairs on the U.S.-Canadian Frontier, October 1789–October 1807." In a jumble of letters many times folded, there is a discussion of the British plan to form alliances with Indians as a hedge against war with the United States. There are translations of formal speeches delivered by Indian diplomats, pledging loyalty to the British they knew and asking the British to honor their word and stop distributing alcohol among the tribes.

Of themselves, the documents in roll 7 would give, at best, a fragmentary history of the region. But coupled with other research the materials could help clarify the Indian/British/American relations of the period.

Such is the case with most of the documents in the "War of 1812 Papers." Alone, they are a curiosity, well worth an afternoon at the microfilm reader. Placed in the context of broader research, however, they may well provide the missing fact, the overlooked perspective. The papers are rich enough to support a variety of approaches but, in the last analysis, their usefulness will depend almost entirely on researcher focus and diligence.

RELATED RECORDS

Probably the best areas of related research are in state and local records. From the detailed personal information in the "War of 1812 Papers," the researcher can trace the early wanderings of an immigrant ancestor from town to town or perhaps turn to county tax and court records to discover the fate of a local manufacturer who benefited from the labor of enemy aliens.

There are, however, easily accessible federal records that amplify the "War of 1812 Papers." Two microfilm publications, both of which come from the Records of the District Courts of the United States, Record Group 21, relate to the efforts of American privateers.

The *War of 1812 Prize Case Files of the U.S. District Court for the Eastern District of Pennsylvania, 1812–1815,* National Archives Microfilm Publication M966, consists of two rolls of film covering 38 cases:

The documents reproduced include libels, monitions, warrants of arrest, interrogations, depositions, claims of owners, claims of parties interested in the cargo, various orders of the court, court declarations, sentences of condemnation, court opinions, private and official correspondence, bills of sale for prize property, copies of court proceedings sent from Drontheim, Norway, and letters of marque from President James Madison. Prize papers presented as exhibits include certificates of registry, British letters of marque, orders to sail, port clearances, ship manifests, bills of lading, receipts, correspondence, indentures, bills of health, British licenses, logs, and other papers.[59]

The cases are arranged numerically, mostly in the order in which they appeared in court, with the documents arranged by date of filing.

The *Prize and Related Records for the War of 1812 of the U.S. District Court for the Southern District of New York, 1812–1816,* National Archives Microfilm Publication M928, is similar in content to M966. Covering nine rolls of microfilm, the case files are arranged alphabetically by name of the prize vessel, with the documents within each case organized primarily by date of filing.

On roll 9 of microfilm publication M928 are privateers' papers, 1812, consisting principally of letters of attorneys and last will and testaments executed by crews of commissioned privateer vessels, as well as "prize tickets," or certificates indicating the number of shares of prize money to which the holder was entitled. The documents are arranged alphabetically by name of privateer vessel. Also on roll 9 are papers relating to the U.S. frigate *Essex,* 1812–16. Arranged chronologically, the documents in this section pertain to the privateering agreements between officers and crew.

There are four lists of impressed American seamen among the printed *American State Papers (ASP),* which can be found in government depository libraries. The local public library will have the address of the nearest depository library.

The first list was presented to Congress March 8, 1806, and was drawn from an application made to the British government in cases of impressment from September 1, 1804, to May 18, 1805. The list includes more than 700 names of seamen, the dates of impressment, the ships of war onto which they were impressed, and remarks relating to citizenship (*ASP,* vol. 2, doc. 196).

A second list was presented to Congress March 2, 1808, and contains the names of 697 seamen, the date and place of impressment, the names of the vessels onto which they were impressed, and the nationality of the seamen (*ASP,* vol. 3, doc. 212).

Congress received two final lists of seamen April 27, 1816. The first shows the names of 1,421 seamen impressed into the service of British public ships and transferred into English prisons as prisoners of war. The second has the names of 219 impressed seamen who were transferred to prisons in the West Indies or Nova Scotia. Both provide the names of seamen impressed, their rank, the name of the British man-of-war that impressed them, the place confined, the date of release, the vessel in which they returned to the United States, and their date of arrival (*ASP,* vol. 4, doc. 282).

NOTES

1. *"War of 1812 Papers"* of the Department of State, 1789–1815, National Archives Microfilm Publication M588 (hereinafter cited as M588), roll 2, fr. 0431.

2. Ibid., frs. 0432–0433.

3. Ibid., fr. 0447.

4. Ibid., fr. 0444.

5. Ibid., fr. 0436.

6. Ibid., frs. 0436–0437.

7. Ibid., frs. 0440–0441, 0453–0454.

8. Ibid., fr. 0456.

9. Leonard D. White, *The Jeffersonians, A Study in Administrative History, 1801–1829* (1951), p. 187.

10. Ibid.

11. Ibid., pp. 184–185.

12. J. Mackay Hitsman, *The Incredible War of 1812* (1965), p. 42.

13. Bernard Bailyn et al., *The Great Republic* (1977), p. 384.

14. John K. Mahon, *The War of 1812* (1972), p. 9.

15. Bailyn, *Great Republic*, p. 384.

16. Mahon, *War of 1812*, p. 255.

17. Marshall Smelser, *The Democratic Republic, 1801–1815* (1968), p. 275.

18. Harry L. Coles, *The War of 1812* (1965), p. 98.

19. Hitsman, *Incredible War*, p. 234.

20. M588, roll 1, frs. 0324–0326.

21. Ibid., fr. 0355.

22. Ibid., fr. 0360.

23. Ibid.

24. Ibid.

25. Kenneth Scott, *British Aliens in the United States During the War of 1812* (1979).

26. Ibid., p. vi.

27. M588, roll 2, fr. 0466.

28. Ibid., fr. 0471.

29. Ibid., fr. 0469.

30. Scott, *British Aliens*, p. 384.

31. M588, roll 3, fr. 0153.

32. Scott, *British Aliens*, p. 384; M588, roll 3, fr. 0153.

33. M588, roll 3, fr. 0161.

34. Ibid., fr. 0139.

35. Ibid., fr. 0141.

36. Ibid., frs. 0444–0446.

37. Ibid., fr. 0480.

38. Ibid., frs. 0571–0574.

39. Ibid., frs. 0617–0618.

40. Ibid., fr. 0829.

41. M588, roll 4, frs. 0126, 0156.

42. Ibid., roll 5, frs. 0539–0540.

43. Ibid., fr. 0073.

44. Ibid., fr. 0074.

45. Ibid., fr. 0160.

46. Ibid.

47. Ibid., fr. 0161.

48. M588, roll 6, frs. 0019–0020.

49. Ibid., fr. 0163.

50. Ibid., fr. 0164.

51. Ibid., fr. 0083.

52. Ibid., fr. 0066.

53. Ibid., fr. 0087.

54. Ibid., fr. 0112.

55. Ibid.

56. Ibid., fr. 0197.

57. Ibid., fr. 0225.

58. Ibid., frs. 0281–0282.

59. National Archives Microfilm Publications Pamphlet Describing M966, *War of 1812 Prize Case Files of the U.S. District Court for the Eastern District of Pennsylvania, 1812–1815* (1974), p. 2.

PART IV

FAMILIES AND COMMUNITIES ON THE AMERICAN FRONTIER

Oklahoma land rush town, circa 1890.

The American frontier is imagined as a scene of log cabins, military forts, trappers, prospectors, Indians, and vast expanses of wilderness. The men and women who settled the frontier are believed to have been a hearty band of independent individuals who had little or no contact with law, order, or government. However, these popular notions obscure a more accurate understanding of frontier families and communities and their extensive involvement with the federal government.

The National Archives has thousands of cubic feet of records that document the lives of individuals, their families, and their communities on the American frontier. One of the essays that follows, Jane Smith's study of Linden Township in Iowa County, WI, draws on more than a dozen record groups to describe the history of this frontier community in the years before statehood was established in 1848. The second essay, by James Oberly, shows how federal bounty-land warrants affected veterans of the Mexican War.

The authors of these essays are well qualified to write on their topics. Until her retirement in 1979, Jane Smith was the director of the Civil Archives Division at the National Archives, where she had supervisory responsibility for most of the records that she used in her essay. Her article was published in the inaugural issue of *Prologue* and has been widely reprinted. A former archivist, James Oberly researched and wrote his essay while still a doctoral student at the University of Rochester. He is currently an assistant professor of history at the University of Wisconsin at Eau Claire.

JANE F. SMITH

Federal Records of the American Frontier: A Case Study

Many scholars probably assume that the records of the federal government in the National Archives contribute mainly to an understanding of broad national policies and problems or to events associated with them. What is not so often realized is that a large proportion of the records of the executive, legislative, and judicial branches of the government are concerned with regional and local issues and events and are therefore essential to the writing of regional, state, and local history. In many ways, such local histories as we now have would need to be rewritten, or at least extensively revised, if the potential value of the relevant federal archives came to be fully appreciated and used.

Almost 50 years ago in an article published in the *Wisconsin Magazine of History,* Prof. Joseph Schafer, Superintendent of the State Historical Society of Wisconsin, asserted that "there should be a plat book or atlas that will give the student of Wisconsin history immediate access to the names of first settlers in each section of the state, together with an ocular account of the lands they occupied, as these are located upon the plats."[1] In this article and in an address entitled "The Microscopic Method

The author wishes to thank James C. Brown, David Gibson, Clarence Lyons, James Paulauskas, James Walker, and Charles Zaid for their help in finding documents used in the preparation of this essay.

Applied to History,"[2] read at the annual meeting of the Minnesota Historical Society on January 17, 1921, Professor Schafer outlined his plans for a "Wisconsin Domesday Book." Briefly stated, by using the original survey plats and the surveyor's notes, the tractbooks preserved in the U.S. land offices, and the census schedules and local records, he proposed "to prepare and publish, partly in the form of an atlas and partly in the form of text, the pioneer history of all the townships of Wisconsin."[3] Four volumes of his "Wisconsin Domesday Book," including a study of the Wisconsin lead region, were eventually published.[4]

This essay employs the microscopic method to show that records in the National Archives can be used to develop the pattern of settlement and pioneer history of a typical township: township 5 N., range 2 E., of the fourth principal meridian, Iowa County, WI (later known as Linden Township).[5] This township was selected because it was more typical of pioneer settlement than the adjacent township 5 N., range 3 E., which includes Mineral Point, the most important town in the entire lead mine area of southwestern Wisconsin during the early 19th century and the residence of many of the most influential business and professional men in Iowa County.[6] It should be noted, however, that the same series of records cited in this essay can be used to develop the pattern of settlement and pioneer history not only of a Wisconsin township but of any township in any or all of the 30 public land states.

The David Dale Owen report and manuscript map of southwestern Wisconsin provide an excellent starting point for detailing the history of township 5 N., range 2 E. The appendix to the report describes the township as "About half rolling prairie; good timber in the southeast, chiefly white oak; well watered by streams and springs. Soil: poor, clayey, second rate; surface broken. Sub-soil: Clay. . . . The most important diggings in this township are on 8; they extend east and west for about half a mile, and are called the '*Pedlar's* [sic] creek diggings.' The amount of ore raised could not be ascertained. There are several other diggings, of less importance, that are noted on the township map."[7] The map also indicates that there were at least 27 individuals living in the township in the autumn of 1839 (see fig. 1 and the accompanying table).

Confirmation of Owen's findings and more precise identification of most of these pioneers were obtained by an examination of the 1840 census schedules for Iowa County, Wisconsin Territory, and certain records of the General Land Office—principally the tractbooks normally maintained by U.S. land offices and a special lead mine tractbook now in the National Archives.[8] Information regarding 10 of the pioneers whose names were noted on the Owen map appeared in all three of these sources; namely, Paschal Bequette, Michael Poad, John Pryor, William Rabeling, James Rule, John Smith, James B. Terry, Stephen Boyd Thrasher, Robert Vial, and Daniel Webb. The only persons noted on the map for whom no references were found in the sources mentioned above were Costello, Trawteter, and Braddon. The tractbooks, however, do show that a William Brandon purchased land in township 2 N., range 1 W., and that a John Kennedy entered land in township 5 N., range 1E., rather than in township 5N., range 2 E. The General Land Office records contain no information about the land transactions of

James Glanville, Samuel Hill, Richard Arthur, and Rabeling in section 16 as that section in every township on the public domain was reserved to the states for educational purposes.[9] Thus, records of titles to holdings in that section are to be found only in state records.

Since the most valuable lead deposits in the township were located along Peddler's Creek, it is not surprising that the Owen map shows a considerable concentration of pioneer population in the vicinity of that stream.[10] The names Heathcock, Poad, and Webb appear in section 8; Vial, Prior (Pryor), Trawteter, Ruler (Rule), Smith, and Stephenson in section 9; and Braddon, Pond (Poad), Thomas, and Traler (Treloar) in section 17. At least three pioneer operators of smelters were residing in the Diamond Grove area of the township: Terry in section 15, Kirkpatrick about a mile to the east in section 14, and Bequette about a mile to the south in section 22. In addition, the names Glanville, Hill, Rablin (Rabeling), and Archer (Arthur) appear in section 16; Paddock in section 15; Kennedy in section 26; Costello in section 31; and Bradbury, McKnight, and Legget (Legate) in section 36.

Although most of these early settlers arrived in the township after the Black Hawk War, it is interesting to note that at least two of its pioneer families—the Terrys and the Kirkpatricks—are listed in the 1830 census schedules of Iowa County.[11] These and many other pioneers in adjacent townships of the lead mine region were undoubtedly attracted to Iowa County in the 1820s in the expectation of acquiring wealth by exploiting the rich mineral deposits of the area as miners or operators of smelters.

The existence of lead mines in southwestern Wisconsin (now comprising Grant, Iowa, and LaFayette Counties) probably dates back to the earliest explorations in that area. Crude mining was undoubtedly carried on by its Indian inhabitants and possibly by the French during the 18th century. Until at least 1810, lead mining activities in the upper Mississippi region had centered in the area of Dubuque,

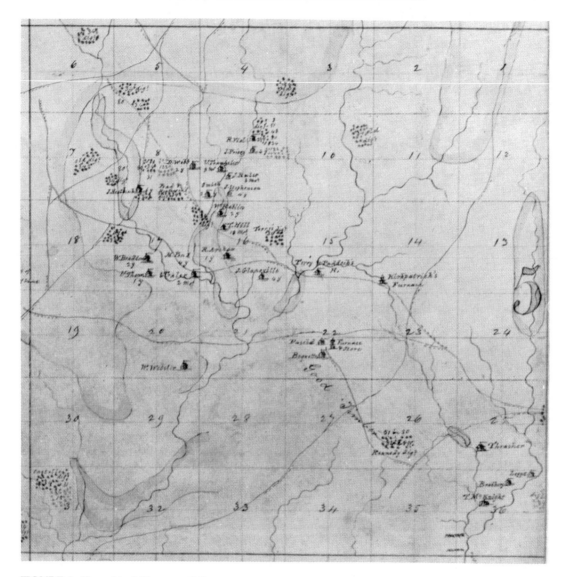

FIGURE 1. Township 5 N., range 2 E., as it appears on the manuscript map of southwestern Wisconsin.

IA. In that year Henry Shreeve is said to have obtained a small cargo of lead on Fever River and floated it back to the towns on the lower Mississippi. The real landmark in the practical, commercial development of southwestern Wisconsin, however, came in 1816 when Col.

George Davenport, agent of the American Fur Co. and Indian trader, "shipped the first flat-boat load of lead to St. Louis." From that time "the Fever River (or Galena) mines may be said to have been definitely known."[12]

Although laws enacted in 1807 directed

Names Appearing in Township 5N., Range 2E., on the Manuscript Map of Southwestern Wisconsin

Names on the map	Verified in other records in the National Archives	Section
Archer, R.	Arthur, Richard	16
Baquette, Paschal	Bequette, Paschal	22
Bradbury	Bradbury, Thomas	36
Braddon, W.	Brandon, William [?]	17
Costello	————	31
Glanoville, J.	Glanville, James	16
Heathcock, J.	Heathcock, John	8
Hill, T.	Hill, Samuel	16
Kennedy	Kennedy, John [?]	26
Kirkpatrick	Kirkpatrick, Richard H. [?]	14
Legget	Legate, Charles F.	36
McNight, T.	McKnight, Thomas	36
Paddock	Paddock, Orman	15
Poad	Poad, Michael	8
Pond, M.	Poad, Michael	17
Prior, J.	Pryor, John	9
Rablin, W.	Rabeling, William	16
Ruler, J.	Rule, James	9
Smith	Smith, John	9
Stephenson, J.	Stephenson, Charles L.	9
Terry	Terry, James B.	15, 16
Thomas, U.	Thomas, William	17
Thrasher	Thrasher, Stephen Boyd	25
Traler, S.	Treloar, Samuel	17
Trawteter, U.	————	9
Vial, R.	Vial, Robert	9
Webb, D.	Webb, Daniel	8
Webster, W.	Webster, William	20

that mineral lands should be reserved from sale and authorized their leasing to individuals for periods not exceeding 3 or 5 years,[13] the federal government made little or no attempt to implement this legislation until the early 1820s. An initial step in that direction was taken on November 29, 1821, when the responsibility for the lead mines formerly exercised by the Secretary of the Treasury was transferred to Secretary of War John C. Calhoun, who through the agency of the Ordnance Department was expected to "render them [the mines] productive."[14]

In his first general report to Secretary of War Calhoun regarding the lead mine lands, Lt. Col. George Bomford of the Ordnance Department cited the existence of rich lead deposits, particularly in the area between the southern boundary of Lake Michigan and the Mississippi River. With regard to leasing policy, however, he informed the secretary that the leases formerly granted had expired and "there are at present no Mines known to be worked, in any of the mining districts, under any regular Leases or authority; but that many were worked in the last year, in the State of Missouri without such authority, chiefly by new settlers & emigrants." He recommended the immediate appointment of an agent or commissioner authorized to grant new leases, adjudicate complaints, and act as a general guardian of the lead mine deposits on the public domain.[15]

Many of Colonel Bomford's specific proposals were later embodied in a "Notice for Leasing the Lead Mines of the United States," which was transmitted on June 15, 1822, to newspapers for publication. It set forth the conditions under which proposals would be received at the Office of the Ordnance Department for leasing the mineral lands of the United States.[16] Almost 5 months later, however, Colonel Bomford again reported to the Secretary of War that no leases had yet been issued despite the fact that almost 80 applications had been received "mostly from the State of Missouri, and with very few exceptions, for the mine lands in the north west or Michigan Territory."[17] He attributed the difficulty primarily to the delay that had been encountered in making the requisite surveys.

Very little progress was made in effectively carrying out existing regulations regarding the reservation of mineral lands until the appointment at St. Louis in August 1824 of Lt. Martin Thomas as Superintendent of U.S. Lead

Mines.[18] Now for the first time an agent of the government authorized to grant leases and permits to operate on U.S. lands was actually stationed in the lead mine region. Shortly after his arrival, Lieutenant Thomas temporarily suspended all mining operations,[19] and, when he permitted work to resume about a week later, he directed the miners to sell their mineral ore only to licensed smelters,[20] thus assuring that the government could collect its rent of 10 percent of the lead the miners delivered.

He also requested the Commissioner of the General Land Office, George Graham, to provide instructions to the registers and receivers of the local land offices on how to proceed when Thomas reported officially the existence of signs of lead ore.[21] The commissioner in reply stated that the registers normally reserved only such lands as the surveyors indicated contained lead mineral and readily admitted that "the partial examinations made by surveyors occasioned numerous omissions of the appearance of lead in the interiors of the sections." In a circular issued on February 21, 1825, Commissioner Graham informed his registers and receivers of Lieutenant Thomas' assignment and directed them to exclude from sale all lands that he determined "ought to be reserved because of lead mineral."[22]

The federal government's long-delayed action to protect its mineral resources came none too soon. Maj. John Anderson, a topographical engineer assigned to survey the lead mine tracts, reported in December 1824 that 20 men "from the lower mines" had in October forcibly entered upon the U.S. lead mine lands at Fever River "for the purpose of removing the mineral therefrom and that in defiance of my remonstrances and authority they still continued their depredations."[23] As a result, the Adjutant General's Office on March 8, 1825, ordered Brig. Gen. Henry Atkinson, the commanding officer of the Western Department, to send "a detachment of a Lieutenant and 15 or 20 men" from Fort Armstrong or Fort Crawford "to be stationed at the Lead Mines on Fever River for the protection of the persons who are working these mines under Leases from the United States."[24]

The most comprehensive statement concerning the value of the lead mine area and the vast increase in mining activity in the vicinity of Fever River is provided in the report of Lieutenant Thomas in 1826 on the operations of the U.S. lead mines in the western country. In describing the lead mines, commonly called the Fever River mines, in the vicinity of the Apple, Smallpox, Fever, and "Sasinawa" Rivers, he stated: "The diggings, or mines, are situated from one to ten miles from the River Au Ferre, where the furnaces are established. Fuel is easily obtained by means of the river. The smelting establishments are immediately on the bank of Fever River about six miles from its mouth. The steamboats which ascend the Mississippi in the spring of the year come close to the lead furnaces, and keel boats at all seasons, when not impeded by ice. Transportation costs less from the Fever River mines to St. Louis than from the mines near Potosi to the depots on the Mississippi." He noted that on his first visit in March 1825 there were only about 30 miners at Fever River but that there were "upwards of one hundred" when he returned on September 30th. He was fully convinced that the estimated 1 million pounds of lead produced in 1825 would be doubled in 1826. Thomas also commented extensively on the failure of the leasing policy and the necessity of supporting the lessees "in the quiet possession of their leases; intruders must be removed."[25] By July 1827 the influx of new settlers had reached such proportions that Colonel Bomford was forced to request authority to employ two new assistants in lead mining work since "our regular business has increased at least four fold."[26]

Among the new arrivals in 1827 was Col. Henry Dodge the future first Governor of Wisconsin Territory and later a U.S. Senator. He was destined to become one of the most powerful and influential figures in the early history of Wisconsin. Accompanied by his family of nine children, Dodge first moved to the lead mining region of Galena, IL, and then on to the lands of the Winnebago Indians near present Dodgeville, WI. From the beginning, he took the initiative in pressing the miners' claims for land against both the federal government and the Indians.[27]

Of particular concern to federal officials was the increasing resentment of the Winnebago at the continued encroachment of the white miners on lands reserved to them in the treaty of June 3, 1816, and the refusal of the miners to comply with the government's demands that the rights of the Indians be respected. Bomford readily admitted in July 1827 that with some 2,000 persons already collected at Fever River, and the boundaries "not yet . . . distinctly marked out," it was quite possible the conditions of the 1816 treaty had been violated.[28]

The long-smoldering resentment of the Winnebago finally erupted into open hostility in the spring and early summer of 1827. Attacks were made on several families in the Prairie du Chien area,[29] and about June 30 a keelboat returning from Fort Snelling was fired on. Gov. Lewis Cass of Michigan Territory, traveling to Green Bay to hold a council with the Winnebago at the time, graphically described the situation at Prairie du Chien where he "found the people in great alarm and consternation, and the whole settlement broken up, men, women and children seeking refuge in the old fort." At Fever River, Cass reported that he "found the alarm had extended there. The miners were quitting the mining districts and fleeing for protection to the town, near the mouth of the River." He urged the miners to send at least 100 volunteers to help protect the Prairie and then proceeded to St. Louis to give a full report to Superintendent of Indian Affairs William Clark and General Atkinson. He informed them that a military force should "be moved immediately to the scene of operations."[30]

The Winnebago War was relatively short and bloodless. General Atkinson with 500 soldiers supported by a volunteer group of 130 miners from Galena led by Colonel Dodge

moved into the Winnebago country.[31] The Winnebago retreated eastward along the Wisconsin River with Atkinson and Dodge in pursuit. At the Fox-Wisconsin portage, where another force from Fort Howard awaited them, the Indians surrendered. At a council on September 9, a temporary settlement with the Winnebago was reached when it was agreed "that the miners should have an unmolested privilege of procuring mineral in the district of country between Fever river and the Ouisconsin, until the Government should appoint a commission to settle all conflicting claims to that section of country."[32] By November 25, 1827, Joseph M. Street, the recently appointed Indian agent at Prairie du Chien, was able to report to the Secretary of War that "at this time, the Winnebago Indians are quiet, and that peace with our Indian neighbours reigns on this frontier."[33] This uneasy peace prevailed throughout the winter, but by spring it was clear that renewed hostilities might be expected unless the miners ceased their intrusions upon Indian lands.

In May 1828 the miners were visited by Thomas McKnight, Assistant Superintendent of U.S. Lead Mines, who carried instructions from his superior, Lieutenant Thomas, directing them to retire immediately to the lands that had been ceded to the government, but to no avail.[34] The encroachments of the miners continued until at last the patience of Superintendent Clark was exhausted. On July 10, 1828, he informed the Secretary of War that he had been compelled to request the commanding general "of this Division of the Army" to provide military force to effect their immediate removal from the Indian lands. He had been much impressed with the forbearance of the Winnebago, but he felt that this military action was necessary "to prevent the most injured among them, from executing vengeance on the invaders of their land:—intruders who have not scrupled to advance into the villages of these people, to dig the mineral from under their feet, & to destroy the corn, which was their only dependence thro' the winter to sustain the lives of their women & children."[35] Although the miners were not actually dispossessed by the contingent of soldiers that arrived to enforce the government's orders, the threat to remove them forcibly, combined with renewed demands that they pay a percentage on all the minerals raised in addition to that paid to the Winnebago, led many of the miners to abandon their claims. A year later the treaty of August 1, 1829, concluded at the village of Prairie du Chien, extinguished Winnebago title to land south and east of the Wisconsin River,[36] thus temporarily satisfying the miners' demands and bringing a measure of peace to the frontier mineral lands.

With peace there was another influx of settlers, chiefly miners, who were attracted by Iowa County's mineral wealth. Linden Township was among the first to attract immigrants. This may be attributed not only to its varied geography, which suggested the presence of rich mineral deposits as well as valuable agricultural lands, but to the actual discovery of lead in the fall of 1827 by Patrick O'Meara, familiarly known as "the Dodgeville peddler." On the banks of what has since been known as Peddler's Creek he accidentally stumbled across the first lead ever discovered in the township.[37]

Another milestone was the discovery in 1828 of the "Heathcock Range" by Bird Millsap and Frederick Dixon of Missouri. These diggings were operated with indifferent success until 1832, when the first practical miners arrived in the township and successfully revealed the riches of this mine. Tom Parish, a smelter at Wingville, purchased the lead mine and worked it for 1 year before selling a one-third interest to William and John Heathcock and Michael Poad. When the government land was opened for sale, the Heathcocks and Poad entered the entire 120 acres of the range and became sole owners. Eventually they sold it to the Pittsburgh Mining Co. for $18,000.[38] The "Old Sam Charles Diggings" discovered in 1833 on land owned by Paschal Bequette, son-in-law of Henry Dodge, also proved very valuable. During succeeding years many different lodes and ranges were discovered, some highly

profitable, others unproductive. In fact, the original township survey plat (1834) and the Owen map (1839) indicate that diggings were to be found in almost every section of the township.

Although the early settlers were predominantly miners, from the first there were some farmers. Indeed it was the combination of mining and farming that gave this region "a potentially permanent population" at an early date.[39] An excellent picture of conditions in the mining district of southwestern Wisconsin and the possibly conflicting interests of the miners and farmers is provided in a "Memorial to the Secretary of War by Inhabitants of the Lead-Mining District," dated January 9, 1832. After reviewing the leasing policy of the U.S. government, the memorialists called attention

> to a subject of great interest and vital importance to them should the Government pass a Law for a Sale of the U.S. Lead Mines the Miners Earnestly hope you will recommend to the Consideration of Congress the Justice and propriety of granting to Each Miner who has complied with the regulations made for the Government of the Mines the privaledge of working out all discoveries made by them Either on Mineral Lotts or Surveys. To sell the mines without making this reservation would deprive the most enterprising and Industrious part of the Mining population of their All, and completely Blast their prospects in this country and leave them here without resources or Means.

The memorial reflected the consensus of a meeting of the citizens of Iowa County and the Territory of Michigan held at the home of John T. Sublett in the town of Mineral Point. Colonel Dodge served as chairman of the meeting and Richard H. Kirkpatrick of Linden Township was appointed to a committee that was "to prepare and report a Memorial to Congress embracing the Objects of the Meeting."[40]

The rapid development in 1831–32 of this lead mine area was interrupted by a new Indian outbreak, one that was far more serious than the 1827 uprising. The instigators this time were the Sac and Fox who still occupied lands in Illinois near the mouth of the Rock River that had been ceded to the U.S. government. As these lands had been surveyed and a part of them settled, new difficulties soon arose between the Indians and the white settlers. Although Superintendent Clark and the Sac and Fox Indian Agent Thomas Forsyth had told the Indians frequently that they must move to their own lands on the west side of the Mississippi, Black Hawk's band persisted in its refusal to leave, even refusing to accept any part of the annuities due members of the tribe who had already moved to their new lands. In mid-April 1832, Henry Gratiot, Sub-agent at Rock River, Prairie du Chien Agency, at the request of General Atkinson, warned the people on the mining frontier to be prepared for an Indian uprising. This alert, combined with other similar rumors, "struck terror into the heart of the mineral regions and paralyzed trade; the pick and gad were forsaken for the more deadly musket and bayonet."[41]

The records of the Bureau of Indian Affairs in the National Archives provide excellent documentation of the events leading up to the outbreak of the Black Hawk War in May 1832. Of particular value is a communication from Clark to the Secretary of War in August 1831 enclosing three folios of background materials on the subject of the Indian hostilities.[42] The records also include a journal of events and proceedings with the Rock River band of Winnebago Indians, January 1832–September 19, 1832, kept by Gratiot.[43]

Colonel Dodge, commander of the Michigan Militia, called attention to the exposed situation of the settlements of the mining district and requested a résumé of Illinois Gov. John Reynolds' plans of operation. Dodge received no response until after the disastrous battle of Stillman's Run, when the governor informed him that Iowa County was in imminent danger of attack. Dodge then spread the alarm through the mining region and advised the inhabitants to unite and fortify themselves for their mutual protection. Some 15 forts and blockhouses were erected at the most exposed points, including Fort Jackson at Mineral Point,

Fort Union at Dodge's residence south of Dodgeville, Fort Napoleon (Bonaparte) at Diamond Grove in Linden Township, Fort Jones in the Blue River district (town of Highland), Fort Defiance in Willow Springs, Fort Hamilton in the town of Wiota, and Fort Gratiot at Gratiot's Grove. Meanwhile, numerous militia companies had been organized, forming the Iowa County Regiment of Michigan Volunteers. Mineral Point, or Fort Jackson, was headquarters for the war effort in the entire lead mine area. It was the distribution center from which supplies were parceled out to the commanders of the county forts under the supervision of U.S. Quartermaster George B. Cole. The contractors for "Sutlers' supplies and munitions of war" were G. W. and John Atchison of Galena and James Morrison and Peter A. De Lorimier of Diamond Grove, Linden Township.[44]

The Black Hawk War is so well known that no attempt will be made to detail it here, but the pioneer history of Linden would not be complete without mention of the short and bloody Battle of the Pecatonica on June 11, 1832. To quote Superintendent Clark, "Genl. Dodge who was ranging between Dixon & Galena, with a party of 21 men [including Paschal Bequette and Richard H. Kirkpatrick], was attacked by eleven Indians on the Peketolica [sic]. The Indians had the first fire and wounded four; a charge was then made upon them and the whole 11 were killed, two of them in the creek, to which the[y] had retreated."[45] It is said that Dodge's son-in-law, Captain Bequette, "in that battle shot and killed two of the war party, and so gained the friendship of the General."[46] Victories in the Battle of Wisconsin Heights and the Bad Axe Massacre, in which Black Hawk was captured, sealed the doom of the Indians. By August the war was over and the frontier settlers were able to return once more to their homes. The compiled service records of three Linden pioneers who are known to have taken part in the Black Hawk War (Terry, Kirkpatrick, and Bequette) are among the records of the Adjutant General's Office in the National Archives.[47] Their bounty-land warrant application files are among the records of the Veterans Administration.[48]

After the Black Hawk War, emigration to Linden Township quickly resumed. The year 1834 marked the greatest influx of miners, many coming from England—particularly Cornwall. Among the new arrivals were John Prior, James Glanville, William and James Rabeling, Mark Smith, and Robert Vial. They were followed in 1835 by Samuel Treloar and Thomas and William Thomas.[49] These new settlers, like the earliest pioneers in Linden Township, were motivated largely by the hope of finding mineral wealth, although many no doubt were also interested in acquiring land for farming purposes.

Before a land office could be established or the first public land sale held, however, it was necessary to prepare an official survey plat of the township. Authorized by the General Land Office under a contract dated October 1, 1832, township 5 N., range 2 E., of the fourth principal meridian (comprising 23,047.52 acres), was surveyed by Hervey Parke and Lucius Lyon during the fourth quarter of 1832.[50] The survey plat, or map, prepared by these surveyors on the basis of their field notes would normally provide the starting point for the study of any township on the public domain, but for Linden Township, as noted earlier, we have preferred to obtain the basic data from the unique Owen map. Nonetheless, the survey plat of this township (approved by the Surveyor General's Office in Cincinnati on August 13, 1834) and the accompanying 41 pages of field notes do contain information of great value in writing the pioneer history of Linden Township.[51] They show not only its geographical features but also the locations of diggings, smelters, residences, and other evidence of land development. For example, the surveyor of the east side of section 25 reported a "lead" worked by Terry, Paul M. Gratiot, and James Brady. "A double cabin stands about 10 ch[ain]s West of line & another about 2 ch[ain]s East of it, both inhabited." The land was "hilly 2d rate & thinly wooded with White & Bur Oak." The sur-

veyor of the north boundary between sections 22 and 23 indicated that the land was "beautifully timbered" and was "supposed to be near the center of Diamond Grove." The surveyor of the east boundary between sections 14 and 23 noted the presence of a stream. "Down this run about 5 chains," he wrote, "is a new Established furnace, near which are several Log dwellings also owned by the Kirkpatricks." Data of this type is, of course, invaluable—particularly when compared with Owen's findings a few years later.

An act of Congress, dated June 26, 1834, established two new land districts in northern Illinois and two in Wisconsin, the latter designated as the Wisconsin and Green Bay districts.[52] The Wisconsin land district embraced all the territory in the then Territory of Michigan south of the Wisconsin River and west of the north and south line "along the range of line next west of Fort Winnebago" (between ranges 8 and 9 E.). The land office for this district was established at Mineral Point, with John P. Sheldon and Joseph Eneix nominated as register and receiver, respectively, on June 28.[53] The location of the land office at Mineral Point further enhanced that place as the most important settlement in the lead region of Wisconsin during the 1830's. To quote from Schafer, this was

> due to her central location, her position as county seat from the year 1830, the construction of roads radiating in all directions, the establishment there of the United States Land Office for the Wisconsin land district, and the richness of the mineral district closely surrounding the town. Next to its mines, the most dynamic of these influences was the land office, an institution whose business affected every settler in the three counties, all of whom had to visit Mineral Point at some time and to all of whom that place symbolized the United States government's relation to settlers on the public domain.[54]

The requisite survey having been completed, the President on May 6, 1835, issued his "Proclamation of Land Sales at Mineral

Point" to be held "commencing on Monday, the seventh day of September next for the disposal of the Public Lands within the limits" of certain townships and fractional townships in the Wisconsin land district north of the base line and east of the fourth principal meridian including townships 1-7 and fractional townships 8 and 9 of range 2. The proclamation specified that "the lands reserved by law, for the use of schools, or for other purposes, will be excluded from Sale." It further provided that "all tracts of land on which lead mines or diggings are indicated to exist, by the official plats of survey, together with such other tracts, as from satisfactory evidence to be adduced to the Register of the Land Office, prior to the date of Sale, shall be shown to contain Lead Mines will be excluded from sale." The proclamation was accompanied by a notice to preemption claimants that "persons claiming the right of preemption to any of the aforesaid lands are required to prove the same to the satisfaction of the Register and Receiver prior to the day of sale."[55] On July 29, 1835, the Commissioner of the General Land Office requested the register and receiver at Mineral Point to likewise reserve from sale "such tracts of timber lands occupied by Smelters as shall be reported to you by the Superintendent of Lead Mines, as necessary for the operation of smelting." They were also instructed not to permit "floating rights" (so called), accruing under the preemption law, to be located on reserved lands.[56]

All of these regulations and instructions represented a concerted effort by the government to implement its established policy of retaining title to all lead-bearing lands and leasing them for a rental of 10 percent of the lead produced. It was apparent, however, that the situation regarding these lands was very complicated and that it would be increasingly difficult to enforce the leasing policy once public sales of land were authorized. The official survey plats only indicated the existence of such lead mines or "diggings" as were observed at the time of survey, more than 2 years before the first sale. Naturally, mineral discoveries made since the survey, as well as those in the interior parts of the sections, were not "indicated to exist by official plats of survey" and very few "other tracts" were reported to the register by "satisfactory evidence" prior to the sale.

As early as December 1834, the register and receiver at Mineral Point, recognizing the nature of the "Pandora's Box" of problems soon to be opened, urged "the propriety of selling the mineral lands in this land district," a proposal in which they were joined by Maj. Charles F. Legate, Superintendent of the U.S. Lead Mines, who had "long entertained the opinion that both the public interests and that of your citizens who inhabit this portion of the country will be advanced by the measure." Otherwise, they warned, "gross frauds can be practiced by 'unprincipled' persons without a possibility of their being detected" and "the most valuable mineral lands in the country may be discovered and entered as ordinary farming lands."[57]

The status of the land they occupied was, of course, a matter of overriding concern to the pioneers from the earliest days of township settlement. The miners usually built their homes on their mineral reserves and counted on eventually acquiring title through a kind of preemption right. Others, particularly those engaged in smelting, wished to enter timber areas that were often remote from their homes. As these presumably contained no minerals, they felt that the reservations announced by the President in 1834 and 1835 were unjust and illegal.[58] Still others, like the Heathcocks and Rules, for example, wished to be miner-farmers or to engage primarily in agricultural pursuits. By 1836 John and William Heathcock, in addition to their mining interests, were cultivating a farm of 160 acres on section 20; the Rule family was farming on section 6.[59]

The concern of the miners and other settlers throughout the lead mining area who were mere squatters on government lands or, at best, held them under lease, is reflected in a "Memorial to Congress by the Legislative Council," referred on March 1, 1836. It asserted that the operation of the recently passed laws made the miners, "a large and respectable portion of the Counties of Ioway and Dubuque," a prey for the speculator and petitioned Congress to recognize that the "first wish of these people is that the mineral lands be sold; that those sales already made be revoked, and that the actual possessor . . . be entitled to the right of pre-emption."[60]

When this appeal fell on deaf ears in Congress, the miners felt fully justified in buying their mineral lands through an ingenious means devised by Register Sheldon of the Mineral Point Land Office, who felt compelled to find a solution to this unfortunate situation. He adopted the practice of reading out, at the public sales, the descriptions of the reserved lands together with the unreserved tracts in the same townships and sections but announced in each instance that no bids would be received on tracts known to contain mines or diggings by the official plats or by "satisfactory evidence." By this device he technically complied with the law that prohibited the private sale of government lands until they had been offered publicly for sale. Immediately after the public sale, Sheldon accepted private offers for the reserved lands whenever the applications were "accompanied by the affidavits of two persons" stating that the lands in question were not mineral-bearing and "were not occupied by any smelter of lead ore."[61]

The result might have been anticipated. The records of the General Land Office show that, beginning with the first public land sales in 1834 and 1835, more than 550 land entries involving reserved lands were filed at the Mineral Point Land Office, including 41 entries in Linden Township filed by pioneers whose names appear on Owen's map. An additional 10 entries were made by these Linden residents on sections outside of the township.[62] An analysis of the entries recorded in the "Special Tract Book of Lead Land in the Mineral Point District, Wisconsin" indicates that speculative transactions involving the reserved lands reached their apex in 1836, when 23 of the 41 disputed entries in Linden Township and all 10 entries outside the township were filed. The

number of such entries dropped to 13 in 1837 and to 3 in 1838.

The pioneer settlers in Linden Township who figured prominently in mineral land transactions were Terry, Poad, and the Heathcocks (often in association with Poad). Terry made nine entries in sections 3, 4, 15, and 22; the Heathcocks, four entries in sections 8, 11, 20, and 21; Poad, four entries in sections 9 and 20; and the Heathcocks and Poad together made two entries in sections 6 and 14. Of course most of the other pioneer settlers named on Owen's map also made entries on reserved lands: Bequette, four entries in sections 21, 22, and 26; Stephen Boyd Thrasher, four entries in sections 25, 26, and 36; Thomas McKnight, two entries in sections 26 and 35; John Pryor, two entries in sections 9 and 21; Henry Rabeling (and Abner Nichols), one entry in section 8; William Rabeling, one entry in section 15; John Smith, one entry in section 10; Mark Smith, one entry in section 7; William Thomas, one entry in section 9; Thomas Thomas, one entry in section 10; Thrasher and McKnight, one entry in section 26; Robert Vial, one entry in section 9; William Webster, one entry in section 25; and Daniel Webb, one entry in section 10.[63] All of these entries involved lands important for mineral deposits or timber needed in smelting operations.

Although the land entry case files for all the transactions involving reserved lands contain the required affidavits regarding the non-mineral character of the land[64] and the register may well have permitted these entries in the firm belief that they were purely agricultural in character, Sheldon was almost immediately denounced as a violator of the law. Unfortunately, some of the lands sold as "agricultural" land proved to contain rich lead deposits while many of the reserved lands were found to be valueless for mining. Under these circumstances, those miners who were still occupying mining lands under leases from the government refused to continue paying the 10-percent rental or to comply with the other conditions of their leases.[65] The General Land Office, greatly alarmed over the charges of fraudulent activities at the Mineral Point office, suspended all entries involving lands in the Mineral Point district that had been reported as lead lands or timber lands "proper to be reserved for smelting purposes."[66] Virtually no entries of this type—even those based on the Preemption Act of 1834—were patented until after the passage of legislation in 1846 permitting the sale of mineral lands.[67]

There followed an extensive investigation by the General Land Office of the allegations made against Sheldon, many of them brought by James D. Doty, leader of the Whig opposition to Governor Dodge. On September 22, 1840, the Commissioner of the General Land Office transmitted to the Secretary of the Treasury a report by the Solicitor of the General Land Office covering his investigation and recommending that Sheldon be discontinued as register. This letter, which is among the Treasury Department records in the National Archives, bears the following endorsement by President Martin Van Buren: "Let Mr. Sheldon be removed and a suitable person reported to supply the vacancy."[68] Although the solicitor's report of September 12, 1840, stated that he was satisfied that "the material charges against Mr. Sheldon are fully sustained and that he should be no longer retained in the public service,"[69] Sheldon vigorously defended the legality of his procedure as register and denounced the allegations of fraud as the work of his political enemies.

No action was taken regarding the controversial suspended mineral entries until 1847, when Richard M. Young, Commissioner of the General Land Office, decided "to make a final disposal of the Mineral Point Sales" under an act approved August 3, 1846, which provided for the "adjustment of all suspended pre-emption land claims in the several States or Territories." On April 12, 1847, he requested Gen. Samuel Leech of Quincy, IL, to undertake a thorough investigation of "the cases designated in the accompanying volume" and provided detailed instructions for carrying out the assignment.[70] The "accompanying volume" to which the commissioner referred contains "A

List of Entries made at Mineral Point, Wisconsin, from the Years 1834 to 46 inclusive that have been suspended at this Office as embracing lead mines, or diggings, which at the time of purchase were interdicted from sale, and which entries were consequently illegally made."[71] For each entry, the General Land Office recorded the certificate number, the case number, a legal description of the land, and the names of the original claimant and present owner. General Leech was instructed to place the affidavits and other testimony for each case in a separate envelope endorsed with the number of the case according to the volume. He was also to enter an abstract of the testimony under the heading provided in the volume and to indicate whether the case should be placed in the first or second class. If the testimony was satisfactory and he believed that the entry should be patented, it was to be designated as first class. If the testimony was insufficient or there was any evidence of fraud, it was to be placed in the second class. When he had completed his investigation he was to return the volume to the commissioner's office with the accompanying papers for final decision.

This unique volume, which is now in the National Archives, bears a notation that it was received August 31, 1847, at the General Land Office from General Leech. A review of the testimony and recommendations it contains shows that only 19 of the 556 cases investigated were placed in the second class and that all 41 cases involving entries made by pioneers of Linden Township were placed in the first class. Leech did state that in some 36 cases (none in Linden Township) discoveries of lead ore had been made before filing the entries "which in all probability was an inducement to purchase but which have since been despoiled of their mineral wealth"[72] or turned out not to be very valuable. As such land was not then worth more than $1.25 an acre, he had placed these cases in the first class.

General Leech's recommendation that all the "fraudulent" entries with the exception of 19 be confirmed to the claimants would seem in some measure to vindicate Sheldon's contention that the allegations against him were politically motivated and that he was not guilty of defrauding the government. Against this background it is interesting to note that his career as a public servant was not yet ended. The records of the Treasury Department include letters from Cass and Jefferson Davis (dated April 1853) recommending him for the position of chief clerk, and they contain his oath of office, dated June 24, 1853, as a clerk in the Third Auditor's Office.[73] Of special interest is Sheldon's letter to Secretary of the Treasury Salmon P. Chase resigning his position because he was opposed to the election of Abraham Lincoln and felt that he must "return to the ranks of the political party whose efforts have always been devoted to the integrity of the Republic and the harmony of the States."[74]

Although Linden was a comparatively old and well-established township long before the settlement of its mineral lands controversy, its prosperity—like that of all the Wisconsin lead mine area—was profoundly affected by the California exodus in 1849–50. Attracted by stories of fabulous discoveries of gold in California, hundreds of miners and farmers—including pioneer settlers—abandoned their diggings and land and disposed of all available assets in order to defray the cost of the transcontinental trip. Mineral Point and Dodgeville were particularly hard hit, but Linden did not entirely escape the fever of emigration. Before the exodus ended, the list of California emigrants included such familiar names as Smith, Webster, Kirkpatrick, and Bequette.[75]

The 1850 census schedules for Iowa County, however, show that at least 15 of the early settlers mentioned on Owen's map in 1839 were still residing in the county, most of them in Linden Township. Of more significance is the fact that the names of at least nine of these pioneer settlers still appear on the 1870 census schedules for Linden: John Pryor, Robert Vial, John Rule, Sr., John and William Heathcock, Michael Poad, James Glanville, Daniel Webb, and Samuel Treloar. Members of the Thrasher and Kirkpatrick families are also listed on the schedules. All of them were

placed in the category of "farmer" or "retired farmer" by occupation. This would seem to provide substantial support for the contention that it was those pioneers who were miner-farmers or interested primarily in agricultural pursuits who made the mineral area of southwestern Wisconsin their permanent home. The most prosperous in terms of property holdings in 1870 was John Heathcock, age 61, who owned real estate valued at $10,000 and had $4,600 in personal property.[76]

In writing the pioneer history of any township on the public domain, it is important to make use of all available postal records, for the development of postal service is an integral part of the story. The registers of postmasters' appointments in the National Archives show that the first post office in Iowa County was established at Mineral Point on March 9, 1829, with Robert P. Gàyard appointed as postmaster.[77] The next post office in the county was established at Wingville on May 23, 1836, with Dawson E. Parish as postmaster. This office was discontinued on September 22, 1837, but it was reestablished and located in Grant County on September 28, 1838. It was again discontinued on June 26, 1845. The first post office in Linden Township was established at Diamond Grove on August 9, 1837, with Stephen P. Hollenbeck as postmaster. The register indicates that he "moved away" and was succeeded by Paschal Bequette, who was appointed postmaster on May 9, 1838. On December 31, 1840, Bequette was succeeded by Orman Paddock, who presumably served until the office was discontinued on August 16, 1842. The second post office in the township was established at Peddler's Creek on March 30, 1843, with John Wasley as postmaster. Its name was changed to Linden on December 28, 1845.[78]

The mail route registers in the National Archives indicate that the earliest mail-carrying contract awarded for service through Linden Township was for the period 1836–37. This route (see fig. 2) extended from Mineral Point by Diamond Grove, Wingville, Blue River, and Parish's to English Prairie (later known as Muscoda). The contract was for "30 miles and back

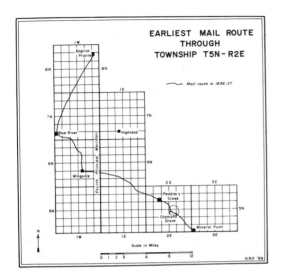

FIGURE 2. The 1836–37 mail route through Linden Township compiled from geographical site location reports among the records of the Post Office Department in the National Archives.

once a week." James Morrison's bid was accepted on December 12, 1836, and he was awarded the contract for $320 a year.[79] For the period 1837–42, the contract was awarded to Samuel Newland for $300 annually with service to begin on July 1, 1838. There was no change from the first contract in the route covered. The post rider was to leave Mineral Point every Wednesday at 6 a.m. and arrive at English Prairie the same day by 5 p.m. The return trip was to be made every Thursday.[80]

The next important mail route was established when a contract was let for the period 1842–46 for a route from Mineral Point by Peddler's Creek, Wingville, Highland (established April 21, 1846), and Blue River to English Prairie. The contract for "40 miles and back once a week" was awarded to Daniel H. Darnall for $250 on April 30, 1842. The post rider was to leave Mineral Point on Wednesday at 6 a.m. and arrive at English Prairie the same day by 6 p.m. The return trip was to be made on Thursday. On September 1, 1842, the route

was changed so that it terminated at Blue River rather than English Prairie.[81]

Of particular value in writing local history are the geographical site location reports in the Post Office Department records. These reports (submitted by the postmasters) show the locations of the post offices and provide other geographical information to assist the department in the preparation of postal maps. They give the legal descriptions of the land on which the post offices are located, terminals of the nearest postal routes, and the mileage to adjacent post offices, rivers, and creeks. Although most of the site location reports date from the 1870s, the reports for a particular office occasionally include a report or site location diagram of much earlier date.

Federal records may be used quite effectively not only in writing local history but also in preparing biographical sketches of pioneer leaders in the area under consideration. The extent to which this can be done is well illustrated in the life of Paschal Bequette, perhaps the most interesting pioneer settler in Linden Township.

He was born in Missouri and spent his youth in St. Genevieve Parish,[82] a member of a family of French immigrants, many of whom were apparently engaged in mining. The private land claims records in the National Archives include extensive documentation on the various land claims of the Bequette family, both in Kaskaskia and St. Genevieve districts.[83] The original claimant, Jean Baptiste Bequette, with several others claimed a concession in 1798 of 1,600 arpents of land from Zenon Trudeau, at that time lieutenant governor of upper Louisiana, a case that became so complicated that heirs were still attempting to secure title to the land in 1850.[84]

Bequette married Elizabeth Dodge, daughter of Henry Dodge. Because Dodge lived in St. Genevieve for many years, serving as sheriff from 1805 to 1821, the two families were undoubtedly acquainted. It is not known, however, whether Bequette married Elizabeth in St. Genevieve or in Michigan Territory, but it may be assumed that he accompanied the Dodge family to Fever River in 1827 and then into the lead mining area of southwestern Wisconsin. In any case, by the early 1830s he had settled in Linden Township.

He played an important role in the Black Hawk War as a first lieutenant in Capt. James H. Gentry's company of the Iowa Mounted Volunteers and won the approbation of his father-in-law, Colonel Dodge, for his valor. His compiled military service record in the National Archives shows that he enrolled in the unit on May 11, 1832, and was mustered out on October 9, 1832, at Mineral Point after serving 4 months and 28 days.[85] The bounty-land warrant application files also include his applications for the bounty land to which he was entitled under acts of September 28, 1850, and March 3, 1855. Bequette's first bounty-land claim, filed in Iowa County on December 24, 1850, shows that he was still a resident of Diamond Grove at that time. The second claim, dated May 30, 1855, was filed at San Francisco, where Bequette was then residing.[86] His bounty-land warrant files among the records of the General land Office show that he sold both warrants instead of locating them and taking title himself.

After the Black Hawk War, Bequette obtained a license from Superintendent of the Lead Mines Legate to smelt lead ore and began to operate a furnace and blacksmith shop at Diamond Grove.[87] As the blacksmith shop was the only one in a radius of many miles, it was "overcrowded with work, principally the mending and sharpening of miners' tools." In 1834 he expanded his business activities by starting a store near his furnace, about a mile south of Captain Terry's store that was the first established in the township.[88]

The *History of Iowa County, Wisconsin,* published in 1881, states that Bequette and Peter A. De Lorimier, with whom he was associated in the smelting business, made the first entry of land in Iowa County; the claim is verified in the General Land Office records.[89] On June 9, 1835, Bequette and De Lorimier entered the west half of the southeast quarter of section 22, township 5 N., range 2 E., at the Mineral Point

Land Office (certificate 268). Later the same day they also entered the west half of the northeast quarter of section 22 (certificate 271).[90] In 1836 Bequette entered the east half of the northeast quarter, section 21, and the west half of the northwest quarter, section 22. In 1837 he completed his land holdings in Linden Township by entering the northeast quarter of the southwest quarter and the west half of the southwest quarter of section 26, which included a part of the Peddler's Creek diggings.[91]

An astute businessman with varied interests, Bequette soon became one of the most active and influential residents of the area. In addition to serving as postmaster at Diamond Grove, he was one of the first inspectors of school district No. 7, which comprised townships 5–8 of range 2 E. Elected with him were Terry, Thrasher, Legate, and Alex Blair. He served as a grand juror when the first term of the U.S. district court was convened in Mineral Point in May 1837, was an incorporator of the Belmont and Dubuque Railroad Co., and was appointed Receiver of Public Monies at the Mineral Point Land Office in 1840. His bond for $50,000 was signed by Robert S. Black, Thomas Jenkins, and his father-in-law, all of Dodgeville; Edward Jones and Legate of Mineral Point; and William J. Madden of Elk Grove. On October 1, 1846, he was appointed to a 4-year term in this position with a bond set at $100,000.[92] Apparently, soon after the expiration of this term of office, he was one of the Iowa County emigrants who undertook the perilous overland journey to California with his family. A contemporary pioneer in the Wisconsin lead region who knew him well characterized Bequette in these words: "He was a gentleman of unimpeachable integrity and honor, enjoying the confidence and respect of all who knew him; for he was a modest, quiet gentleman, and an enterprising business man."[93]

Bequette next appears in the records of the federal government as Receiver of Public Monies at the land office at Benicia, CA, a position to which he was appointed in August 1854. He was reappointed in 1857 but apparently left shortly thereafter to accept appointment as Receiver of Public Monies at the land office in San Francisco.[94] His appointment file for this position includes letters of recommendation from some of the most prominent political figures in California, Wisconsin, and Iowa, including J. B. Weller (Governor of and former Senator from California), Col. Benjamin F. Washington, and Sen. George W. Jones of Iowa.[95] Although his appointment was for 4 years "from the 22nd day of December, 1858," he served only until May 1861.[96] It appears that his resignation may have resulted from indignation over certain suspended vouchers (2d quarter 1860) for office stationery that were disallowed "as unauthorized, extravagant in quantity and price, and some of them unnecessary."[97] On May 24, 1861, he transmitted his accounts to the Commissioner of the General Land Office and requested him "to forward to my address at Visalia, California, a treasury draft . . . for the balance due me of $4,215.85 which will close my accounts as Receiver of Public Moneys and disbursing agent."[98] This episode closes the career of Paschal Bequette as reflected in the records of the federal government at the National Archives.

There are those who are impatient with local history—so many unknown names, so many details about a small bit of earth only 6 miles square. But there are others who realize that the parochial is not without broader meaning and that the well-told story of a township reveals much also about the history of the country of which it is a part. The pioneer experience especially cannot be well understood by later generations except as we can watch pioneers moving on to and developing new lands into homes and communities, and to study it properly we need to focus our microscope on the township—that cell of organized living in the nation's heartland—and observe it closely for at least a generation. Federal records should be used together with local records and published works, of course, for they supplement local holdings, especially in the pioneer years before local governments were in full operation or able to make and preserve adequate records. At all periods in our history, federal records have provided the broader framework needed to give local records greater meaning.

In writing this essay no attempt has been made to exhaust printed and manuscript sources relating to southwestern Wisconsin. The purpose has been, using Linden Township as an example, to illustrate the type and variety of manuscript records in the National Archives that can be used in the writing of regional, state, and local history. Many of the documents used in this study have been published by the National Archives in the Territorial Papers of the United States.

NOTES

1. Joseph Schafer, "The Wisconsin Domesday Book," *Wisconsin Magazine of History* 4 (1921–22): 63.

2. Joseph Schafer, "The Microscopic Method Applied to History," *Minnesota History Bulletin* 4 (1921–22): 3–20.

3. Ibid., p. 3.

4. Joseph Schafer, *Town Studies*, vol. 1 of General Studies, Wisconsin Domesday Book (Madison, 1922); *Four Wisconsin Counties, Prairie and Forest*, vol. 2 of General Studies, Wisconsin Domesday Book (Madison, 1927); *The Wisconsin Lead Region*, vol. 3 of General Studies, Wisconsin Domesday Book (Madison, 1932); and *The Winnebago-Horicon Basin, A Type Study in Western History*, vol. 4 of General Studies, Wisconsin Domesday Book (Madison, 1937).

5. The township with which this essay is concerned comprises the 36 sections in T. 5 N., R. 2 E., of the fourth principal meridian as surveyed by the General Land Office and *not* the 56 sections in townships 4 and 5 constituting the "Town of Linden" as organized in 1849. See *History of Iowa County, Wisconsin* (Chicago, 1881), pp. 807, 810. The village of Linden, originally known as Peddler's Creek, has always been located in T. 5 N., R. 2 E., identified in this essay as "Linden Township."

6. Schafer, *The Wisconsin Lead Region*, pp. 48–49, 187.

7. David Dale Owen, "Report of a Geological Exploration of Part of Iowa, Wisconsin, and Illinois, Made Under Instructions From the Secretary of the Treasury of the United States, in the Autumn of the Year 1839; With Charts and Illustrations," S. Doc. 407, 28th Cong., 1st sess., p. 132, Serial 437.

8. Iowa County, WI, vol. 1, 1840 Population Schedules, Records of the Bureau of the Census, Record Group 29, National Archives (hereafter records in the National Archives will be cited as RG____, NA); "Special Tract Book of Lead Land in the Mineral Point District, Wisconsin," Records of the General Land Office Relating to Leasing and Operation of Lead Mines, Records of the Bureau of Land Management, RG 49, NA. The original tractbooks of the local land offices in Wisconsin are in the custody of the State Historical Society of Wisconsin, but microfilm copies have been retained by the National Archives.

9. Act of April 30, 1802, 2 Stat. 175; act of March 3, 1803, 2 Stat. 226.

10. Although Peddler's Creek is located chiefly in sections 6–8 and 17 of the township, the tractbooks and other records of the General Land Office (RG 49, NA) relating to leasing and operation of lead mines and lands in Mineral Point District, WI, cite "Pedlar's Creek Diggings" in sections 4, 5, 9, 16, 26, 31, and east halves of 25 and 36.

11. Iowa County, MI, vol. 1, 1830 Population Schedules, RG 29, NA.

12. Schafer, *The Wisconsin Lead Region*, pp. 27, 35; Reuben G. Thwaites, "Notes on Early Lead Mining," *Wisconsin State Historical Society, Collections* 13 (Madison, 1895): 285.

13. Acts of March 3, 1807, 2 Stat. 446, 449. The latter act specifically provided that "any grant which may hereafter be made for a tract of land containing a lead mine, which had been discovered previous to the purchase of such tract from the United States, shall be considered fraudulent and null."

14. W. H. Crawford to John C. Calhoun, November 29, 1821, p. 1, vol. 1, Letters Sent Relating to Mineral Lands (hereafter cited as Mineral Lands Letters), Records of the Office of the Chief of Ordnance, RG 156, NA.

15. George Bomford to Calhoun, March 30, 1822, pp. 9–10, vol. 1, Mineral Lands Letters, RG 156, NA.

16. Bomford, "Notice for Leasing the Lead Mines of the United States," June 15, 1822, pp. 15–16, vol. 1, Mineral Lands Letters, RG 156, NA.

17. Bomford to Calhoun, November 12, 1822 (Second Report on the Lead Mines of the U.S.), p. 61, vol. 1, Mineral Lands Letters, RG 156, NA.

18. Bomford to Martin Thomas, August 18, 1824, pp. 114–122, vol. 1, Mineral Lands Letters, RG 156, NA.

19. *History of Iowa County, Wisconsin*, p. 409.

20. On January 31, 1825, Bomford wrote to Calhoun concerning possible changes

in the system for leasing and working the lead mines, including a proposal to license persons "specially to do smelting." He contended that this would "augment the amount of rents, and render their collection much more certain." Bomford to Calhoun, January 31, 1825, pp. 129–130, vol. 1, Mineral Lands Letters, RG 156, NA. On February 17, 1825, Bomford informed Thomas that the Secretary of War had approved this proposal; p. 130, vol. 1, Mineral Lands Letters, RG 156, NA.

21. Thomas to George Graham, January 21, 1825, p. 136, vol. 1, Mineral Lands Letters, RG 156, NA.

22. Graham to Thomas, February 22, 1825, pp. 278–279, vol. 14, Miscellaneous Letters, Division "C" (hereafter cited as Miscellaneous "C" Letters), RG 49, NA. Graham to registers and receivers, February 21, 1825, p. 277, vol. 14, Miscellaneous "C" Letters, RG 49, NA.

23. Bomford to Calhoun, March 27, 1825, p. 140, vol. 1, Mineral Lands Letters, RG 156, NA.

24. Acting Adjutant General to the Commanding Officer, Western Department, March 8, 1825, p. 141, vol. 1, Mineral Lands Letters, RG 156, NA.

25. Thomas' report entitled "General Operations and History of Lead Mines in Missouri and the Upper Mississippi Country," dated "January 1826," was transmitted by Bomford to James Barbour on Feb. 7, 1826. Barbour forwarded it to the Senate on February 18, 1826. The original report is now filed as 19A-E2, Records of the U.S. Senate, RG 46, NA. It is published in U.S., Congress, *American State Papers, Class 8, Public Lands* 4 (1859): 555–561.

26. Bomford to Barbour, July 14, 1827, p. 216, vol. 1, Mineral Lands Letters, RG 156, NA.

27. The standard biography is Louis Pelzer, *Henry Dodge* (Iowa City, 1911).

28. Bomford to Barbour, July 31, 1827, p. 223, vol. 1, Mineral Lands Letters, RG 156, NA.

29. John Marsh to Lewis Cass, July 4, 1827, Letters Received, Michigan, 1827, Records of the Bureau of Indian Affairs, RG 75, NA. The Marsh letter is an enclosure to a letter from Cass to Barbour, July 4, 1827. See also report of Henry Atkinson to George Gaines, September 28, 1827, H. Doc. 2, 20th Cong., 1st sess., p. 155, Serial 169.

30. Cass to Barbour, July 4 and 10, 1827, Letters Received, Michigan, 1827, RG 75, NA.

31. Atkinson to Gaines, H. Doc. 2, 20th Cong., 1st sess., p. 156, Serial 169. See also *History of Iowa County, Wisconsin,* pp. 461–462.

32. Atkinson to Gaines, H. Doc. 2, 20th Cong., 1st sess., p. 157, Serial 169.

33. Joseph M. Street to Barbour, November 15, 1827, Letters Received, Prairie du Chien, 1827, RG 75, NA.

34. *History of Iowa County, Wisconsin,* p. 492.

35. William Clark to Barbour, July 10, 1828, Letters Received, Prairie du Chien, 1828, RG 75, NA.

36. Documents relating to the negotiation of the treaty of August 1, 1829, with the Winnebago Indians, Ratified Treaty No. 156, RG 75, NA.

37. *History of Iowa County, Wisconsin*, pp. 466–467, 807.

38. Ibid., p. 808.

39. Schafer, *The Wisconsin Lead Region*, p. 42.

40. "Memorial to the Secretary of War by Inhabitants of the Lead-Mining District," January 9, D-Misc. 1832, Letters Received by the Secretary of War, Unregistered Series, 1789–1861, Records of the Office of the Secretary of War, RG 107, NA.

41. Henry Gratiot to George B. Porter, May 11, 1832, Letters Received by the Michigan Superintendency, 1932, RG 75, NA; see also *History of Iowa County, Wisconsin*, p. 479.

42. Clark to the Secretary of War, August 12, 1831, Letters Received, St. Louis, 1831, RG 75, NA. Clark enclosed copies and extracts from the reports of Indian agents to the Superintendent of Indian Affairs "relating to the continued occupancy by the Sacs & Foxes of the ceded lands on the East of the Mississippi" (folio A); copies and abstracts from his instructions to the agents of the tribes engaged in the hostilities (folio B); and copies of talks with the Indians (folio C).

43. The journal is with a letter from Gratiot to Cass, September 30, 1832, Letters Received, Prairie du Chien, 1832, RG 75, NA.

44. *History of Iowa County, Wisconsin*, pp. 480–481.

45. Clark to John Robb, June 26, 1832, Letters Received, Sac and Fox, 1832, RG 75, NA.

46. John Carl Parish, *George Wallace Jones* (Iowa City, 1912), p. 120.

47. Compiled Military Service Records of the Indian Wars (Volunteer Organizations), Records of the Adjutant General's Office, RG 94, NA.

48. Bounty-Land Warrant Application Records, Post-Revolutionary War Series, Records of the Veterans Administration, RG 15, NA.

49. *History of Iowa County, Wisconsin*, pp. 809–810.

50. This information appears on the original survey plat, which remains in the custody of the Bureau of Land Management, Eastern States Office, Status Section, Washington, DC. See also copy of letter from Sam Williams to Hervey Parke, October 2, 1832, Letterbook D, Surveyor General of the Territory Northwest of the River Ohio, RG 49, NA. This letter transmitted the survey contract to Parke, "together with diagram of the township lines, and instructions relating thereto." The instructions in part directed him to ascertain "as near as practicable, the *exact situation* of all *Lead Mines* which have been worked, called 'diggings,' and of the furnaces, houses and improvements, and every other object worthy of note, and describe them in your field book."

51. The field notes for surveys in Wisconsin have been retained by the Bureau of Land Management, Eastern States Office, Status Section, Washington, DC.

52. Act of June 26, 1834, 4 Stat. 686.

53. Sheldon and Eneix were confirmed on June 30: U.S., Congress, Senate, *Executive Journal*, 4: 436, 442. Their commissions, which were sent to Mineral Point July 30, 1834, are recorded on p. 28, vol. 5, Letters Sent to the Registers and Receivers (New Series), Division "C," RG 49, NA.

54. Schafer, *The Wisconsin Lead Region*, p. 187.

55. "Proclamation of Land Sales at Mineral Point," No. 196, vol. 1, Record Copies of Proclamations, Public Land Sales, Division "C," RG 49, NA.

56. Elijah Hayward to Sheldon and Eneix, July 29, 1835, p. 16, vol. 6, Letters Sent to the Registers and Receivers (New Series), Division "C," RG 49, NA.

57. Sheldon and Eneix to Lucius Lyon, December 19, 1834, LC: HR 23A-G22.2, Records of the U.S. House of Representatives, RG 233, NA.

58. Schafer, *The Wisconsin Lead Region*, pp. 118–121.

59. *History of Iowa County, Wisconsin*, p. 810.

60. "Memorial of the Legislative Council of Michigan Territory," Mar. 1, 1836, LC: HR 24A-G16.4, RG 233, NA.

61. *History of Iowa County, Wisconsin*, p. 497; see also Schafer, *The Wisconsin Lead Region*, p. 83.

62. This information is based on an analysis of the "List of Suspended Entries Made at Mineral Point, Wisconsin," and the "Special Tract Book of Lead Land in the Mineral Point District, Wisconsin," RG 49, NA.

63. "List of Purchases of Lead Lands in Wisconsin and Iowa, 1834–39," and the "Special Tract Book of Lead Land in the Mineral Point District, Wisconsin," RG 49, NA.

64. The land entry papers of the former General Land Office, RG 49, NA, are now maintained in the General Branch at the Washington National Records Center, Suitland, MD.

65. *History of Iowa County, Wisconsin*, p. 497.

66. "A complete list of all the lands in the Mineral Point District which have been reported as lead lands, or timbered lands proper to be reserved for smelting purposes," Records Relating to Leasing and Operation of Lead Lands in Mineral Point District, WI, RG 49, NA. See also J. M. Moore to Register, Mineral Point, p. 208, vol. 9, Letters Sent to the Registers and Receivers (New Series), Division "C," RG 49, NA; Acting Commissioner, General Land Office, to the Secretary of the Treasury, July 31, 1840, Letters From the Commissioner of the General Land Office to the Secretary of the Treasury (hereafter cited as GLO to Secretary of the Treasury) (June 23–Dec. 31, 1840), General Records of the Department of the Treasury, RG 56, NA.

67. Act of July 11, 1846, 9 Stat. 37.

68. James Whitcomb to Levi Woodbury, September 22, 1840, GLO to Secretary of the Treasury (June 23–Dec. 31, 1840), RG 56, NA.

69. Solicitor of the General Land Office to Whitcomb, September 12, 1840 (enclosure to Whitcomb to Woodbury, Sept. 22, 1840), GLO to Secretary of the Treasury (June 23–Dec. 31, 1840), RG 56, NA.

70. Richard M. Young to Samuel Leech, April 12, 1847, Record of Suspended Entries in the Mineral Point District of Wisconsin, RG 49, NA.

71. This volume is in the Records of the General Land Office Relating to Leasing and Operation of Lead Mines, RG 49, NA.

72. This statement is recorded in Record of Suspended Entries in the Mineral Point District of Wisconsin as part of Leech's certification, dated August 22, 1847, concerning such matters as the authenticity of the testimony produced by the claimants.

73. Jefferson Davis to M. F. Burt, April 23, 1853; Cass to Burt, April 26, 1853; and oath of office, Applications for Positions in the Treasury Department (hereafter cited as Treasury Department Applications), RG 56, NA.

74. Sheldon to Secretary Chase, March 7, 1861, Treasury Department Applications, RG 56, NA.

75. *History of Iowa County, Wisconsin*, p. 679.

76. Iowa County, WI, vol. 3, 1850, and vol. 10, 1870, Population Schedules, RG 29, NA.

77. P. 23, vol. 7, Registers of Appointments of Postmasters, Records of the Post Office Department, RG 28, NA.

78. P. 772, Vol. 12-B, Registers of Appointments of Postmasters, RG 28, NA.

79. Route No. 3458, Mail Route Register, 1836–37 (KY, MO, WI), RG 28, NA.

80. Route No. 2914, Mail Route Register, 1837–42 (IL, WI), RG 28, NA.

81. Route No. 4416, Mail Route Register, 1842–46 (IL, WI), RG 28, NA.

82. George W. Jones to the President of the United States, April 17, 1858, Presidential Appointments File, Appointments Division, Records of the Office of the Secretary of the Interior, RG 48, NA.

83. Decisions of Land Commissioners in Louisiana Territory (now Missouri), vol. 2 (Book 53), and Report of Recorder of Land Titles at St. Louis, MO, under Act of May 26, 1834, vol. 43, Division "D," Private Land Claims Records, RG 49, NA. Extensive documentation on the Bequette claims has been published in U.S., Congress, *American State Papers, Class 8, Public Lands*, vols. 2 and 3 (1834), vol. 4 (1859), and vol. 6 (1860).

84. Private Land Claim Dockets 102 (Survey 3204) and 172, RG 49, NA. These dockets are now maintained in the General Branch at the Washington National Records Center, Suitland, MD.

85. Paschal Bequette, Compiled Military Service Record (Black Hawk War), RG 94, NA.

86. Paschal Bequette, Act of 50-80-Wt. 19661; Act of 55-80-Wt. 25998, Bounty-Land Warrant Application Records, Post-Revolutionary War Series, RG 15, NA.

87. Paschal Bequette, License Bond, December 1, 1832, in Bonds and Leases for Mines of Lead Ore (Unnumbered), RG 49, NA.

88. *History of Iowa County, Wisconsin*, p. 810.

89. "List of Purchases of Lead Lands in Wisconsin and Iowa, 1834–39," and "Special Tract Book of Lead Land in the Mineral Point District, Wisconsin," RG 49, NA. The first land entry at Mineral Point was made on October 20, 1834, by George Wallace Jones, who filed for the southwest quarter of section 30, T. 1 N., R. 1 W. The first public land sale at Mineral Point, held in November 1834, covered certain lands *west* of the fourth principal meridian (Grant County).

90. Land entry case files (certificates 268, 271), and "Special Tract Book of Lead Land in the Mineral Point District, Wisconsin," RG 49, NA.

91. Land entry case files (certificates 3268, 3269, 4758, and 4790), RG 49, NA.

92. *History of Iowa County, Wisconsin*, pp. 476, 516. Official bonds of Paschal Bequette, November 18, 1840, and October 1, 1846, Surety Bonds, Records of the Bureau of Accounts, RG 39, NA.

93. Theodore Rodolf, "Pioneering in the Wisconsin Lead Region," *Wisconsin State Historical Society, Collections*, 15 (Madison, 1900): 371.

94. Executive Commissions Confirmed, p. 45, vol. 1, Appointments Division, RG 48, NA; official bond of Bequette, October 4, 1854, Surety Bonds, RG 39, NA; Commissioner Hendricks to Bequette, December 30, 1858, vol. 10, Appointments Division, RG 48, NA.

95. Paschal Bequette, Presidential Appointments File, Appointments Division, RG 48, NA.

96. Special record, vol. 1, Appointments Division, RG 48, NA. See also J. M. Edmunds to Royal H. Waller (notified Waller of his permanent appointment from July 15, 1861), vol. 12, Appointments Division, RG 48, NA.

97. Paschal Bequette to Joseph Wilson, March 19, 1861, Letters Received From Registers and Receivers, Division "D," Mail and Files, RG 49, NA.

98. Bequette to Commissioner, General Land Office, May 24, 1861, Letters Received From Registers and Receivers, Division "D," Mail and Files, RG 49, NA.

Military Bounty-Land Warrants of the Mexican War

Before 1861, the U.S. military suffered chronic manpower shortages. For military manpower during the Revolutionary War and the War of 1812, the United States relied most heavily on patriotism and a recruiting device called the military bounty-land warrant, whereby the government offered a warrant, or certificate, for land in return for enlistment. For both Revolutionary War and War of 1812 veterans, Congress decided that the land warrants could be used only in specified areas of the public domain known as military districts. This meant that a veteran had to move to the frontier (Ohio in the 1790s, Illinois in 1817) to take advantage of the federal bounty.[1]

The execution of President Polk's war against Mexico, declared May 12, 1846, was hindered by the familiar problem of too few troops. Nine months after war broke out, in an effort to increase military manpower, Congress passed an act to raise 10 regiments of troops by granting 160-acre bounty-land warrants to regulars and volunteers (but not officers) who served a year or the war's duration, whichever came first, or died trying.[2] Under this new legislation, warrants could be used to select land anywhere on the public domain. Congressional discussion of the 10-regiments bill centered on two questions: the minimum length of service for eligibility and whether the warrants should be made assignable. Congress quickly decided that 1 year's service (rather than the 5 years required of soldiers in the War

of 1812) was sufficient for eligibility. However, the assignment (transfer by sale) of land warrants provoked more heated debate. Senator Thomas Hart Benton from Missouri so feared land speculation that he sought to limit "occupancy" of a parcel of land patented under a land warrant to blood descendants of the veteran upon whose service the land warrant was originally granted. Benton argued that if warrants were assignable, speculators would buy them for a pittance. Opponents of Benton and his scheme for something resembling an American entail understood that a warrant without the option to sell was useless to most veterans. This group, led by Senator Simon Cameron from Pennsylvania, prevailed in 1847 with a simple compromise: veterans were given the choice of selecting a $100 treasury note instead of the warrant. Since public land sold at $1.25 an acre, a 160-acre land warrant bore a face value of $200. This treasury scrip option in effect set a minimum price at which bounty-land warrants would be sold. The arrangement satisfied critics who worried that veterans who wanted to sell their warrants might not receive fair value for them.

Many veterans circumvented the rule requiring an applicant to actually receive the warrant before selling it.[3] For example, in New Orleans, the chief port of discharge for Mexican War veterans, many warrant brokers offered a rewarding shortcut around the regulation requiring veterans to wait for the warrant.

Agents helped thousands of veterans file warrant application forms; then many of the veterans signed over power-of-attorney rights to dispose of the land warrants. Each party benefited from the arrangement: the veteran was paid immediately for the transaction, and the broker received the warrant directly from Washington. While no one was hurt by the subterfuge, Benton's fear that speculators would dominate land-warrant exchanges seemed confirmed.

Interested contemporaries of Benton and an occasional historian have suggested that most veterans and their heirs chose to sell the warrants rather than use them to obtain land in the public domain. The question "what did veterans do with their bounty-land warrants" can be answered by analyzing a random sample of the warrants that are preserved in the National Archives.[4] I analyzed a ½ of 1 percent random sample (or 441 cases) of the 88,269 people who received bounty-land warrants under the 1847 act (more than 90 percent of whom had served in the Mexican War). This essay is based on the findings of that analysis. The warrants are numbered consecutively in two series: 80,689 160-acre warrants, and 7,580 40-acre warrants awarded to a special group of 90-day volunteers. Two facts about the army provide us with a yardstick to measure the sample's reliability. First, we know the approximate composition of the troops, whether they were in the U.S. Army or belonged to state volunteer regiments. Approximately two-thirds of the men served as state volunteers, while one-third campaigned as U.S. regulars. The corresponding figures for the sample are 295 volunteers (66.8%), 143 U.S. regulars (32.4%), and 3 unknowns (0.8%). Second, we know that approximately 14 percent who served in the war died as a result of combat-related injuries. The corresponding figure for the sample was 60 dead or about 13 percent of the sample. On the basis of the close match between known figures about Mexican War forces and the sample, we may proceed with some confidence that findings for the sample apply generally to the whole population of Mexican War veterans.

The findings of my analysis show how veterans and their heirs used the land warrants. From the 441 files (381 veterans and 60 heirs), just 26 veterans and heirs used their land warrants to select and take title to 160 acres of public land. In other words, 94 percent of the 1847 warrantees sold their land warrants. Of the 26 veterans and heirs who did not sell, 24 lived in public land states and, as a rule, used their warrants close to home within their state of residence.[5] The vast majority of veterans in the sample (94.5%) sold their warrants, and heirs of veterans behaved much the same as the veterans. Ninety-two percent of the 60 heirs found in the sample sold their warrants.[6]

The physical form of the 1847 warrants is a folio with the front page containing a letterpress form to be filled in with pertinent eligibility information (information about the applicant: name, rank, and unit of the veteran, and relationship to veteran if the warrantee was an heir), date the warrant was issued, address or depository of the warrantee, the signatures of the preparing clerk in the Pension Bureau and the Commissioner of Pensions, the warrant number, and the appropriate acreage. The inside and back pages were reserved for handwritten information about transfer of the warrant by sale.

Transfers had to follow a regular form that consists of three paragraphs. In the first paragraph the warrantee acknowledged transfer of both the warrant and all rights to the land to another person in exchange for an unspecified "value received." There was space for the transfer to be dated and signed by one witness, a notary public, and the warrantee.

The second paragraph consists of a simple statement from the notary public that the warrantee was known to be himself and had executed the assignment on the date specified. The handwriting of this paragraph almost always matches that of the first, suggesting that the notary wrote both. The third paragraph is a statement from a judge or clerk of the local circuit court to the effect that the notary was in fact authorized as such in that county. The purpose of all these sworn statements was to

WAR DEPARTMENT,

Office of the Commissioner of Pensions.

IT HEREBY CERTIFIED, that the Land Warrant No. *33755 for 160 acres* has been issued in the name of *Thomas Mitchell — Private*, *Capt. Preston's Comp.y 9 Reg. U.S. Infantry*

under date *of October 27 1848* and will be deposited in the GENERAL LAND OFFICE, at the Seat of Government; and that, pursuant to the provisions of the subjoined ninth section of the Act of Congress, approved on the 11th day of February, 1847, entitled "*An act to raise for a limited time an additional military force, and for other purposes,*" this Certificate of right to locate said warrant on any *Quarter Section* of land subject to private entry, will be received at any of the Land Offices of the United States, under the regulations and restrictions set forth in the accompanying statement of the Commissioner of the General Land Office.

After the location of this Certificate, it is to be surrendered to the General Land Office, whence the PATENT will issue.

GIVEN under my hand, at the **Pension Office,** this *27* day of *October 1848*

One of
Chubb & Schenck
President

J. L. Edwards
Commissioner of Pensions.

By J. G. Hunt

G. Alexander, Printer, Washington.

Military bounty-land warrant of Thomas Mitchell.

prevent fraud. These precautions probably worked since the sample reveals only three cases of known fraud.[7]

The most unusual case was that of a Mississippi widow, Ellen Reed. She and her children Thomas and Susan applied for a land warrant in 1849 in the name of her late husband Richard Reed, a private in D Company of the First U.S. Artillery Regiment. The warrant application was in order, and on June 22, 1849, Mrs. Reed was issued warrant number 61,656. In August, she sold the warrant. Unfortunately for Mrs. Reed, Richard Reed's mother applied for a land warrant in her son's name, claiming next-of-kin status. When she insisted that Richard had never married and had no children, the Pension Office questioned Ellen Reed about the particulars of her marriage. Ellen answered that she married Richard in Columbus, MS, on a certain date. Private Reed's mother had little difficulty proving that Richard had gone fishing near his home on the Kennebec River in Maine the day of his "wedding" in Mississippi. Ellen's warrant was canceled and a new one was issued to Reed's mother.

Unlike earlier bounty-land acts, the 1847 warrants could be used anywhere on the public domain. This freedom to select land in one of the 13 states containing public domain did not result in an even distribution of claims in those states. Warrant holders used them primarily in the upper Mississippi region. Table 1 presents a summary of warrant usage by state, and the figures show two-thirds of the sample warrants being used in Iowa, Illinois, and Wisconsin. As table 2 demonstrates, three of the five busiest land offices were situated in the old lead-mining area long the Mississippi.

Veterans and heirs assigned their land warrants without filling in the name of the buyer on the assumption that the warrant might change hands several times before some ultimate purchaser took the paper to a land office and selected a quarter-section of public land. Most of the end users were farmers who bought warrants on credit at high rates of interest from frontier land bankers. The war-

rants themselves bear no trace of such "time-entry" arrangements, but the practice made brokers wealthy and, in the absence of western banking facilities responsive to farmers' needs, probably helped thousands of farmers get a start in landownership.

Capitalists could obtain warrants for less than the $1.25 an acre charged by the government for public land and save themselves

TABLE 1
Sample Warrant Location By State*

State	Number	Percent
Ohio	6	1.4
Indiana	24	5.6
Illinois	117	27.1
Michigan	15	3.5
Wisconsin	68	15.8
Iowa	104	24.1
Minnesota	6	1.4
Kansas	3	0.7
Missouri	40	9.3
Arkansas	13	3.0
Louisiana	20	4.6
Mississippi	1	0.2
Alabama	14	3.2
Total	431	99.9

*Ten warrants are not included, three because of fraud and seven for administrative cancellations.

TABLE 2
The Ten Busiest Land Offices for Warrant Locations

Office	Number	Percentage of Sample
Dixon, IL	40	9.2
Fairfield, IA	36	8.4
Green Bay, WI	31	7.2
Dubuque, IA	30	7.0
Mineral Point, WI	27	6.3
Iowa City, IA	24	5.6
Palestine, IL	15	3.5
Vandalia, IL	14	3.2
Natchitoches, LA	12	2.8
Springfield, IL	11	2.6
Total	240	55.8

money when locating large quantities of land. Some of the speculators were southerners or easterners working through western agents.[8] Robert Ives ran a banking house in Providence, RI, that was associated with the mercantile powers in that city, and in 1852 he purchased thousands of acres of public land through the eastern Illinois land offices at Danville and Vandalia. He bought warrant number 76,985 from Philadelphia's Edward McCarty in November 1852 and quickly redeemed it for land through the Danville Land Office.[9] Another of the great eastern capitalists who bought one of the warrants was Elias White of Baltimore.[10]

Several buyers of warrants in the sample were western land brokers whose activities have received attention from historians of land speculation. John Culbertson of Iowa City and Horatio Sanford of Dubuque were prominent resident Iowa speculators.[11] Cyrus Woodman, the biggest speculator in early Wisconsin history, bought a warrant, as did Fond du Lac's Keyes Darling and Mark Guggenheim of Green Bay.[12] John Dement and his brother Charles obtained over 150,000 acres, mainly with warrants, in Illinois during the Fillmore-Taylor years. The buyer of three of the warrants in the sample, Dement had served as register of the Dixon Land Office for every Democratic President from Jackson to Pierce.[13]

Several congressmen found warrants an attractive investment. John Sherman of Ohio bought one of the earliest land warrants issued in 1847 and obtained land through the Winamac, IN, Land Office.[14] Two of the three Washburn brothers in Congress at various times before the Civil War bought warrants in the sample. Israel of Maine selected land in Minnesota, while Elihu of Illinois stayed within his own district and used his warrant at the Dixon Land Office.

In addition to contributing to our knowledge of the distribution of public lands, the 1847 warrants are also a useful source for other aspects of local and family history. For example, as part of every warrant assignment the notary public listed the county or city where the transaction took place. In about 90 percent of the warrants in the sample, the site of the assignment is a good approximation of the home of the warrantee.[15] Thus, a genealogist can use these warrants to gain a more specific geographical location for an ancestor's home.

Researchers in family history should also be aware that in the 1850s the federal government made additional bounty land grants to veterans of the War of 1812, the Mexican War, and the various Indian Wars. A comparison of the land grant application files of veterans with their military service records will pinpoint the whereabouts of these individuals at two points in time—as young men serving their country and as veterans applying for bounty land grants.[16]

Genealogists also may be able to learn of the literacy or illiteracy of an ancestor who was a warrantee. In order to locate a warrant at the land office or sell a warrant to a buyer, the veteran or heir had to take an oath and sign his or her name. In approximately 25 percent of the cases in the sample, warrantees "made their mark" (usually a ragged "X") which generally is an indication of illiteracy.

Finally, the application files also may include a variety of other information of interest to genealogists. If a veteran applied, the application usually provides a date of birth and residence at the time the application was completed. If an heir applied, the file should reveal the name of the heir and his or her relationship to the deceased veteran. Applications from widows and children, the most common heirs, often provide dates of birth for all of the applicants.

Access to the military bounty-land application files is relatively easy and the search for the application file of a specific veteran can be done by mail. The staff of the National Archives will conduct a search for the file if the researcher can provide the full name of the veteran and the state regiment in which he served. Since there were many veterans with the same or similar names, the more specific identification provided, the more likely that the Archives staff will find the correct individual.

Copies of individual application files are available for a modest fee; requests should be submitted on National Archives Trust Fund Form 80. (These forms are available free from the Reference Services Branch upon request.) Completed forms should be submitted to the Military Service Branch (NNMS), National Archives and Records Administration, Washington, DC 20408. Following these procedures will insure that family and local history researchers locate the application files they want and the information they need as quickly as possible.

NOTES

1. Jerry O'Callaghan, "The War Veteran and the Public Lands," *Agricultural History* 28 (1954):163–168; Rudolph Freund, "Military Bounty Lands and the Origins of the Public Domain," in Vernon Carstensen, *The Public Lands* (1963), p. 14; Theodore Carlson, *The Illinois Military Tract* (1951).

2. Act of February 11, 1847, 9 Stat. 125.

3. The ban on assignment of the warrants before receipt is stated in section 9 of the 1847 Act: "All sales, mortgages, powers or other instruments of writing, going to affect the title or claim to any such bounty right, made or executed prior to the issue of such warrant or certificate, shall be null and void."

4. See Richard S. Maxwell, "The Public Land Records of the Federal Government, 1800–1950, and Their Statistical Significance," paper presented at the Conference on the National Archives and Statistical Research, May 1968, p. 11. The warrant files are part of Records of the Bureau of Land Management, Record Group 49, National Archives (hereafter cited as RG_____, NA). See Clarence S. Peterson, *Known Military Dead During the Mexican War, 1846–48* (1957).

5. One Kentuckian used his warrant to move to Missouri, and Peter McGlew, a Troy, NY, carpenter, moved to Iowa to take up farming.

6. Of the 60 applicants for warrants of next-of-kin status, 11 were widows and 49 were either parents or siblings.

7. Frauds were more likely in the absence of good records. Mexican War veterans usually had their discharge papers available when making their applications to the Pension Office. Later bounty-land acts in 1850, 1852, and 1855 rewarded older veterans of Indian wars and the War of 1812. Most of these veterans had lost their discharge papers, and many had forgotten the particulars of their service. The grants of the 1850s were more generally plagued by sharpers and swindlers than the 1847 grant. The pattern in 1847 was that the warrants issued to heirs were the most susceptible to fraud; detection came about only upon a second, legitimate application.

8. Paul Gates, *History of Public Land Law Development* (1968), ch. 11; Gates, "The Role of the Land Speculator in Western Development," *Pennsylvania Magazine of History and Biography* 65 (1942):314–333; Robert Swierenga, *Pioneers and Profits: Land Speculation on the Iowa Frontier* (1968), chs. 5, 6.

9. For details on Robert Ives's land speculations, see General Land Office cash entry books for the Vandalia and Danville land offices, 1852, RG 49, NA.

10. For the White family business, see Paul Gates, "Southern Investments in Western Lands," *Journal of Southern History* 5 (1939):155–185.

11. Swierenga, *Pioneers and Profits*, tables 2–1 and 2–6.

12. Details on Woodman's speculations may be found in Larry Gara, *Westernized Yankee* (1956) and Paul Gates, "Frontier Land Business in Wisconsin," *Wisconsin Magazine of History* 53 (1969):307–327.

13. Paul Gates, *The Illinois Central and Its Colonization Work* (1934), p. 115.

14. Sherman's brother William Tecumseh resented the fact that officers were expressly left out of the bounty provisions of the 1847 act. See his 1850 letter on the subject to Persifor Smith, reprinted in *Pennsylvania Magazine of History and Biography* 75 (1951):248.

15. About 10 percent of the warrantees cannot be identified by geographical home at the time of the assignment. For the most part, unknowns were regulars in the U.S. Army who promptly sold their warrants in New Orleans. The only other instances where the place of assignment may not reflect the home state is in the case of certain river cities (Cincinnati, St. Louis, New York, or Washington), which drew warrantees from neighboring states because of the concentration of warrant brokers offering good prices.

16. The land warrant files of the congressional acts of the 1850s as well as the possibilities of using them for research are discussed in James W. Oberly, "Westward Who? Estimates of Native White Interstate Migration After the War of 1812," *Journal of Economic History*, 46 (1986):431–440.

PART V

COUNTING AMERICAN FAMILIES AND COMMUNITIES

Randolph Street, Chicago, 1898.

112

For the past two centuries, one of the fundamental activities of the federal government has been to take a census of the American population every 10 years. As stated in section two of the first article of the U.S. Constitution: "The actual Enumeration shall be made within three Years after the first Meeting of the Congress of the United States, and within every subsequent Term of ten Years, in such a manner as they shall by Law direct." This simple statement made the United States the first nation in the world to provide for a census by law.

Little did the framers of the Constitution realize that the schedules compiled by the census takers would become an extraordinarily important source for family and local history research in the United States. Beginning in 1790, census takers recorded a wide variety of data about the American people—for example, their names, addresses, occupations, places of birth, and age. For many Americans the census is the only documentary record of their lives in America. "The manuscript federal population census," notes Keith Schlesinger in his essay, "offers a combination of depth, breadth, and continuity unmatched by any other historical document."

But the population census is not the only general record that documents individual families. The passage of a law requiring a tax on individual income during the Civil War years resulted in a body of records that rivals census schedules in the quality and quantity of family and local history information. For the years from 1862 to 1866, at least, the documentation on who lived where and owned what is quite complete.

The authors of the three essays that follow provide guidance on the use of census schedules and income tax records. Sarah Larson is a family and local history consultant who worked for the National Archives for several years. Keith R. Schlesinger received his doctorate in history from Northwestern University and has worked as an editor on the Adams Papers. Cynthia G. Fox is an archivist in the Civil Archives Division of the National Archives.

SARAH LARSON

The Census and Community History: A Reappraisal

In 1859, Sandy Bowers, a "superlatively illiterate but very generous man," discovered that 10 feet of the mining claim he was working outside Virginia City, NV, covered a portion of the rich Comstock silver lode.[1] The adjacent 10-foot claim, belonging to a widow variously reported as "Mrs. Cowan" and "Eilly Orrum," also overlapped the lode. Being practical, after a fashion, Bowers married the widow and spent a halcyon 8 years running through a little over a million dollars. For a time the wealthiest couple in Virginia City, the Bowerses entertained lavishly and constantly, built themselves a $300,000 granite palace in the Washoe Valley complete with silver doorknobs and a brass piano with mother-of-pearl keys, and took an 8-month tour of Europe, after which Eilly claimed she had met Queen Victoria.[2] By 1866, the Bowerses' mine was exhausted, and Sandy died in 1868 at the age of 35, leaving his wife nothing except the granite mansion.[3] Eilly survived by gradually selling the furnishings and fixtures of the palace and then running it as a picnic resort. By 1892, the mansion was a "habitation for owls, bats, and spooks," while the widow earned a meager living telling fortunes.[4]

This is local history at its most hearty and most familiar, spinning the tales of eccentricities and memorable events that seem to capture the spirit of an era. What could be more evocative of the jerry-built nature of a boomtown, for example, than the history of the Virginia City Methodist Church, which lost four buildings to wind and fire and two ministers to romance and spirits in under 15 years?[5] And, who better than Sandy and Eilly Bowers sums up the early years of Virginia City, which was established in 1859, had a peak population of 25,000 in 1876, and a mere 2,695 by 1900?[6]

But, before the Bowerses found their way into retrospective newspaper articles and history books, their story was part of the local folklore, quite possibly gaining a bit in the telling over time. To check reliability, the researcher must go back to contemporary records, the most accessible of which may well be the microfilmed census schedules. The census is particularly useful for the study of frontier communities, which had no formal government body to gather and preserve community records.

For instance, in 1860 Nevada did not exist either as a state or territory, but Virginia City was definitely in place, housing the miners busy burrowing into the Comstock Lode for gold and silver. The researcher must go to maps of the period to discover that Virginia City was part of Carson County, Utah Territory. Contemporary maps also reveal outlying districts, vital information for both genealogist and local historian, no matter whether the search is for specific individuals like the Bowerses or for an overall community profile. Americans are characteristically mobile, but many migrations are from one small community to the next

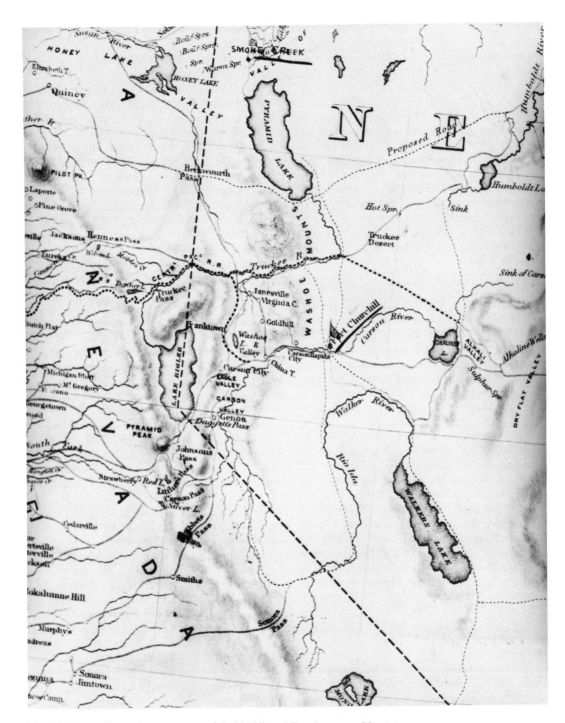

This 1860 map shows the proximity of Gold Hill and Franktown to Virginia City, suggesting how miners could easily move from one small community to the next as their fortunes fluctuated.

rather than coast to coast. This was particularly true for brand new towns where the sap still leaked from wooden store fronts.

Virginia City sat directly atop the Comstock Lode, as did Gold Hill, a short distance away. In between were mining camps and isolated claims; the two towns were linked together by a scraggly chain of tents. In 1860, Gold Hill had a population of only 638, Virginia City one of 2,345.[7] Miners ranged back and forth between the two as they staked out new claims, hoping to tap into the rich Comstock Lode. Thus, while histories say that in 1859 Sandy Bowers struck it rich in Virginia City, the most likely Bowers in the 1860 Utah Territory census is in Gold Hill. There is an S. S. Bowers, age 27, male, born in Illinois, occupation miner. Significantly, this Bowers owned $115,000 in real property, a striking contrast to most of the other miners listed, who were recorded as having virtually no real or personal property. This census entry, then, would seem to fit the story handed down in the histories, of a young man just beginning to take incredible wealth from the mountain, who was to die 8 years later at age 35.

However, if the researcher doesn't stop in triumph with S. S. Bowers, but continues to read the census, just eight pages later he will find an L. S. Bowers, also age 27, male, born in Illinois, occupation miner. But this Bowers has no property, real or personal, recorded. Two different miners? An enumerator's error? In some histories, Sandy Bowers is identified as Lemuel S. Bowers, so the initials would fit in either case. And both men are recorded as living with a Marion, age 33, female, born in Scotland. However, one schedule was filled out August 22, 1860, and the other the next day; and different people are listed as sharing a dwelling with Bowers and Marion in the two entries.[8]

The problem is not resolvable merely by looking at the census. But it should be clear at this point that the researcher who carefully examines the census, rather than abandoning the hunt prematurely, will find questions that don't quite fit contemporary accounts, the resolution of which would add much to historical accuracy. For example, the histories say that Sandy Bowers married Eilly Orrum or Cowan. But they don't say when. While a Bowers was living with Marion in 1860, the census does not indicate whether or nor she was his wife. Could Marion and Eilly be the same person?

In the 1870 census, there is an Allason Bowers in Franktown, Washoe County—also near Virginia City.[9] Allason was 42, female, white, keeping house, born in Scotland of foreign-born parents. And, importantly, Allason was worth $7,500 in real property and the same amount in personal property. She shared her house with Olive Leisley, age 14; Frank Worren, age 32, farm laborer; Wm. McPherson, age 37, farm laborer; Margaret Bowers, age 8; Susan Sullivan, age 28, domestic; and Joshua Jones, age 19, teamster. This entry also might fit the story of the twice-widowed Eilly Bowers, of dwindled means, living in a granite mansion in the Washoe Valley. Olive Leisley might be the child of the first marriage, Margaret Bowers the child of the second, and the other residents, boarders. Even the names fit; the traditional nickname for Allason is Ally, which could easily be misspelled as "Eilly."

By 1880, Franktown had a population of only 113, one of whom was Ella Bowers, a white female aged 49, born in Scotland of Scots parents, widowed, keeping house.[10] She had only one boarder, 32-year-old Joseph Kennedy, a contract laborer who had been out of work for 6 months.[11] Is this Eilly Bowers? Again, the name is probable, and the diminished fortunes are consistent with the story. She didn't age a full 10 years from one census to the next, but this is not unheard of. On balance, while the census alone could never supply proof positive, the information in the two Franktown entries is sufficiently close to indicate further digging into contemporary materials, such as land records, vital records (Did Olive Leisley or Margaret Bowers get married?), and any existing tax records. It's more problematical as to whether the Marion in Gold Hill was the Allason Bowers or Ella Bowers in Franktown. The ages would be fairly consistent, and all entries list

Scots nativity, but the names are very different. However, even if Marion was a separate person, this sheds new light on the history of the Bowerses because it suggests Sandy did not immediately marry the widow with the adjacent mining claim.

Genealogists are accustomed to grappling with the problems the census raises, such as names changing, individuals being listed twice, ages and household composition changing. The solving of these puzzles is the very substance of genealogy. But what could the local historian gain by wading into this morass of contradictory information? Fundamentally, the census triggers constructive skepticism. Any good researcher knows that folklore and oral tradition cannot be relied upon blindly. But it is not always easy to determine how to test the stories, how to distinguish the constructive questions from the nitpicking. The census will either support traditional accounts, indicating reliability, or raise specific questions that will direct the historian toward particular related records. Without the census, a researcher interested in the Bowerses of Virginia City would be unlikely to delve into the records of Gold Hill or of Franktown, which was in another county.

Likewise, the story of Sandy and Eilly Bowers should convince the genealogist not to rely solely upon printed local histories for specific information on communities in which ancestors lived. The same skepticism that is brought to good genealogy should be transferred to the use of local history, not to discard the histories scornfully on the basis of unreliability, but to double check. Even more important, traditional accounts that do not make use of the census cannot give a full portrait of the community.

Local history has tended to focus on the records left behind by community residents; government and court documents; city directories and maps; records of businesses, churches, fraternal organizations; manuscript and photograph collections; and, above all, contemporary newspapers. While not at all inaccurate, the history that emerges from these sources inescapably emphasizes the doers, the

wealthy, the fractious and flamboyant. This traditional approach tends to overlook ordinary people, such as the vast number of Virginia City residents who drifted through, following rumors of silver and gold, who, in their obscurity, did not appear in court records, were never killed in a mining accident, never became rich, never ran for office. These people contributed just as much to the rhythms of the community history as did those who bombastically made their way into local folklore. However, the stories of ordinary people do exist, preserved in the scrabbly handwriting of the census enumerator.

Almost as though conjured up by sleight-of-hand, Virginia City crops up on the 1860 census with a population of over 2,000. Many of those listed in the 1860 schedules arrived in Virginia City after the Comstock Lode was discovered in 1859. The earliest prospectors came on foot over the Sierra Nevada Mountains from California to find themselves snowed in for the winter. The range was covered with tent camps, regularly blown down by the "Washoe Zepher," as there was no road for the transportation of lumber and the slopes were bare of timber. Eventually, the men dug holes in the hills for shelter. Food and water "were at such a premium that everyone lived on whiskey, the one staple that seemed to come through even better than the mail."[12] Brush was the only fuel, and by spring the miners were sick from filth, scurvy, and lack of food.

But once the snows melted on the Sierra passes, more prospectors hurried into Virginia City, bringing in their wake the rudiments of boomtown civilization: roads, real estate speculators, mining stockbrokers, newspaper editors, lawyers, doctors, gamblers, saloon keepers, grocers, and even a few ministers. By the time of the Virginia City census in August 1860, the town was duly christened, sharing the Comstock Lode with Gold Hill.

Growth was phenomenal. By 1870, Virginia City had a total population of 7,048, almost equally native and foreign born. Of that total, 6,418 were "white," 91 "colored," and 539 "Chinese."[13] (Although the term "black" was

POPULATION OF CIVIL DIVISIONS LESS THAN COUNTIES.

TABLE III.—STATE OF NEVADA—Continued.

COUNTIES.	1870 Total.	Native.	Foreign.	White.	Colored.	Chinese.	1860 White.	Colored.	1850 White.	Colored.	COUNTIES.	1870 Total.	Native.	Foreign.	White.	Colored.	Chinese.	1860 White.	Colored.	1850 White.	Colored.
ESMERALDA—Cont'd.											LINCOLN—Cont'd.										
4 and 5	235	145	90	218	1	16					St. Thomas	252	197	55	252						
6	625	404	221	612	1	12					West Point	138	124	14	135		(b)				
Pine Grove	305	214	91	301	1	3					LYON.										
PineGrove Rockland	40	20	20	40							Churchill	40	19	21	40						
Rockland	120	68	52	113		7					Dayton	918	457	461	843	1	74				
7. Mason	158	120	38	157		1					Silver City	879	417	462	836	1	42	636	1		
HUMBOLDT.											NYE.										
Battle Mountain	261	146	115	244	2	15					Belmont	244	154	90	243	1					
Buena Vista	520	306	214	464	2	54					Duckwater	145	105	40	145						
Unionville	470	271	199	414	2	54					Ellsworth	54	41	13	53		1				
Central	23	10	13	15		8					Hot Creek	40	33	7	40						
Fish Creek	11	3	8	10	1						Ione	52	37	15	52						
Golconda	80	50	30	66		a13					Patterson	40	27	13	40						
Grass Valley	27	26	1	26	1						Reveille	80	52	28	78		2				
Humboldt	136	69	67	106		30					Silver Park	263	189	74	260		3				
Lake	117	49	68	93	1	23					Smoky Valley	57	33	24	57						
Paradise Valley	230	152	78	228		a1					Washington	49	33	16	49						
Queen's River	76	41	35	76							White River	63	56	7	63						
Sacramento	25	13	12	24							ORMSBY.										
Sierra	84	51	33	68		a15					Carson City	3042	1436	1606	2316	29	697				
Star City	36	11	25	30		6					Carson City							701	13		
Winnemucca	290	138	152	234	3	53					Empire City	626	324	302	552	2	72				
LANDER.											STOREY.										
Austin	1324	754	570	1281	27	16					Gold Hill	4311	1965	2346	4096	5	210	637	1		
1st ward	92	44	48	88		4					1st ward	2800									
2d ward	308	168	140	285	23						2d ward	1511									
3d ward	697	405	292	687	4	6					Virginia	7048	3592	3456	6418	91	539	2337	8		
4th ward	227	137	90	221		6					1st ward	1000									
Battle Mt. Station	150	81	69	103	2	45					2d ward	2300									
Beowawe	54	23	31	33		21					3d ward	2500									
Cortez District	46	22	24	45		1					4th ward	1248									
Eureka District	640	375	265	624	2	14					WASHOE.										
Garden Valley	28	24	4	27		1					Clark's Station	16	1	15	15		1				
Grass Valley	26	20	6	26							Crystal Peak	120	90	30	108	1	11				
Northern Reese River Valley	106	72	34	105		1					Franktown	271	139	132	264		7				
Palisade	39	22	17	26		13					Geiger Grade	55	19	36	50	1	4				
Secret Cañon	95	57	38	95							Glendale	129	94	35	125		4				
Smoking Valley	19	11	8	19							Long Valley	45	39	6	45						
Southern Reese River Valley	113	81	32	112		1					Mill Station	129	76	53	124	3	2				
Tuscarora, Independence Valley	119	12	107	15		104					Ophir	110	91	19	109		1				
Yankee Blade	56	26	30	55		1					Pea Vine	10	9	1	10						
LINCOLN.											Red Rock	6		6			6				
Hiko	110	83	27	108	1	(a)					Reno	1035	695	340	929	22	81				
Hiko	54	40	14	53		(a)					Truckee Meadows	320	224	96	293	1	26				
Pahranagat Valley	39	35	4	38	1						Verdi	40	27	13	40						
Tampinte	17	8	9	17							Wadsworth	253	173	80	209	8	36				
Panaca	493	379	114	488	2	(b)					Washoe City	552	320	232	510		42				
Bullionville	96	73	23	96							WHITE PINE.										
Clover Valley	32	29	3	32							Diamond Valley	26	16	10	26						
Meadow Valley	365	277	88	360	2	(b)					Egan Cañon	93	45	48	93						
Proche	1620	1067	553	1587	8	c23					Hamilton	3913	2147	1766	3698	55	160				
Dry Valley	133	105	28	131		a1					Kern	36	16	20	36						
Eagle Valley	159	139	20	158		(a)					Newark Valley	75	53	22	75						
Highland	21	15	6	21							Piermont	18	9	9	18						
Proche City	1144	665	479	1116	6	22					Pinto	51	31	20	51						
Rose Valley	27	19	8	27							Robinson	67	42	25	67						
Spring Valley	136	124	12	134	2						Shermantown	932	583	349	930	1	1				
Rio Virgin	762	619	143	754		(d)					Spring Valley	19	13	6	19						
Colville	4	3	1	2		(c)					Steptoe Valley	39	26	13	39						
Junction of Rio Virgin	13	13		13							Treasure	1929	791	1129	1778	11	131				
Las Vegas Valley	8	8		5		(b)															
Overton	149	117	32	149																	
St. Joseph	198	157	41	198																	

(a) Also 1 Indian.   (b) Also 3 Indians.   (c) Also 2 Indians.   (d) Also 2 Indians.

From *Statistics of the Population of the United States*, vol. 1, Census Office (1872).

the racial designation used on the census schedules, "colored" was used in the statistical compilations for 1870.) The Comstock Lode had been one of the richest mineral finds to date, internationally, and a glance down one page of the 1870 return indicates the extent to which people poured into Virginia City from around the world and throughout the country.

Under place of birth were listed New York, Alabama, Michigan, France, Georgia, Ireland, England, Nevada, Virginia, Massachusetts, Ohio, Sweden, Louisiana, Pennsylvania, Kentucky, California, Indiana, Canada, and Vermont.[14] Also in the census were people from Wales, Scotland, Germany, Norway, Switzerland, Mexico, and Denmark.[15]

Occupations were as varied as the population, although miners obviously held sway until the lode ran out. The boomtown atmosphere of Virginia City is clearly reflected in what was probably a row of lodging houses recorded in the 1870 census. Ages range from 19 to 57, and the occupations listed give some sense of the social mixing: "fast freight line," "clerk," "hostler," "driver," "miner," "keeps house," "milk business," "life insurance," "gambler," "policeman," "billiard saloon," "barkeeper," "laborer," "mechanic," "stockbroker," "actor," "painter," "carpenter," and "keeps lodgers." Though most boarders were single, one boarding family of four was supported by a mechanic father, while the mother kept house and the 27- and 25-year-old sons were professional gamblers.[16]

Though there seems to have been great residential mixing among people from various parts of the United States and northern Europe, the same cannot be said for those from China and Latin America. Noticeable for its difference from other parts of the Virginia City census is one long 1870 list of separate dwellings—most probably tents—in which residents with Latin last names noted their place of birth as Mexico, California, the Argentine Republic, Panama, Chile, Nevada, and Peru.[17] While a few natives of Mexico were interspersed with the Virginia City population, most Latin Americans apparently lived in an ethnic enclave.

Likewise, though some of the 539 Chinese in the 1870 census were scattered throughout the community, most as household servants, the majority lived in a neighborhood apart. The census suggests what an enormous cultural and language gap existed between the Chinese and the enumerators. Most of the Chinese reported have similar last names. However, making allowances for American spelling, this similarity is not beyond the realm of possibility, given that most Chinese immigrants to America at this period came from the same western province. Yet, the similarity of the first names, with a surprising number of Charlies and Sams, suggests that the enumerator either couldn't differentiate the sounds of the Chinese language or followed the prevalent custom of giving all "Chinamen," be they Chinese or Japanese, the same name.[18]

There is great repetition in the occupations of the Chinese, reflecting the customs of community and employee. Perhaps no other immigrant group to America was received with as much violence as the Chinese. Many west coast states attempted to limit or prohibit the ownership of land by orientals, and well into the 1950s the Chinese were bounded by a unique set of immigration restrictions. Yet, in frontier towns and mining communities in which there were many single men or fathers and sons forging ahead without their women, the personal services such as cooking and laundering and sewing that the Chinese performed were invaluable. With such a ready market, it is no surprise that just one page of the 1870 Virginia City census listed 30 Chinese with the occupation "wash house," and the others "wood chopper," "bar tender," "cook," and "waiter."[19]

Oddly, virtually every Chinese woman included in the 1870 Virginia City census was listed with the occupation of "harlot." Even in families, where, for instance, the father was a cook and there were several children "at home," the wife was recorded as a "harlot." Only a small handful of white women had the occupation of "prostitute," and they were obviously grouped together in a particular area of town in which they shared their census schedule with gamblers, saloon keepers, and miners. Also in that neighborhood was one forlorn "milk man," a native of Switzerland.[20]

Single white women who lived scattered throughout Virginia City, usually in lodging houses, were rarely recorded as plying the oldest profession. Many were listed as "seamstress," with the overwhelming number "keeps house." There were, however, a fair number of single Mexican women living outside their ethnic neighborhood who were listed as "prostitute."

This is the stuff to pique a researcher's curiosity. Why were Chinese women listed as "harlots" and women of other ethnic groups as "prostitutes?" As the profession was supposedly illegal, reference to any existing court records might reveal whether an official distinction was made between the two words; newspaper articles might reveal any unofficial social distinction, as might contemporary dictionaries.

It would also be interesting to check how many women hauled before the bar for prostitution were listed in the census as "seamstress" or "keeps house." Of course, it would be highly unreasonable for the researcher to assume that all women living without a father or spouse were prostitutes. Many in the census had children in their homes and might have been supported by prospector-husbands who sent money back to Virginia City. Or they might have been widowed; mining was a harsh and dangerous profession. By the same token, many prostitutes had children who were buffed and polished and sent off to school with everyone else. Thus, while it would be foolish to extrapolate information solely on the basis of the census, judicious use of census and local records would illuminate not only the histories of specific individuals but also community attitudes toward particular groups of people and professions.

Population peaked in Virginia City at an estimated 25,000 in 1876. But the mines were exhausted as quickly as they had grown up, and some 15,000 people left the city in the next four years.[21] Unlike other frontier towns that had grown rapidly on the strength of one economic activity, Virginia City had little hope of diversifying; due to location, agriculture was virtually impossible and an inability to obtain the railroad ruled out large-scale commercial enterprise.[22] As the city shrank, some shopkeepers stayed behind, some miners labored in outlying mines.[23] Significantly, though the mines died out suddenly, Virginia City still had a population of 10,917 in 1880.[24]

The popular image of the frontier boomtown has always been one of single, young, and usually rowdy men making their fortunes outside the bounds of staid Eastern "civilization."

In actuality, though, migration always initially involved a high number of single young men; families quickly followed. A high proportion of men married as soon as possible, many bringing brides from their former communities. In addition, many migrants traveled in at least partial family groups, with fathers and sons sharing lodgings. Even unattached men without fathers or brothers often boarded with families and, therefore, took their meals and smoked their pipes in pretty conventional settings.[25] By the time the Comstock Lode began to peter out, many Virginia City residents had thus put down roots too deep to yank up at the rumor of rich mining fields elsewhere.

By 1880, the boomtown atmosphere of Virginia City had greatly diminished. The census suggests that there was more residential separation, with mining lodgers living apart from lodgers who worked as skilled laborers or in service industries. Fewer families took in lodgers and a greater percentage of families lived in individual homes apparently set apart from the boarding district. The Chinese population had dwindled appreciably and, importantly, there were scarcely any Chinese women recorded in the 1880 census. Most of the Chinese remaining still lived in an ethnic neighborhood, but the Latin American enclave seems to have disappeared. As in 1870, what few blacks there were lived scattered throughout the Virginia City population.

The real boomtown occupations had almost evaporated by 1880. In place of dozens of real estate speculators and mining stockbrokers and the innumerable gamblers, there were paperhangers, upholsterers, butchers, bookkeepers, teamsters. From the census, there appears to have been more police per capita in 1880. Some new occupations turn up that reflect the change in fortunes, such as scavenger and rag picker. In place of the many Chinese in washhouses, there were women doing washing and ironing, presumably in their homes, as most were married and had children "at home." Almost all of these women were Irish. There were few doctors and attorneys in the 1880 Virginia City census, and the huge lists of foundry workers had disappeared, to be replaced by the roster of children housed in the Nevada Orphan Asylum.

Apparently, there was a specific red light district where scarlet women, now listed as "prostitute," regardless of race or nationality, lived among the gamblers and saloon keepers. The gamblers seem to have been mostly in their late 20s to mid-30s, while the prostitutes ranged from the late 20s to late 30s. Thus, even those who trafficked in "vice" appear to have been aging, with few youngsters entering the community. Many of the prostitutes had several children each; all who were old enough were sent to school.

Although the census returns for 1890 were destroyed by fire and water, the compiled statistics indicate that the population of Virginia City, which then included Gold Hill, had shrunk to 8,511. Of that 2,078 lived in the two Gold Hill wards.[26] By 1900, Gold Hill was once again a separate jurisdiction, with a complement of 872 individuals, while Virginia City was reported with 2,695.[27] Since its heyday, Virginia City had lost over 22,000 residents.

Residential and occupational patterns in the 1900 census resemble those of a small, stable community rather than a mining boomtown. A review of the schedules shows an attorney, a dentist, a physician, and only a handful of lodging house owners. There were some new professions, reflecting new American technology: a typist or two, some electricians. Most of the occupations were unremarkable, except that prostitutes had become "courtesans" and there were several "capitalists" and a French "orchardist." During its 41 years, Virginia City had changed radically, but, significantly, it had survived into the 20th century.

Once the researcher has completed a rough portrait of a community, such as this for Virginia City, it is then possible to fill in the features. Of more importance than broad trends are the specific people. Who, exactly, stayed in Virginia City from 1860 to 1900? What were the people like who left? Were they single or younger or responsible for smaller families? Did they pursue any particular occupations or belong to any specific ethnic or nationality groups? Of those who stayed, who purchased housing, who remained in lodgings? Did neighbors from the earlier years tend to move to the same parts of town as their fortunes improved?

It is on this highly specific level that the genealogist could benefit from a reevaluation of census use. By looking at an entire neighborhood, rather than searching for individual names, the genealogist may be able to solve rather tough research problems. For instance, a lost daughter is more apt to have married a neighbor's son than a stranger passing through. Particularly for stable communities, the genealogist could look for a new household in which the wife has the first name of the lost ancestor and the husband has the same last name as the ancestor's former neighbors. Armed with these hints, marriage records could then be searched under the husband's name.

Likewise, handwriting is not always legible. So the genealogist can double-check a hunch by examining past and future censuses. If the neighbors remain the same from one census to the next and all the rest of the information matches, this is not proof positive that the illegible name is the right ancestor. Still it is a very good indication that it might be correct.

Frequently, a genealogist reaches a point at which an ancestor can be traced back no further. However, careful study of the other people in the community might indicate a mass migration. A large number of miners listed as born in Pennsylvania, of which the problem ancestor was one, might suggest that a number of people left an exhausted Pennsylvania mine in search of one newly opened. Reference to local histories of Pennsylvania would pinpoint those mining communities that had recently fallen on hard times, and then the census records for those areas could be combed for the elusive ancestor.

Some people may have been part of a mass migration yet have a different place of birth than those with whom they traveled. The genealogist must take into account the possibility of an interim stop. A miner from Cornwall may have helped exhaust that Pennsylvania mine before moving on to Nevada. Likewise, a Virginia-born man living in Indiana in the midst of a Kentucky-born community may well have moved first to Kentucky.

But, of course, the census can only provide inklings and indications for further research; census information is as fallible as that in any historical source. Just as the researcher can refer to the census to check the stories handed down in local histories, the census can be checked against traditional local history sources. Verification and expansion of census data can be found in probate records; mortgage records; deeds; real and personal property tax assessment schedules; real and personal property tax books; school censuses; cemetery interments; birth, marriage, and death registers; building permits; welfare or charity records; voting abstracts; pollbooks; and reports of county or city superintendents of schools.

Particularly rich sources for local history are church records. Many churches had mechanisms for the transfer of membership from one community to the next; the records of these transfers detail migration patterns.[28] Parish records also contain information on baptisms, marriages, funerals, and general membership. Records of the political parties, available on the local level when they have been preserved, are particularly useful for 19th-century research because party membership was high and the parties were extremely active in defining and focusing enthusiasm on community issues.

Voluntary and fraternal organizations also left behind valuable records that are still turning up in forgotten attic corners. These organizations helped define status and leadership within a community as well as served as a training ground for local entrepreneurs and politicians.[29]

Newspapers, read with the appropriate measure of skepticism, are outstanding sources for local history, particularly any stories that list people. Unfortunately, newspapers become so brittle with age that their use has been re-

stricted by custodial institutions. However, there are ongoing microfilming projects designed to preserve and make accessible community newspapers. Some of this microfilm is available for purchase commercially and some through interlibrary loan. The reference librarian at a public library should be able to locate microfilmed newspapers throughout the country.

City directories and manuscript collections held by local libraries and historical societies are common local history sources. But many researchers have not considered the possibility of title insurance records, sometimes made available by insurance companies, and out-of-date financial and employment records of other community businesses.[30] Obviously, for these records the historian is dependent upon the good will of the business in question, except when such materials have been donated to a historical society.

City maps are wonderful sources. Early street patterns can indicate the presence of strong political, religious, or business authority. For instance, many religious communities were laid out in a precise grid by church leaders, just as railroad companies imposed the grid pattern on towns they scattered across the plains. By contrast, Virginia City grew up all haphazard, with streets conforming more to the slope of the mountain and the location of the Comstock Lode than the convenience of the residents. Maps also indicate distribution of wealth. There is great geographic mobility within a city as immigrants and newcomers crowd into older areas and the wealthy move away in distaste. It has been said the history of New York City can be charted by the movement of Delmonico's Restaurant up Manhattan Island. The location of firehouses, schools, churches, and parks all suggest the relative importance of a particular neighborhood in the eyes of the city fathers.

Examination of a neighborhood can suggest other research clues as well. Did an ancestor switch religious denominations? Check for the predominant religion of his or her community. Curious as to why a border state ancestor chose the side he did during the Civil War? Hunt up the enlistment history of his neighbors. The influence of community should always be considered when trying to untangle what an ancestor did and why.

All of which dovetails back to the census, the detailed record of who, exactly, was building those roads, setting up business, and promenading in the park. The census is the historian's Edward R. Murrow, introducing the people responsible for the growth and development of America's communities.

Those decennial population schedules for 1790 through 1910 that still exist are available on microfilm for public use at the National Archives and its field branches. As the microfilm is available for purchase, many public libraries, universities, and historical and genealogical societies throughout the country have at least part of the census in their holdings. All decennial census schedules are arranged geographically. There are federally prepared indexes for parts of the 1880, 1890, 1900, and 1910 censuses on microfilm; local indexes for other years have been compiled and published by various organizations and individuals. These are most readily accessible through local genealogical societies.

It is important to keep in mind that the census has changed greatly over time. Different questions have been asked with each new decade, and definitions of basic terms, such as rural and urban, have changed. Perhaps the most succinct explanation of the instructions given to enumerators is *Twenty Censuses: Population and Housing, 1790–1980*, prepared by the Bureau of the Census, U.S. Department of Commerce.[31]

Reference to *Twenty Censuses* will reveal that the 1910 census lists for the first time the mother tongue in addition to nativity. By comparing the two, the researcher may well be able to pinpoint not only what country an immigrant was from but what part of that country. This information will be invaluable for those tracking individuals or groups back beyond the boundaries of America.

Mother tongue was recorded specifically for those born in a foreign country and for those native born, 10 years and older, who did not speak English. By focusing on language, the researcher will get some indication of the degree of Americanization of immigrant households and communities. It is illuminating to learn if the children, but not the parents, of a specific family spoke English. In such cases, children often translated the unfamiliar American experience, as well as language, for their parents. Retention of the mother tongue in ethnic communities suggests the preservation of other old ways as well. The researcher should be alert to particular records that would have been generated by the following of traditional customs in a new American setting.

The 1910 census also distinguishes between first and subsequent marriages; between trade or profession and the general industry or business in which a person was occupied; whether an individual was an employer, employee, or self-employed; whether the person was a Union or Confederate Civil War veteran; and whether he or she was blind in both eyes or deaf and dumb.

Nowhere else but in the census is the demographic, ethnic, and socio-economic composition of a community revealed in such detail in a consolidated group of records.[32] Nowhere is there such a wealth of information about individuals and institutions. Easily accessible and well organized, the census should be a mainstay of both genealogical and expanded local history research.

NOTES

1. Marvin Lewis, ed., *The Mining Frontier: Contemporary Accounts From the American West in the Nineteenth Century* (1967), p. 177.

2. William S. Greever, *The Bonanza West: The Story of the Western Mining Rushes, 1848–1900* (1963), pp. 97–98.

3. Ibid., p. 98.

4. Lewis, *The Mining Frontier*, p. 179.

5. Rose Marian Shade, "Virginia City's Ill-Fated Methodist Church," *Journal of the West* 8 (1969): 447–452.

6. Lawrence H. Larsen, *The Urban West at the End of the Frontier* (1978), p. 14; U.S., Census Office, *Census Reports: Population, 12th Census*, vol. 1 (1901), pp. 264–265.

7. U.S., Census Office, *The Statistics of the Population of the United States, 9th Census*, vol. 1 (1872), p. 199.

8. *Eighth Census of the United States, 1860*, National Archives Microfilm Publication M653, roll 1314, pp. 1004–1012.

9. *Ninth Census of the United States, 1870*, National Archives Microfilm Publication M593, roll 835, p. 460.

10. U.S., Census Office, *The Statistics of the Population of the United States, 10th Census* (1883), p. 256.

11. *Tenth Census of the United States, 1880*, National Archives Microfilm Publication T9, roll 759, p. 309.

12. Nevada State Historical Society, *Nevada: A Guide to the Silver State* (1940), p. 273.

13. U.S., Census Office, *Statistics of 9th Census*, p. 199.

14. *Ninth Census*, roll 835, p. 91.

15. U.S., Census Office, *Statistics of 9th Census*, p. 364.

16. *Ninth Census*, roll 835, p. 13.

17. Ibid., p. 164.

18. Ibid., pp. 41 & 45.

19. Ibid., p. 41.

20. Ibid., p. 116.

21. Larsen, *The Urban West*, p. 14.

22. Ibid., p. 106.

23. Ibid., p. 44.

24. U.S., Census Office, *Statistics of 10th Census*, p. 256.

25. Don Harrison Doyle, "Social Theory and New Communities in Nineteenth-Century America," *Western Historical Quarterly* 8 (April 1977): 156.

26. U.S., Census Office, *Report on the Population of the United States at the Eleventh Census* (1895), p. 236.

27. U.S., Census Office, *Report on 12th Census*, pp. 264–265.

28. Doyle, "Social Theory," p. 160.

29. Ibid., pp. 161–162.

30. Mark Friedberger and Janice Reiff Webster, "Social Structure and State and Local History," *Western Historical Quarterly* 9 (July 1978): 302.

31. For a list of all government publications regarding the census, write the Superintendent of Documents, U.S. Government Printing Office, Washington, DC 20402, or contact any of the Department of Commerce field offices.

32. Friedberger and Webster, "Social Structure," p. 299.

KEITH R. SCHLESINGER

An Urban Finding Aid
for the Federal Census

The New Social History seeks to carry certain ideas and approaches into the mainstream of American historical studies and examine politics, institutions, and ideas while considering the influence of social forces. One of the New Social History's most innovative features is its attempt to reconstruct and interpret the lives of ordinary people. In order to accomplish this task, scholars must study aggregate populations, communities, and associations as they developed and changed over time. Most of the quantitative methods developed to support such research have, however, functioned imperfectly because of their reliance upon an essential historical source that nevertheless contains serious flaws. The manuscript federal population census offers a combination of depth, breadth, and continuity unmatched by any other American historical document, but its unique stature instantly becomes a liability whenever it fails to perform effectively. No recent quantitative study of 19th-century America has entirely escaped this predicament. Thus, improving the research value of the census represents one of the most important challenges now confronting the New Social History.

Researchers have long realized that the manuscript schedules provide a social geography of enumerated localities. Historians of aggregate populations have utilized systematic sampling of the census to recapitulate the social characteristics of political units ranging from small towns to urban wards to entire cities. By selecting every hundredth household, for instance, census users can assemble a man-

ageable yet highly accurate representation of a larger society.[1]

Although the census contains enough of a geographical foundation to permit sampling of aggregate populations, it is quite insufficient for historians who wish to study communities.[2] The manuscript schedules are arranged politically by state, county, municipality, and ward. This approach not only ignores intrinsic social groupings but tends to fragment them within the census. The unpredictability of enumerators' routes further aggravates the problem. No convenient sampling method like the one for aggregate populations exists at present to mitigate the uncertainty this creates for community studies.

Even greater difficulties await historians of associations. Membership lists and related sources have recently been unearthed for a variety of groups ranging from clubs to unions to the "criminal element."[3] The discovery of detailed information about the people contained in these lists would make possible a more sophisticated reconstruction of past society. The census by itself is completely unsuited to this task. The search for a particular person requires a line-by-line search of the schedules that can take hours or even days. Alternative sources like city directories and municipal records facilitate the location of information about individuals, but they invariably lack the depth and coverage of the census. The same discouraging prospects await social historians who attempt to trace members of aggregate populations, communities, or associations from one census year to another.

Although three recent technical innovations now permit improved access to census information for individuals, they have by no means completely solved the problem. Privately developed computer-process "accelerated" indexes, the official "Soundex" index, and computerized catalogs for selected cities cover only a part of the schedules now available for public use.[4] The publisher of accelerated indexes has after nearly a decade managed to transcribe those parts of the census that have survived for the years 1800–50. The Soundex was the product of a temporary New Deal project that undertook only a partial compilation for 1880 and complete transcriptions for 1900 and 1920. High costs and complex procedures have restricted computerized cataloging to a mere handful of towns and cities for the period 1860–80.[5]

Unreliability represents a far more intractable problem. Genealogists continue to debate the merits of accelerated indexes, but it now seems clear that any project that catalogs millions of names under budget and time constraints will produce its share of errors.[6] Even the Soundex, with its complex coding system that groups letters by sound rather than rigid spelling rules, can fall far short of expectations.[7] The limited size of computerized urban catalogs presumably renders them less subject to technical error, but they share with the larger indexes a complete dependence upon the census's unreliable spelling. Users will encounter difficulties when they attempt to compare names derived from other sources with those listed in an index or catalog.

Census users need a tool that can 1) locate individuals economically as well as efficiently in the schedules and 2) permit more effective reconstruction of geographical communities. If historians could use residential information available in reasonably comprehensive and prevalent city directories to locate households in the manuscript census, then such a tool would at last be within reach. This essay will present two different methods that seek to provide the kind of link between city directory addresses and manuscript census data that re-searchers need. The first will cover enumerations for 1900 and 1910; the second will provide less consistent yet still impressive results for the remaining censuses dating back at least to 1850. Together, the two approaches constitute what will hereafter be referred to as an urban finding aid. Each part of the finding aid will be presented in the form of a demonstration involving a single individual.

The case of Jacob Jacobs, a 19th-century Chicagoan, illustrates the value of the post-1880 urban finding aid. A brief discussion with a surviving relative revealed that Jacob's wife Sarah bore him at least six children: Hyman, David, Goldie, Mollie, Dora, and Emanuel. The family arrived from Russian Poland sometime in the 1880s and almost immediately settled in Chicago. Assuming that no oversight occurred, the 1900 census should have recorded the family there.

Since no accelerated indexes presently exist for Illinois after 1850, the 1900 Soundex is the only device that can help locate Jacob Jacobs. The Soundex assigns a numerical code to each surname.[8] More than one surname can occur in each code, and forenames are alphabetized without regard to surname. Thus, "Jacob Jacobs" would be found after "Albert Josephs" under the code "J212." Yet even when the search was extended beyond the forename "Jacob" to alternative spellings (Yiakov, Jakof), nicknames (Jake), and initials (J) in J212 and other likely surname code groups, no household like the one Jacob Jacobs headed could be found in the Soundex. This raises an important question: Did the census fail to record Jacob Jacobs, or is the Soundex alone at fault? The answer will have a decisive impact on the course of research utilizing the census. If longtime residents like Jacobs were overlooked, then the reliability of census data and census-related research would come under suspicion.

The search for Jacob Jacobs begins in the Chicago city directory. Like most urban directory publishers, the Lakeside Press of R. R. Donnelley & Sons sought to include all males of employable age, whether or not they lived with their families. Those younger than 20 were not listed unless they actually held a job, while those older than 20 were included even if they did not. The publisher also recorded a smattering of male students attending business school and college, working women, widows, and marriageable girls. Lakeside's claim to comprehensiveness and accuracy arose from economic necessity as well as abstract pride. Local businessmen, who used the directories most frequently and purchased advertising space in them, expected the publisher to produce a reliable source of names and addresses. The true measure of the historical value of any directory, however, is its ability to reveal the whereabouts of a clearly difficult case for which the Soundex and perhaps the census itself cannot account.

Jacob Jacobs did not obligingly leap from the pages of the Chicago directory. No less than eight candidates appeared in the volumes for the years 1899, 1900, and 1901. All 3 years were checked in order to account for every individual and address that the census takers might have visited. To reduce the amount of work involved, the names of Jacobs' wife and children were checked in the directory on the chance that one or more met the criteria for inclusion and also lived at home. Referring to the list of names in figure 1, it is highly probable that the "Miss Dora" and "E" (Emanuel) who lived together at 309 West North Avenue actually resided in their father Jacob's household.

The chief obstacle to the use of directory addresses in census research is the uncertainty surrounding their contemporary geographical location. In a booming prairie metropolis like Chicago, house numbering schemes varied from street to street and changed with great rapidity. Fortunately, the confusion this must have caused directory users prompted publishers in Chicago and many other cities to include a "street and avenue guide" (hereafter referred to as a street guide) as a regular feature of their directories. The typical form that these guides took is shown in figure 2. Streets were listed in alphabetical order. Under each street name, both the names of the cross-streets and the cor-

Jacobs Dora* Miss c[ler]k 76 Illinois
  h[ome] 309 W North av
Dora wid[ow] h 813 School
Emanuel insp[ector] h 1481 Lexington
E* clk 250 Madison h 309 W North av
EJ salesman h 215 Indiana
  •
  •
  •
Jacob ag[en]t b[oar]ds 480 S Sangamon
Jacob tailor 2508 Canal
Jacob tinsmith h 149 W 12th pl
Jacob J painter h 175 Mohawk
Jacob O constable h 1249 George
  •
  •
  •
J Frank bkpr [bookkeeper] 70 Adams

*Probable offspring of subject Jacob Jacobs.

FIGURE 1. Extract from *Lakeside Directory of the City of Chicago, 1900.*

responding house numbers for the intersections were provided.

The part of the street guide covering "North Av W." (i.e., West North Avenue) in 1900 indicates that number 309 fell between

NORTH AV [east]
  •
  •
  •
NORTH AV W. fr river w to city limits.
Even nos. s.s.
    The River.. 1
      •
      •
    Ashland av 241
    Marshfield... 271
    Paulina... 297
    Hermitage av.................................... 327
    Wood.. 353
      •
      •
NORTH PARK AV

FIGURE 2. Extract from the "Street and Avenue Guide," *Lakeside Directory, 1900.*

Paulina and Hermitage streets. Both retain these names today, so it is possible to locate the desired section of North Avenue on any sort of Chicago street map. Had one or both of the cross-streets been renamed since 1900, the street guide listing for West North Avenue in figure 2 would still have revealed the necessary information about physical location. If Paulina had been named "Main" in 1900, this would not have altered the fact that it was the only street between Marshfield and Hermitage, whose names have remained unchanged. Interpolation of this sort will rarely mislead a researcher who properly uses the contemporary and modern maps at his disposal.

Establishing the precise geographical location of a probable residence represents only half the struggle involved in discovering Jacob Jacobs in the manuscript census. How does the patch of ground along North Avenue between Paulina and Hermitage relate to a vast census of nearly two million Chicago residents? Fortunately, the census is not as inaccessible as it first appears. Beginning in 1880, urban wards were further subdivided into "enumeration districts" (EDs). These normally covered two or more city blocks and were arranged in numerical order in the bound manuscript census volumes. Within each ED, enumerators recorded the addresses of every household. A researcher could quickly find an address in the census if he knew of a way to determine which ED it belonged to.

The National Archives and Records Administration (NARA) maintains a collection of census records well suited to this purpose. "Office copy" district boundary maps for the period 1880–1950 permit the user to plot a known address and thereby identify the appropriate ED. One social historian has recently made effective use of this previously untapped source.[9] The NARA holdings are, however, neither complete nor available outside Washington, DC.[10] Scholars lacking time and funds would welcome the development of locally available sources and portable materials that could achieve comparable, or even superior, results.

Improved availability of certain noncartographic census records and more effective exploitation of urban documentary sources should offer scholars as much-needed alternative to the Archives in Washington. NARA has for some time distributed microfilm copies of the unrestricted part of the manuscript census. In addition to the complete sets available for loan or examination in National Archives field branches, many public and research libraries purchase selected rolls of film containing the locality or state in which they are situated. Early in 1980, NARA completed the microfilming of ED boundary descriptions for the period 1880–1950.[11] A researcher armed only with a modern street map, a street number guide, and the appropriate boundary descriptions can reconstruct detailed census maps for even the largest cities within a fairly short period of time.[12]

Since EDs often followed precinct lines in 1900 and occasionally did so in 1880, contemporary precinct maps can serve as substitutes for the original Census Bureau maps. Researchers can then use the ED boundary descriptions to assign the correct ED number to each precinct. The frequent inclusion of precinct numbers as part of the boundary descriptions greatly facilitates the process. Many municipal archives and libraries may possess detailed precinct maps, as those in Chicago do for the year 1900.[13] These maps largely eliminate the need for laborious cartographic work.

One further refinement will often render unnecessary the precise matching of each precinct with the appropriate ED number. In many metropolises and even some smaller cities, the Census Bureau clearly intended that EDs should rigorously follow the numbering as well as the boundaries of wards and precincts.[14] In Chicago, ED numbering began with "one," which corresponded to the first precinct of the first ward. The EDs then ascended through all the wards (one through 35) and all the precincts within each ward (the number varying with population density). This means that a "conversion table" between ward and precinct numbers on the one hand, and ED numbers on the other, can be constructed in a matter of minutes. A part of the table for Chicago in 1900 is reproduced in figure 3. Only 42 interruptions like the ones included in the figure occurred in over 1,100 EDs.

The impact that locally obtainable documents have on the speed and accuracy of census research becomes clear in the case of Jacob Jacobs. Chicago precinct maps (figure 4) clearly show that 309 West North Avenue belonged in either the second precinct of the 14th ward or the fourth precinct of the 15th. According to the conversion table (figure 3), the address is located in either ED 419 or 462. Since even and odd house numbers were usually ranged on opposite sides of a street, a brief visual check

I Ward	II Precincts	III Enumeration Districts
14	1–41*	418–458*
15	1–43	459–501
16	1–34	502–535
•	•	•
•	•	•
•	•	•
19	1–33	584–616
20	1–19	617–635
21	1–13	636–648
	14**	649,650**
	15	650,651
	16–23***	652–659***
22	1–25	660–684

*Use the following formula to compute a target precinct's ED number:

Target ED = (first ED in column III)
            + (target precinct no.) − 1

E.g., Ward 15, Precinct 4 = 459 + 4 − 1 = ED 462
**Special case; enumeration district(s) listed for each precinct
***Normal progression resumes; for the remainder of the affected ward, use the formula:

Target ED = (first ED listed in column III)
            + (target precinct no.)
            − (first precinct listed in column II)

E.g., Ward 21, Precinct 20 = 652 + 20 − 16 = ED 656

FIGURE 3. Parts of the precinct-to-ED conversion table for Chicago, 1900.

FIGURE 4. Sections of precinct maps for Wards Fourteen and Fifteen, Chicago (1900).

of addresses in the manuscript census should determine which ED actually contains the Jacobs household.

The Chicago street guide contains a rather unusual feature that renders even this relatively simple procedure unnecessary. Each street entry in the guide contains a written description indicating the disposition of house numbers. In figure 2, "even nos. s.s." means that all even-numbered buildings were located on the south side of West North Avenue. The number 309 therefore fell on the north side of the street, in the fourth precinct of the 15th ward. Thus, ED 462 should contain the Jacobs family.

Once ED 462 is located on the appropriate roll of microfilm, the task of visual searching begins. Since census takers tended to cover one square block at a time, longer streets will appear in several different places, including the end of the enumeration where previously overlooked households were recorded. Each time the name "West North Ave." appeared in ED 462, the house numbers were checked to see if the number 309 occurred. Within minutes, the presumed residence of Jacob Jacobs was located on roll number 263, ED 462, page 14, beginning with line 6. The entire process from directory to doorstep for this unusually difficult case took about 45 minutes, not including the time involved in assembling the documentary tools.

Census information recorded for the household residing at 309 West North Avenue provides a clear demonstration of the urban finding aid's superiority over the Soundex. The head of the family was listed as "John Punskovsky," a name bearing no resemblance to Jacob Jacobs. Yet this man was born in Russian Poland, had married a woman named Sarah, and had two children in residence named Dora and "Emil" (i.e., Emanuel). Close examination of the manuscript entry resolves the issue. Beneath the surname Punskovsky lies the clear outlines of the name "Jacobs," which the enumerator had obviously attempted to erase. Since the census taker gave neither Dora nor Emanuel the surname Jacobs, they were not considered eligible for separate Soundex entries as household members with a differing surname. Unlike the city directory, the Soundex would have required advance knowledge of the *original* family name in order to locate the Jacobs household.

The Soundex in this instance clearly inhibited the location of an individual's census data, but how often will this occur? The Soundex and the urban finding aid need to be tested together on a larger group of people. Chicago's municipal reformers, for example, were overwhelmingly middle or upper class, and exceptionally persistent in the community—in other words, the people most likely to be the census taker's "best customers."[15] Of 251 selected reformers residing in Chicago in 1900, 20 percent failed to appear in the Soundex. Thirty-nine of these were subsequently located using the urban finding aid, which raised the total proportion of cases found in the census to 95 per-

cent. Of those retrieved without the use of the Soundex, half suffered from misspellings that prompted incorrect Soundex coding. The other half were either in the same position as the Jacobs children (listed under their parent's name only) or victims of human error on the part of government clerks dealing with literally millions of names requiring Soundex coding.

Still poorer Soundex results were obtained for a group of immigrants. A Catholic parish in Cleveland conducted a rare private census of its predominantly Czech communicants in 1880.[16] Of 357 parish households enumerated, 342 (96 percent) were manually traced in the federal census. The Soundex, on the other hand, reliably located only 187 (52 percent). The latter could perhaps be excused its poor performance, since in 1880 it included by deliberate design only families that contained a child under the age of 11. The object of the parish census, however, was to determine the future parochial educational needs of the Czech neighborhood. It therefore contained a disproportionate number of families with young children and hardly any who could be termed "mature." The 1880 Soundex's unique procedural shortcomings can be blamed for only a small fraction of its demonstrable failure. The Chicago city directory, in contrast, correctly listed the addresses of more than 75 percent of a sample of families drawn from a comprehensive Czech parish census performed in 1880. Had additional information such as occupation (which the Soundex does not record) been available to distinguish between identical directory names, the success rate for the sample could have risen as high as 90 percent.

The three samples from Chicago and Cleveland substantiate Olivier Zunz's conclusion that the census is a reasonably complete source, typically covering over 90 percent of the population.[17] They also show that the Soundex is indeed primarily responsible for the large number of apparent oversights. Its shortcomings are actually more serious than outright failure of this sort would suggest. Even when individuals are successfully located, it often requires a sizable investment of time to trace alternate spellings on several cumbersome micro-film rolls and carefully sift dozens of entries in each surname code group. Wherever possible, the faster, more thorough urban finding aid should supplant the Soundex as the primary device for tracing names in the census.

Other census years besides 1900 should benefit from the urban finding aid. The 1910 census was the first to incorporate census tracts. Only the very largest cities (e.g., New York and Chicago) were originally involved. Tracts did not normally follow precinct lines or other minor civil boundaries. Researchers will have to reconstruct tract maps from the microfilmed boundary descriptions or use the census maps kept in Washington.

The prospects for developing an urban finding aid grow increasingly bleak as the decades recede into the 19th century. The 1890 census is, of course, nearly a complete loss due to the disastrous Commerce Building fire of 1921.[18] The 1880 enumeration benefited from EDs, but their boundaries (as Chicago attests) often bear no relationship to precinct lines. Virtually no pre-1900 census maps have survived, and the boundary descriptions that historians need to reconstruct maps for 1880 fail to cover several states and territories.[19] The censuses for 1850 through 1870 not only lacked subdivisions smaller than entire wards but street names and house numbers as well. Searches would involve hundreds of manuscript pages, and without the aid of recorded addresses the process could require several hours for each name.

Despite such problems, the 1850–70 enumerations possess several important advantages. They contain the names of all persons enumerated, whereas earlier censuses only recorded the heads of households. Full information about occupation and nativity was also made available for the first time beginning with the 1850 census. Equally important, though its significance has gone unrecognized, was the requirement that the census taker record the date on which he began each manuscript page. Researchers clearly need a method quite different from the one for the period 1900–10 that can

take advantage of the mid-19th-century enumerations' strengths in order to overcome their weaknesses.

Controlled sampling forms the basis for the second part of the urban finding aid. The selection and plotting of a few names from each ward on a contemporary map provides a guide that can establish the approximate location of other addresses. Chicago's regular coastline and checkerboard street grid presumably improve the chances for obtaining good results, but researchers cannot always count on such conveniences occurring elsewhere. A city like Boston provides a better environment for assessing the value of controlled sampling. Old Boston's complicated street patterns and jagged peninsular shoreline make it the virtual antithesis of a prairie boomtown like Chicago. The seventh ward in 1850, containing an unusually broad socioeconomic range, will serve as the actual test site for controlled sampling.[20] Once again, the search for a single person will demonstrate the procedures involved.

Arthur Hathaway, a porter by trade, appeared in the Boston city directory for 1849, 1850, and 1851. Like many laborers, he was highly mobile. In 1849, he lived outside the seventh ward at 18 Wall Street; for the next 2 years, he resided at 3 Morton Court. He could conceivably have been enumerated at either address, but for the moment the latter seems most promising, since it was listed in the directory corresponding to the census year of 1850.

Locating Hathaway's residence on a map essentially follows the procedure developed for the Chicago finding aid. Boston lacked a comprehensive street number guide before 1867, but the 1850 directory did contain one for a few main thoroughfares as well as an alphabetical listing that often indicated the house number at which streets terminated. Comparison of house numbers in the seventh ward for 1850 and 1867 revealed that they remained practically unchanged over the years. The publisher of the directory forthrightly told his readers that such stability, along with the predominant pattern of very short streets, rendered a detailed street number guide unnecessary.[21] The appearance of a complete guide coincided with the commencement of the first serious campaign to renumber Boston's streets. This means that researchers can in most cases apply the 1867 guide to the 1850 street grid.

Once the house numbers have been recorded for each cross-street on a map of the seventh ward, the task of collecting the sample that will be used to locate Arthur Hathaway can begin. A careful examination of the manuscript census must now be made. The page number on which each new enumeration date begins should be written down. Although the partly commercial seventh ward had an unusually small population, it nevertheless took the enumerator 11 days to complete his task. Figure 5 reveals a series of daily "runs" averaging 10 pages each, a convenient size for a brief visual search. These "enumeration dates" determine how the sample shall be selected.

An enumerator on foot in a densely populated city would presumably choose to record a geographically compact area on any given day. This would prove true even if the official census taker hired assistants to cover parts of his ward. The selection of at least one household from each date offers the best opportunity of recapturing the enumeration routes. To increase the sample's representativeness further, one household should be chosen for every 10 pages in longer date runs. Rigid application of these criteria can, however, produce close clustering of two or more cases, thereby reducing the sensitivity of the sample to complex geographical patterns. Above all, common sense must prevail from the sample to succeed.

The actual selection of names for the sample occurs after the target pages have been chosen. The following rules should permit the selection of names that can be located with relative ease in the city directory:

1. Select a fairly unusual name; avoid common names like "Smith."
2. Choose a person with an occupation; this maximizes the chance of reliable identification in the city directory.
3. Avoid poorly transcribed or spelled names; the deliberate selection of a more reliable name will rarely if ever reduce the predictive power of the sample.

Effective sampling requires definite information about physical locations as well as distinctive names. Many people, particularly laborers like Arthur Hathaway, moved frequently over short distances. In these cases the researcher must determine which directory address the census taker actually visited. Guesswork will not suffice because the sample must above all else be reliable.

The problem in nearly every case can be solved by selecting one or two proximate names from the manuscript census in addition to the name intended for use in the sample. Joseph Weatherby, for example, was selected to represent the enumeration date of October 7. The directory identified his residence as 11 Crescent Place in 1849, but the volume for 1850 indicated that it was 11 Montgomery Place. As figure 6 indicates, Weatherby's dwelling was listed as No. 318 in the manuscript census. Joseph Butler, recorded immediately below

Recorded date	Begins on page	Length (pp.)	Sample page(s) chosen
Sept. 30	1	5	3
Oct. 1	5	10	8,13
2	15	5	18
3	20	7	23
4	27	5	29
5	32	25	37,44,52
7	57	20	59,66,72
8	77	15	79,83,88
9	92	17	94,102
10	109	7	110
11	116	11	118,124
END	127	—	—

FIGURE 5. Enumeration dates for Ward Seven, Boston, 1850.

Sample no.	Date	Page no.	Line no.	Dwelling no.	Family no.	Name	Occupation	Address
6C	10–5	52	12	232	298	Welch Follonsby J	merchant	9 Morton pl
7A	10–7	59	31	259	342	Davenport Samuel S.	hack driver	8 Providence
7B	10–7	66	5	288	379	Hale Nathan	editor	6 Hamilton pl
7C	10–7	72	9	318	409	Weatherby Moses H	stone contractor	11 Montgomery pl
[7C]*	10–7	72	23	319	410	Butler James	hardware merchant	12 Montgomery pl

*Redundant case used for address verification

FIGURE 6. Part of the worksheet used to compile the sample for the seventh ward, Boston.

Weatherby, resided at dwelling No. 319. It is not absolutely certain that the two were physical neighbors, but since the census takers tended to go from door to door, there is a high probability that they were. The directory bears this out: Butler lived at 12 Montgomery Place in 1850, next to Weatherby at No. 11. Weatherby would therefore take his place in the sample, rather than be discarded because of a questionable address.

Once the sample names have been collected, they must be assigned numbers in the same order as they appeared in the census, checked in the city directory, and plotted on the street map of the ward. The entire process will normally proceed at the rate of about 30 names per 8-hour working day. Figure 6 presents a part of the worksheet used to organize and code the seventh ward's 20 sample names. Figure 7 comprises the entire working sample, plotted on a ward map containing house numbers obtained from the 1850 and 1867 street guides. Since several long enumeration dates are represented by more than one point, letters are used to distinguish the different points (e.g., 6A, 6B, 6C). If a desired address were to fall nearer one lettered point than another, then the pages immediately surrounding that point would be examined first.

A cursory examination of the numbers reveals that a recognizable progression of points along several distinct paths does indeed exist. Sudden jumps (between 2B and 3, 5 and 6A, 6C and 7A, 7C and 8A) occur when the census taker evidently began to enumerate a different section of the ward. The selection of a few additional cases not shown in figure 7 reveals that the enumeration for October 11 (including points 11A and 11B) contains households scattered throughout the ward. If Boston and Chicago are fair examples, then it was common for the last enumeration date to serve as a "cleanup" section for families missed on the first visit. Since less than a dozen pages make up the cleanup section for the seventh ward, manual searches or special indexing should pose little difficulty. Otherwise, the sample points do not seriously overlap, so that an obvious order of priority exists for searching any address in the ward.

Arthur Hathaway's Morton Court address falls very near point 6C. The number corresponds to a name drawn from page 52 of the manuscript census. An examination of the immediately surrounding pages quickly reveals Hathaway, who was recorded on page 53.

The ease with which Hathaway was found is not unusual for the ward as a whole. Of 30

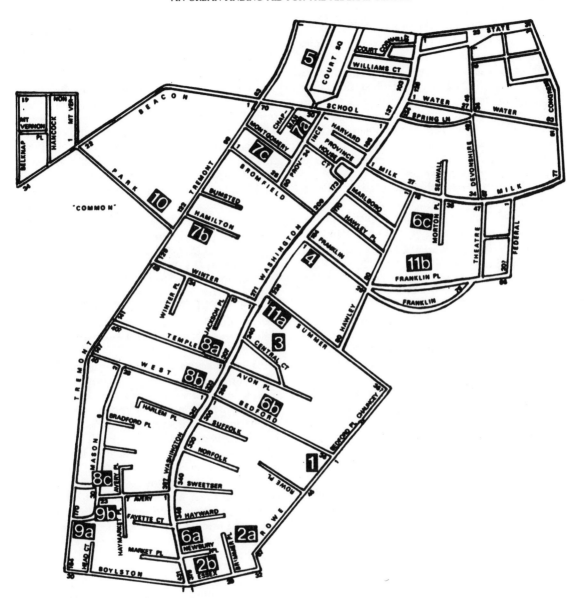

FIGURE 7. Map of the seventh ward, Boston (1850), with plotted sample points.

names drawn at random from the census for the seventh ward, more than half were located with the aid of the sample after visually examining fewer than six pages.[22] All but one of the 30 were discovered well below a search limit

of 50 pages, which corresponds to about 30 minutes of unhurried work.

Similar random tests of controlled samples assembled for one high-status and one lower-status ward in Chicago unexpectedly produced less remarkable but still impressive results.[23] From 80 to 83 percent of each set of 30 names were located after searches of less than 50 pages per case. Increasing the number of names drawn for the original controlled sample in each ward from one to two per enumeration date produced a discovery ratio of over 90 percent. The modest disparity between the Chicago wards and Boston's seventh ward apparently has more to do with street grid patterns than socioeconomic factors.

The sampling technique used in Boston and Chicago will prove increasingly effective after 1850, but will have only limited applications before that year. The period 1850–70 saw many rapidly growing cities develop the comprehensive city directories that census users must have in order to create urban finding aids. Controlled sampling will prove most successful in those places lacking ED boundary descriptions in 1880.[24] Since ED numbers and street addresses are recorded on each page of the 1880 manuscript census, a fairly large sample can be drawn in a very short time for each ED. Once the samples are plotted on a map, they should approximate the actual boundaries of EDs, which normally conformed to marked streets. Although performing this task for a large city like Chicago might take several days, the ability to locate addresses almost as precisely as with written boundary descriptions makes it well worth the effort.

The trouble really begins with the years before 1850. City directories, where they existed at all, appeared infrequently and were relatively exclusive. From 1790 to 1840, the census did not provide the names of all the individuals it enumerated or the date on which the enumeration occurred. Since the major improvements in transportation occurring at the time did not greatly influence the methods that a census taker used to cover his ward, it is quite possible that the 10-page-per-day average found in Boston's seventh ward in 1850 could with certain necessary alterations be applied to earlier enumerations of the city. Although quality will undoubtedly vary from place to place, a

finding aid based on controlled sampling offers the only sensible recourse in those instances where pre-1850 census indexes fail to perform properly.

The value of the urban finding aid lies chiefly in its ability to locate census information about individuals in precisely those places where scholarly inquiry most demands it and population density makes the task most difficult. The study of communities will also benefit substantially from census records and controlled samples that permit researchers to map the schedules and thereby establish with greater confidence the boundaries of neighborhoods, ethnic concentrations, and other types of social geography. Social historians will at last be in a position to study aggregates, communities, associations, or some combination of the three across much of urban America and through time as well. Genealogists and social scientists should also profit from a device that increases their control over urban enumerations.

Challenges as well as opportunities await users of the urban finding aid. Those who wish to link census data with other sources providing information on selected individuals will desire improved access to the plethora of records kept by governmental bodies at all levels. Researchers will also wish to use a wide range of documents that banks, hospitals, libraries, businesses, charities, unions, and other important institutions presently tend to discard or treat as privileged information.[25] In order to realize the finding aid's potential, scholars must be prepared to work in concert with archivists and government officials to facilitate the transference of old documents onto microfilm and to identify and make available significant bodies of material in private hands. All those involved in the process must also confront honestly and sensibly the potential threat to constitutional guarantees of privacy posed by the growth of linked computer databases filled with information about individuals. Otherwise, efforts to curb the abuse of such data may well lead to the condemnation of all research utilizing personal records, regardless of its purpose. Devices like the urban finding aid can provide the technical means by which determined and well-organized researchers can greatly expand the horizons of quantitative social research.

The author wishes to thank Professors Josef Barton and Henry Binford of Northwestern University, Mr. Arthur Miller of Lake Forest College, and Mr. Gunther Pohl of the New York Public Library for their advice and support in the preparation of this essay.

NOTES

1. "Systematic sampling" in the present context refers to the sequential selection of individuals, households, etc., which disregards the identity and personal characteristics of the subjects involved. The model for the application of systematic sampling to quantitative history remains Stephan A. Thernstrom, *The Other Bostonians: Poverty and Progress in the American Metropolis, 1880–1970* (1973). For a thorough bibliographical survey of social mobility studies and other categories of quantitative social history, see Kathleen N. Konzen, "Community Studies, Urban History, and American Local History," in Michael Kammen, ed., *The Past Before Us: Contemporary Historical Writing in the United States* (1980). For a review of systematic sampling, see William G. Cochran, *Sampling Techniques* (1977), especially pp. 212–213.

2. Richard Sennett, *Families Against the City: Middle Class Homes of Industrial Chicago, 1872–90* (1970), was among the first to use census records in the study of geographically defined communities. Other recent examples include Josef J. Barton, *Peasants and Strangers: Italians, Rumanians, and Slovaks in an American City [Cleveland], 1890–1950* (1975); Herbert G. Guttman, *The Black Family in Slavery and Freedom, 1750–1925* (1976), app. B, "Black, Jewish, and Italian Households in New York City in 1905"; Jeffrey S. Gurok, *When Harlem Was Jewish, 1870–1930* (1979); Robert Arthur Burchell, *The San Francisco Irish, 1848–80* (1979).

3. Eric H. Monkkonen, *The Dangerous Class: Crime and Poverty in Columbus, Ohio, 1860–85* (1975), demonstrates the usefulness of police records in social research.

4. Accelerated indexes provide the name, county of residence, and manuscript page number for each household head recorded in a particular state's enumeration. Accelerated Indexing Systems, Inc., of Bountiful, UT, will supply upon request a current pricelist of published indexes. For an assessment of the Soundex, see Charles Stephenson, "Tracing Those Who Left: Mobility Studies and the Soundex Indexes to the U.S. Census," *Journal of Urban History* (Nov. 1974): 73–81. Richard Jensen et al., "Social Predictors of American Mobility: A Census Capture-Recapture Study of New York and Wisconsin, 1875–1905" (1978), provides the most thorough explanation and demonstration of the Soundex's value in tracing individuals over vast distances as well as time. Michael B. Katz, *The People of Hamilton, Canada West: Family and Class in a Mid-Nineteenth Century City* (1975), provides a brief explanation of machine-readable coding and computer-assisted record linkage.

5. An index for the 1910 enumeration was prepared by the Census Bureau in 1960, covering the 11 states constituting the former Confederacy and an additional 10 states that received extensive immigration from the Old South; the index has been filmed as

1910 Census Soundex and Miracode Indexes, National Archives Microfilm Publications T1259 through T1279, 4,642 rolls. The following American cities and towns have thus far been manually or electronically cataloged; the years indicate the censuses covered: Binghamton, NY, and Johnstown, PA—1850-80 (Dennis Kelly, 1973); Kingston, NY—1860 (Stuart M. Blumin, 1976); Poughkeepsie, NY—1850-80 (Clyde and Sally Griffen, 1978); Jacksonville, IL—1850-70 (Don Harrison Doyle, 1978); and Holland, MI—1860-80 (Gordon W. Kirk, 1978). Social history projects have cataloged the cities of Philadelphia—1850-1900 (Theodore Hershberg); Pittsburgh—1850-70 (Laurence Glasco); and Buffalo—1850-60 (Glasco).

6. Two convincing demonstrations of the accelerated indexes' deficiencies may be found in David Kendall Martin, "The New York 1800 Census Index," *The American Genealogist* 54 (Jan. 1978): 53-54, and Lynn C. McMillion, "An Index Can Be a Roadblock," *The Virginia Genealogist* 21 (July-Sept. 1977): 205-206. Historians have thus far shown little inclination to use any type of genealogical index, and no scholarly criticism has found its way into print from that quarter.

7. A battery of tests designed to evaluate the Soundex's performance appears later in this essay.

8. For the rules of Soundex coding, see National Archives and Records Service, *Federal Population Census, 1790-1890: A Catalog of Microfilm Copies of the Schedules* (1979), p. 96.

9. Joel Perlmann, "Using Census Districts in Analysis, Record Linkage, and Sampling," *Journal of Interdisciplinary History* 10 (Autumn 1979): 284-286.

10. An inventory of available maps by state and city for 1880-1940 is provided in James B. Rhoads and Charlotte M. Ashby, *Preliminary Inventory of the Cartographic Records of the Bureau of the Census* 103 (Washington, DC: National Archives and Records Service, 1958). Hardly any maps for 1880 have survived, and the structure of the inventory implies that unexpected gaps may occur in later years for those cities presumably covered by the map collection.

11. *Descriptions of Census Enumeration Districts, 1830-90 and 1910-50,* National Archives Microfilm Publication T1224, 146 rolls (hereafter cited as T1224); *Census Enumeration District Description Volumes for 1900,* National Archives Microfilm Publication T1210, 10 rolls (hereafter cited as T1210).

12. The construction of a reproducible set of boundary outline maps based solely on written boundary descriptions for the borough of Manhattan in New York City (1900 pop. 1.85 million) took less than 40 hours. The same procedure for Kansas City, MO (1900 pop. 164,000) required about 7 hours.

13. Old precinct maps are accorded rather low priority even among municipal archivists, so coverage is likely to be spotty. On the other hand, since the Census Bureau relied on precincts in so many cities before the introduction of tracts (see note 14), even a few fortuitous matches between surviving precinct maps and ED boundary descriptions would save a great deal of time and effort.

14. In 1900, 86 of 161 cities with a population of 25,000 or more benefited from complete, systematic enumeration district-precinct number matches. Only 2 of the 24 cities of over 150,000 (Detroit and Washington, DC) did not exhibit this relationship. Seven cities (all under 40,000, with the exception of Columbus, OH) possessed ED de-

scriptions that indicated precinct numbers but *not* the actual street boundaries. Locating precinct boundary documentation for these cities becomes essential, if the controlled sampling technique described later in this essay is to be avoided. T1210, U.S. Bureau of the Census, *Twelfth Census of Population, 1900*, 10 vols. (1901–03). 1:lxix–lxx.

15. This conclusion and the data that follow are derived from the author's examination of Chicago reform groups for the period 1880–1910.

16. I wish to thank Prof. Josef Barton of Northwestern University for providing the data and preliminary analysis for the Cleveland and Chicago parish samples used in this essay.

17. Olivier Zunz et al., "Sampling for a Study of the Population and Land Use of Detroit in 1880–1885," *Social Science History* 1 (Spring 1977): 326–328.

18. Katherine H. Davidson and Charlotte M. Ashby, *Preliminary Inventory of the Records of the Bureau of the Census* 161 (Washington, DC: National Archives and Records Service, 1964), p. 102. The inventory also provides a description of the few remaining schedules for 1890.

19. The following states and territories completely lack boundary descriptions for the year 1880: Alabama, Arizona, Arkansas, California, Colorado, Connecticut, Montana, Ohio, Oregon, Pennsylvania, and Wisconsin. T1224, roll 4, "Introduction."

20. Edward Pessen, *Riches, Class, and Power Before the Civil War* (1973), pp. 195–198, identifies Ward Seven as the wealthiest per capita in antebellum Boston. Pessen also observes that the rich clustered along certain fashionable streets. A survey of the manuscript census confirms the hypothesis that between these elite "islands" there lived a sizable number of more ordinary Bostonians. More accurately, Pessen's findings suggest that the elite formed a ring of wealth that followed the streets constituting the borders of the ward (Beacon, Tremont, Mt. Vernon, Boylston). Such a peculiar pattern largely offsets any advantage controlled sampling derives from the presence of Boston's "first families."

21. Introduction to the "Street Directory," *Boston City Directory*, ca. 1850. Exact page locations are provided in each volume's table of contents.

22. Four of the 30 names originally selected for the Boston test sample lacked directory entries. Substitutes were selected so that the performance of the directory would not influence the assessment of controlled sampling procedures. Common names were retained in the test sample with the aid of proximate households.

23. The fifth ward in 1860 and the fourth ward in 1870 served as the test wards in Chicago. The fifth was primarily given over to laborers, with a small, isolated colony of elite residents settled on the periphery. Conversely, the fourth was a largely upper-class ward, with a small "ghetto" inhabited solely by factory operatives and artisans. The development of a finding aid for the 1870 enumeration in Chicago is described in Keith Schlesinger and Peggy Tuck Sinko, "Urban Finding Aid for Manuscript Census Searches," *National Genealogical Society Quarterly* 69 (Sept. 1981): 171–180.

24. See note 19.

25. Only a handful of institutional collections now available to scholars contain materials suitable for record linkage. See, for example, the patients' files of Harper Hospital, Detroit, MI (1872–1965), in the Burton Historical Collection, Detroit Public Library; Boston Central Labor Union delegate book (1899) and Boston Penny Savings Bank account ledgers (1864–ca. 1886), both in the Massachusetts Historical Society. A model

for the development of sources useful in record linkage is the collection of fire-insurance maps in the Library of Congress. For an assessment of the collection and the social data they can provide, see Walter W. Ristow, "United States Fire Insurance Maps, 1852–1968," *Quarterly Journal of the Library of Congress* 25 (July 1968): 194–218. The value of public and private records containing data on individuals is suggested by the use made of fire-insurance maps and housing records in Roger D. Simon, *The City-Building Process: Housing and Services in New Milwaukee Neighborhoods, 1880–1910*, American Philosophical Society, Transactions, No. 68, pt. 5 (July 1978); divorce case files in Elaine Taylor May, *Great Expectations: Marriage and Divorce in Post-Victorian America* (Chicago: University of Chicago Press, 1980); a union dues book in Paul G. Faler, *Mechanics and Manufacturers in the Early Industrial Revolution: Lynn, Massachusetts 1780–1860* (Albany: State University of New York Press, 1981); and public school academic files in Joel Perlmann, "Who Stayed in School? Social Structure and Academic Achievement in the Determination of Enrollment Patterns, Providence, Rhode Island, 1880–1925," *Journal of American History* 72 (Dec. 1985): 588–614.

CYNTHIA G. FOX

Income Tax Records of the Civil War Years

Ask any adult American the significance of April 15th and the response will almost always be, "income tax." April 15th is a magic date, the last date that can appear on the outside of the envelope we mail to some remote tax center by the all-powerful Internal Revenue Service. By and large, we American taxpayers are an honest lot. We fill out our 1040 forms, make out the check, are grateful to have tax time over, and pray we don't get audited.

What else do we know about the income tax? We were taught in school that the Constitution as originally written did not include permission for the federal government to levy direct taxes on individual citizens. To correct this deficiency the 16th amendment was proposed, and it was ratified on February 25, 1913, giving Congress the power to tax incomes "from whatever source derived." Many people believe that this was the first income tax that Americans had to pay. However, the first income tax was actually levied almost 51 years earlier by act of Congress on July 1, 1862 (12 Stat. 432). The records of that first income tax are a valuable source for family and local history.

The Civil War income tax was the first tax paid on individual incomes by residents of United States. It was a "progressive" tax in that it initially levied a tax of 3 percent on annual incomes over $600 but less than $10,000 and a tax of 5 percent on any income over $10,000. In 1864, the rates increased and the ceiling dropped so that incomes between $600 and $5,000 were taxed at 5 percent with a 10 percent rate on the excess over $5,000. Passed as

an emergency measure to finance the Union cause in the Civil War, the first income tax generated approximately $55 million in government revenues during the war. Paying the taxes was viewed as a part of a patriotic war effort and the whole country was proud when the merchant prince A. T. Stewart paid $400,000 in taxes on an income of $4 million.[1]

Taxes were levied on residents of all states and territories not in rebellion. In the South, some states operated under reconstruction governments while the war went on. Virginia, for example, the site of the Confederate capital, was largely controlled by federal forces, and northern and western Virginians were subject to the income tax from the beginning. States that seceded were included in the tax base as soon as Union troops established control. Georgians paid income taxes in 1865 even though their state was not officially readmitted to the Union until 1870.

The Civil War taxes were not immediately repealed at the end of the war but continued in force until 1872, when the Grant administration sponsored the repeal of most of the "emergency" taxes. The tax on whiskey remained in force. Between 1868 and 1881, the U.S. Supreme Court responded to challenges regarding the validity of the Civil War taxes on dividends, real estate, inheritances, and income by upholding the constitutionality of those taxes.[2] Fifteen years later the Populists attempted to revive the income tax and Congress passed a law providing for a new 2 percent tax on incomes over $4,000. But the Supreme Court surprised the nation by reversing

141

its earlier decision and declaring the law unconstitutional in 1895. This ruling, declaring that an income tax is a direct tax and therefore unconstitutional, led to the ratification of the 16th amendment in 1913.

The Civil War income tax was only a small part of a very complicated system of federal duties, stamp taxes, and fees that the government collected from individuals and businesses. David A. Wells, appointed the Chairman of the U.S. Revenue Commission in 1865, described the tax structure as being based on a principle "akin to that recommended to the traditionary Irishman on his visit to Donnybrook Fair, 'whenever you see a head, hit it.' " Congress was guided, Wells wrote, by a similar principle, "whenever you find an article, a product, a trade, a profession, or a source of income, tax it!"[3] Wells believed that the universal system was based on nothing in past experience and would likely never be repeated. In fact, the 1862 tax law served as the basis for the present internal revenue system, both in articles taxed and organization for collecting taxes.

Congress passed the Internal Revenue Act on July 1, 1862, "to provide Internal Revenue to support the Government and to pay Interest on the Public Debt," but the taxes, including the income tax, were not actually levied until September 1, 1862. Like tax legislation today, the 1862 law was extremely complicated. Monthly specific (or fixed) and ad valorem (a percentage of the market value) duties were placed on articles and products ranging from ale to zinc. Monthly taxes were levied on gross receipts of transportation companies, interest paid on bonds, surplus funds accumulated by financial institutions and insurance companies, gross receipts from auction sales, and sales of slaughtered cattle, hogs, and sheep. Annual licenses were required for bankers, auctioneers, wholesale and retail dealers, pawnbrokers, distillers, brewers, brokers, tobacconists, jugglers ("Every person who performs by sleight [sic] of hand shall be regarded as a juggler under this act."), confectioners, horse dealers, livery sta-

ble keepers, cattle brokers, tallow-chandlers and soapmakers, coal-oil distillers, peddlers, apothecaries, photographers, lawyers, and physicians. Hotels, inns, and taverns were classified according to the annual rent or estimated rent, from a first-class establishment with a yearly rental of $10,000 to an eighth-class hotel with a yearly rental of less than $100, and charged license fees from $200 to $5 accordingly. Eating houses paid $10 per year for a license, theaters $100, and circuses $50. Bowling alleys and billiard rooms paid according to the number of alleys or tables belonging to or used in the building to be licensed. Stamp duties were imposed on legal and business documents and on medicines, playing cards, and cosmetics.[4]

The new Office of the Commissioner of Internal Revenue in the Treasury Department supervised the collection of taxes and duties and prepared regulations, instructions, directions, and forms used in assessing and collecting taxes. President Abraham Lincoln issued a series of Executive orders dividing all of the states and territories under Union control into collection districts. The number of collection districts could be as few as one, as in the case of the Territory of New Mexico, but it could not exceed the number of its congressional representatives. Subsequent Executive orders may have altered the collection districts either in number or geographical coverage. Lincoln also appointed a collector and an assessor for each district. Local officials, or assistant assessors, compiled lists of taxpayers used by collectors to collect the taxes.

All persons, partnerships, firms, associations, and corporations submitted to the assistant assessor of their division a list showing the amount of their annual incomes, articles subject to special tax or duty, and the quantity of taxable goods, made or sold. The assistant assessors then compiled two alphabetical lists: (1) the names of persons or entities residing in the division who were liable for taxation and (2) names of persons or entities residing outside the division who owned property in the division. Under each name are recorded the value, assessment (or enumeration of taxable income or items), and the amount of duty or tax due.

Reflecting the government's need for money and the difficulty of collecting income taxes, the Internal Revenue Act of June 30, 1864 (13 Stat. 223), raised tax rates and put some teeth into the law. This act made it the duty of any person liable to the annual tax (anyone with an income in excess of $600 or owners of certain luxury items) to file a list of income and taxable property with the assistant assessor in the division in which he or she resided on or before the first Monday in May. Failure to file on time resulted in the assistant assessor estimating a taxpayer's worth plus a penalty of an additional 25 percent of the tax due. A false or fraudulent list or statement resulted in having the assessor or assistant assessor estimate the true value and setting the tax due accordingly. In addition, the fine was 100 percent of the tax. From this assessment, the tax form specifically stated, "there can be no appeal." The assessment lists were turned over to the collector of internal revenue, who then posted a notice in each county within the district. In the notice he specified a time and place when he would be collecting the taxes due.

Taxpayers submitted their lists of income and property on a Form 24, "Detailed Statement of Income, Gains, and Profits." The Civil War tax form included spaces for reporting income and listing deductions. "Proper deductions" from income derived from business or trade included rent, insurance, freight and expressage, wages of employees, and other expenses. Rental income from lands and buildings were reported separately. The only proper deduction from income derived from the rent of lands was repairs to fences, while rent from buildings could be reduced by the cost of repairs and insurance. Farm income from the sale of livestock and produce was taxed after deductions for labor, repairs, the farmer's livestock costs, insurance, and interest on incumberances. Profits from the sale of property; interest collected on debts; dividends on any

stock, capital, and bank deposits; and interest on U.S. bonds or any other source were taxable. Minors with incomes exceeding $600 were also liable through their guardians. In case something had been missed, the form includes spaces to enter all other income.

There were five supplementary deductions authorized. Losses on real estate; interest paid; national, state, and local taxes; rent paid for a homestead; and, interestingly, all salaries of officers or payments to persons in service in any branch of the U.S. government were free of tax. The 1862 tax law had not exempted federal salaries, and the Treasury Department had deducted the amount of the tax from the paychecks of federal employees. On February 16, 1863, Roger B. Taney, Chief Justice of the U.S. Supreme Court, wrote to Secretary of the Treasury Salmon P. Chase complaining that deductions from the salaries of federal judges constituted a violation of the constitutional doctrine of separation of powers. The Secretary of the Treasury forwarded the letter to the Attorney General. As a result, all federal salaries were exempt from taxation in the 1864 revision. In 1872, the administrator of the estate of Abraham Lincoln applied for a refund of taxes improperly assessed on Lincoln's salary as the President of the United States.

Schedule A of Form 24 listed certain categories of personal property that were subject to an annual tax. Carriages of any size and shape not used exclusively in farming or in transporting merchandise were taxed from $1 to $6 depending on their value. Also based on value, gold watches were taxed either $1 or $2 and pianofortes or other parlor musical instruments were taxed at either $2 or $4. Billiard tables (not licensed) carried an annual tax of $10. Gold and silver plate were taxed by the Troy ounce at 50 cents and 5 cents respectively. Yachts and pleasure and racing boats were taxed based on tonnage, between $5 for 10 tons or less and $100 for more than 110 tons.

An act of December 24, 1872, abolished the offices of assessors and assistant assessors.

On May 20, 1873, these offices were closed and the records relating to the Civil War taxes were shipped to the Commissioner of Internal Revenue in Washington, DC. Following the 1895 Supreme Court decision that declared income taxes unconstitutional, Congress approved a joint resolution requiring that income tax returns be destroyed. The Secretary of the Treasury appointed a committee to carry out the congressional instructions. The Commissioner of Internal Revenue delivered all of the individual tax returns and collectors' lists of income tax paid to the committee on May 5, 1896. The records were then burned. Because the assessors lists contained information on business licenses and other taxes, they were retained. Some of these original assessment lists survived and are now part of the holdings of the National Archives.

As part of an ongoing publications program, the assessment lists for the Civil War period are being converted to microfilm publications.[5] The records from 34 states and territories are currently available on microfilm. Most of the publications reproduce the records for the period 1862 to 1866. However, there were so few records for some of the territories that all of the assessment lists have been included. The records for the Territory of Montana, for example, cover the period 1864–72 and the records for the Territory of New Mexico date from 1862 to 1874, with a gap in the records in 1872. The lists are not complete for all collection districts, and there may be other significant gaps like the one in the New Mexico records.

The lists are bound into volumes, and they have been microfilmed in that order. The lists are generally arranged by collection district, thereunder by divisions within the districts, and thereunder chronologically whenever possible. In order to make the lists easier to use, descriptive pamphlets have been prepared that list the counties included in each collection district.

The assessment lists are divided into three categories: annual, monthly, and special. Entries in the annual and monthly lists are for taxes assessed and collected in those specific periods. The special lists augment incomplete annual and monthly lists and include special taxes, such as a special income tax levied in October 1864. In the descriptive pamphlets, the three types of lists are identified by the symbols A (annual), M (monthly), and S (special).

These records can prove very useful to local historians, family historians, and researchers interested in specific industries within a geographical area. The lists usually provide the names of the persons or business firms liable for taxes, their addresses (city lists often include street addresses), the taxable period, pertinent remarks on the assessment, the article or occupation taxed, and a notation of payment. Besides detailing revenue brought by the general income tax, these various lists show levies against many diverse items, such as inheritances and gold watches as well as larger tax liabilities against capital stock, circulating bank notes, and businesses subject to excise duties.

Using the tax lists to determine the degree of an individual's wealth is relatively easy since the Statistics Bureau of the Treasury Department published tables showing the average cost of provisions, consumer goods, board, and rent by state in 1869. These publications also provide information on average wages generally paid by profession or skill.[6]

Take, for example, a Baltimore banker, Thomas Splicer, Jr., of 82 McCulloh Street in the first division of the third Maryland collection district. Splicer had a taxable income of $7,750 in 1865. He owned two gold watches, one of which was valued at more than $100, and a pianoforte valued between $100 and $200. Splicer had also paid income tax on an inheritance of $2,700 during 1865.[7] Splicer must have been wealthy. According to the Treasury Department tables, the average rent on a six-room house in Maryland was $10 per month. Consumer goods and food were also very reasonable in Maryland. Extra fine flour sold for $8 per barrel, roasted coffee was 35 cents per pound, beef was 15 cents per pound, butter was 40 cents per pound, eggs were 22 cents per dozen, coal was $8.50 per ton, medium quality satinets were 50 cents per yard, and men's heavy boots could be had for $5.25 a pair. In 1865 gold sold for $145 per ounce.

Some information in the assessment lists is not duplicated elsewhere. For example, persons who had no fixed address may not be included in census records. Some of these individuals, traveling retail dealers and peddlers, were required to obtain licenses under the Civil War tax laws. The assessment list that shows Abraham Lincoln's taxes for 1864, for example, includes the names of several retail dealers whose addresses are "long boats." These river and canal merchants may not have been enumerated in the census. Similarly, itinerant peddlers are listed on monthly and special lists showing payment for retail licenses.

Local business history is well documented in the assessment lists. For example, the giant Anheuser-Busch Company, brewer of nearly one-third of all beer sold today in the United States, has its corporate headquarters at 721 Pestalozzi Street in St. Louis, MO. The corporation dates from 1875, but the assessment lists for St. Louis show an E. Anheuser operating a brewery on Pestalozzi Street over a decade earlier. By 1867 the lists show a G. Busch paying the brewer's license fee at the same address, while Anheuser appears to have gone into liquor importation and soapmaking. Anheuser had a daughter who married Gus Busch, and the business remains a family-owned operation to this day.

Local historians should seriously consider the assessment lists as a source. Take New Orleans under the Union occupation as an example. By examining the annual license list for 1862, one can draw an image of life in that cosmopolitan city. D. M. Hildreth's St. Louis Hotel between Chartres and Royal Streets was a first-class place to stop while in the city. For entertainment, one might attend the Varieties Theater on Gravier Street or visit E. B. Eastman's Exhibition at 1 Conti Alley. For some quick cash, one might visit the pawnbroker C. Docteur at 145 Royal Street.

The assessment lists also provide information about professionals and tradespeople in the city. There were numerous physicians in New Orleans, including one named Mrs. Smith. Perhaps not surprising during war time, there were a number of women engaging in retail business, running eating houses, and operating hotels; and one apothecary on Orleans Street. On Bienville Street, two dentists had offices at #4 and #66; and between them, at #30, P. Gisclon had his chocolate factory. Along Chartres Street, factories produced shoes and furniture. The lists will even tell you which butcher occupied which booth at Treme Market.

These income tax records can also be used in conjunction with later tax records. The National Archives in Washington has records relating primarily to corporate and business taxes dating to 1910 and corporate assessment lists, 1909–15. The corporation assessment lists are available on microfilm as publication M667.

Post-Civil War income tax records, 1867–73, are available in the National Archives field branches. Several of the field branches have additional records relating to post-Civil War taxes. The Denver Branch, for example, has original monthly assessment lists created by district collectors in what are now the states of Arizona, Colorado, New Mexico, and Wyoming as late as 1917. Some of these records document miscellaneous and regular revenue taxes, mostly those imposed on the retail sale of liquor and the manufacture of tobacco products. They also concern taxes on brewers, oleomargarine sales, and, after 1899, telephone messages. Because the assessment lists include the reported net income of firms, they can be used to augment statistical studies of corporate profits and to compare the growth of companies engaged in like activities. Many other field branches have similar records.

The Civil War income tax records are not only a valuable source of information for biographical, genealogical, and local history research but should also be considered when conducting regional and area studies of business and industry or quantitative studies of demographics during the 1860s. They can be used in conjunction with census records, later tax records, and with state and local records to document the growth of industries, shifting patterns of wealth, migration patterns, and even women in the work force.

NOTES

1. Samuel Elliot Morrison and Henry Steele Commager, *The Growth of the American Republic*, Vol. 1 (New York, Oxford University Press, 1962), p. 748.

2. *Pacific Insurance Company* v. *Soule* (7 Wallace 433); *Veazie Bank* v. *Femno* (8 Wallace 533); *Scholy* v. *Rew* (23 Wallace 331); and *Springer* v. *US* (102 US 586).

3. Herbert Ronald Ferleger, *David A. Wells and the American Revenue System, 1865–1870* (New York, Columbia University, 1942), p. 44.

4. For a full discussion of the law see Charles F. Estee, comp., *The Excise Tax Law Approved July 1, 1862; and all Amendments* (New York, Fitch, Estee & Co., 1863).

5. The Internal Revenue assessment lists, 1862–74, for the following states and territories are currently available as microfilm publications:

M754 Alabama, 1865–66, 6 rolls; M755 Arkansas, 1865–66, 2 rolls; M756 California, 1862–66, 3 rolls; M757 Colorado, 1862–66, 3 rolls; M758 Connecticut, 1862–66, 23 rolls; M759 Delaware, 1862–66, 8 rolls; M760 District of Columbia, 8 rolls; M761 Florida, 1865–66, 1 roll; M762 Georgia, 1865–66, 8 rolls; M763 Idaho, 1865–66, 1 roll; M764 Illinois, 1862–66, 63 rolls; M765 Indiana, 1862–66, 42 rolls; M766 Iowa, 1862–66, 16 rolls; M767 Kansas, 1862–66, 3 rolls; M768 Kentucky, 1862–66, 24 rolls; M769 Louisiana, 1863–66, 10 rolls; M770 Maine, 1862–66, 15 rolls; M771 Maryland, 1862–66, 21 rolls; M773 Michigan, 1862–66, 15 rolls; M775 Mississippi, 1865–66, 3 rolls; M776 Missouri, 1862–66, 22 rolls; M777 Montana, 1864–72, 1 roll; M779 Nevada, 1863–66, 2 rolls; M780 New Hampshire, 1862–66, 10 rolls; M603 New Jersey, 1862–66, rolls 1–17 (with New York); M782 New Mexico, 1862–70, 1 roll; M603 New York, 1862–66, rolls 18–218 (with New Jersey); M784 North Carolina, 1864–66, 2 rolls; M787 Pennsylvania, 1864–66, 107 rolls; M788 Rhode Island, 1862–66, 10 rolls; M789 South Carolina, 1864–66, 2 rolls; M791 Texas, 1865–66, 2 rolls; M792 Vermont, 1862–66, 7 rolls; M793 Virginia, 1862–66, 6 rolls; M795 West Virginia, 1862–66, 4 rolls.

6. There are two publications that are particularly useful. The first is *Cost of Labor and Subsistence in the United States for 1869 as Compared with Previous Years*, compiled by Edward Young and published in 1870. The second is entitled *Special Report on Immigration*, also compiled by Edward Young. This second report, published in 1871, was designed to provide cost-of-living information to newly arrived immigrants. It also includes information on the types of jobs available in the southern and western states.

7. Thomas Splicer, Sr., died March 12, 1864, leaving his son mortgaged real estate. Splicer sold his father's property to pay the debt. His share of the profits was $2,700.

PART VI

DISCOVERING AMERICAN MINORITIES

Example of Black life in America in the 1930s. (*From the William Harmon Foundation Collection, National Archives*)

148

America is a nation of immigrants. Virtually every American can trace his or her lineage to ancestors who arrived in this country over land or by sea from some other part of the world. Thousands of years ago the ancestors of American Indians traveled over a land bridge from Asia to Alaska and migrated down to what is now the lower 48 states. In the 17th and 18th centuries, religious dissenters and economic opportunists came from England seeking a better life. Also during these years came black people from Africa, bound in chains, to be used as slaves in the southern colonies. Beginning in 1820 and for the next 100 years, tens of millions of peasants from Europe and Asia traveled to this country in packet ships. Together these diverse peoples came together to form a unified culture and nation. "E Pluribus Unum," reads the motto on our currency, "Out of many, one."

Recording the arrival of new immigrants and tracking their adjustment to American society has been a function of the federal government since the early days of the republic. The arrival of Europeans and Asians on board packet ships was duly recorded in custom passenger lists and ship passenger lists. The government also took note of these foreigners when they applied for citizenship and became Americans. The National Archives has thousands of cubic feet of naturalization records.

The government also documented its relations with American minorities who were the victims of persecution and injustice. The often violent relations between native American Indians and white settlers are documented in the records of the Bureau of Indian Affairs and in federal court records. The tumultuous transition of black people from slaves to freedmen in the years after the Civil War was noted by the federal government in the records of the Bureau of Refugees, Freedmen, and Abandoned Lands and of other agencies. These records are invaluable sources of family and local history information on these Americans.

The authors of the following essays provide an introduction to immigrant, black, and American Indian family history. Frank H. Serene is a specialist in immigration history and an archivist on the staff of the National Archives and Records Administration. Barry A. Crouch is associate professor of history at Gallaudet College in Washington, DC, and Larry Madaras is an associate professor of history and government at Howard Community College in Columbia, MD. Cynthia G. Fox is an archivist in the Civil Archives Division of the National Archives and Records Administration.

FRANK H. SERENE

American Immigrant Families: Ship Passenger Lists

The National Archives holds many sources related to individual immigrants and aggregate immigration movements. Among the most complicated and valuable of these sources are passenger lists. Compiled on a ship-by-ship basis, the lists document millions of immigrants who arrived in this country between 1820 and 1945. These records contain information that may be used by historians and genealogists to document the history of individuals, families, or entire ethnic groups. The vast majority of passenger lists are available on microfilm at the National Archives Building in Washington, DC.

THE SCOPE AND CONTENT OF SHIP PASSENGER LISTS

The compilation of ship passenger lists in America began in the late 18th century, but most of the extant lists cover the years from 1820 to 1945. The so-called customs passenger lists, part of Records of the U.S. Customs Service (Record Group 36), span the years from 1820 to 1905. They were created in response to an 1819 act of Congress that required the master of a ship entering an American port from a foreign country to file a list of passengers with the district collector of customs. The customs passenger lists include the original lists, copies and abstracts, and State Department transcripts.

The original lists were prepared at the port of entry. The lists contain the name of the vessel, the name of the master, the name of the port of embarkation, the date of arrival, and the port of arrival. For each passenger, they include the passenger's name, age, sex, occupation, name of country of origin, country of intended settlement, and data and circumstances of death en route if applicable. Such passenger information was also recorded for tourists and American citizens. Unfortunately for researchers, however, only a small part of the original lists has survived, and only the lists for the port of New Orleans are complete.

When the original lists are not available, researchers may find adequate information in extant copies and abstracts. Prepared by customs collectors at each port in accordance with the 1819 act, the copies and abstracts served as quarterly reports to the State Department. Some collectors submitted a copy for each list, while others incorporated abstracts of the information into a quarterly report. The copies and abstracts contain the names of passengers, usually in an abbreviated form. In addition to the passengers' names, the copies contain the name of the vessel, the port of embarkation, the port or district of arrival, the date of arrival, and sometimes the name of the master. The abstracts usually contain, along with the names of the passengers, the name of the district or port of arrival, quarter and year of arrival, and, occasionally, the port of embarkation. Because the copies and abstracts were sent to Washington, a large part survived the ravages of time and neglect. Researchers are far more likely to find copies or abstracts for particular ports of entry than they are to find original lists.

Information from the copies and abstracts was transcribed into ledgers by personnel at the State Department, thus generating the State Department transcripts. There are eight volumes of transcripts covering the years 1819 to 1832. Entries are arranged by quarter and year of arrival, thereunder by district or port of arrival, thereunder by name of vessel, and thereunder by name of passenger. The transcripts include for each passenger: the passenger's name, sex, age, occupation, country of emigration, and country of intended settlement. These records are part of Records of the U.S. Customs Service (RG 36). Use of the State Department transcripts can be troublesome. Entries for some quarters begin in one volume and end in the next, and sometimes passengers arriving months apart can be found in the same volume. These problems are compounded by the fact that volume two of the original nine-volume set is missing.

The so-called immigration passenger lists, part of Records of the Immigration and Naturalization Service (RG 85), had meager beginnings. They were initiated in response to provisions of an immigration act passed on August 3, 1882, which directed the Secretary of the Treasury to coordinate a program of passenger registration through existing state commissioners, boards, or officers.

Under the program coordinated by the Secretary of the Treasury, state forms were used during the 1880s to register incoming passengers, and these forms serve as the early immigration passenger lists. The National Archives holds microfilm copies of the Pennsylvania state forms used to register passengers who entered the port of Philadelphia in 1883. For vessels, these forms contain the name of the captain, name of the vessel, port of arrival, and date of arrival. For passengers, they have the passenger's name, sex, occupation, last legal residence, place of birth, and remarks.

The records created were called immigration passenger lists because the vast majority of individuals arriving in this country by ship

were, in fact, immigrants. But it would be wrong to assume that every passenger was an immigrant. In fact, the lists also record the names of U.S. citizens returning to America as well as the names of tourists arriving for a visit to the United States. For purposes of this article, however, the terms immigrant and passenger will be used interchangeably except when otherwise noted.

Because of the immigration law passed by Congress on March 3, 1893, passenger lists were standardized and their informational content was increased. During the ensuing decade additional personal information was requested so that by 1907 the informational content currently associated with passenger lists was in place. Each list (which includes the name of vessel, its captain, port of entry, date of entry, and port of embarkation) includes each passenger's name; age; sex; occupation; marital status; ability to read and write in any language; nationality; last legal residence; destination beyond the port of entry; town, city, or county of birth; and previous U.S. residence if the passenger was returning to the United States. Illiteracy was not a bar to admission until 1917; before that date the record of an alien's ability to read and write was kept for statistical purposes only.

Passenger lists also contain information regarding a passenger's self-reliance and moral character. Such information relates to whether a passenger had a ticket to his or her intended destination, whether a contractor had paid for the ticket, the amount of money under 30 dollars held by the passenger, the name of any relative or friend that the immigrant hoped to join, whether the passenger had been in an almshouse or prison, and whether the passenger was a polygamist. The reason for the 30-dollar plateau is not clear. A financial test was proposed for the immigration law in 1906, but was dropped from the final draft. Although a financial test was never formally enacted, immigration officials were given wide discretion to identify potential paupers and bar their admission.

Further information relates to the health

Upon entering an American port, the ship captain delivered a ship passenger list, such as the one above, to the district collector of customs. Each list included specific information on passengers including name, age, sex, occupation, and nationality.

and physical appearance of immigrants. This information concerns the condition of the passenger's mental or physical health; whether the passenger was crippled or deformed, the cause of the infirmity, whether it was permanent, and the length of time the passenger had been afflicted; the passenger's height in feet and inches; the passenger's complexion; the color of the passenger's eyes and hair; and whether the passenger had any identifying marks.

Like customs passenger lists, immigration passenger lists include names of tourists and citizens of the United States. At a few ports, lists for tourists and citizens were maintained separately from lists for immigrants. The amount of information for citizens and tourists is not as detailed as that for immigrants. For non-immigrant passengers, the information includes each passenger's name, age, sex, marital status, and date and place of birth if born in the United States or the date of naturalization with the name and location of the court where naturalization occurred.

Both customs and immigration passenger lists are arranged by port and thereunder chronologically by date. To use these lists, researchers should know the port of entry, the exact date of arrival, and the name of the vessel. Within each list, passengers' names are entered randomly, so the researcher will have to read through the list until the desired name is found.

GUIDES AND INDEXES
TO SHIP PASSENGER LISTS

Two guides published by the National Archives are particularly useful. Both can be purchased from the Publications Services Branch of the National Archives. The *Guide to Genealogical Research in the National Archives* (1982) includes a general introduction to ship passenger lists and an excellent table of information on the availability of original lists, copies, and abstracts and on pertinent indexes for specific ports or districts. *Immigrant and Passenger Arrivals: A Select Catalog of National Archives Microfilm Publications* (1983) provides details on the availability of passenger lists and on the 23 card and book indexes that have been made into microfilm publications by the National Archives. The card and book indexes were prepared for specific ports and specific periods of time; thus, researchers must know the port of entry and the approximate date of entry before using these indexes.

One very useful index uses the Soundex system. Developed by the Remington Rand Corporation for searching large name indexes, Soundex is a coded surname index based on the way a surname sounds rather than the way it is spelled. Surnames that sound the same but are spelled differently have the same code and are filed together. Soundex is most useful, therefore, when a researcher is uncertain about how a name was spelled at the time of immigration. Within the Soundex system, surnames are listed according to code and then alphabetically by first name. A pamphlet explaining the use of the Soundex system is available from the Publications Services Branch.

Of all the indexes, the most valuable seem to be the card indexes, which can be used as sources of information and as finding aids. For passengers, they contain name, age, occupation, nationality, and last permanent residence. For vessels, they contain the vessel's name, port of entry, and date of arrival.

Information in the book indexes and the Soundex system is not nearly as complete as in the card indexes. Book indexes are arranged chronologically by date of arrival and contain each passenger's name, age, and intended destination. Soundex index cards may contain only each passenger's name, age, and sex. The Soundex index may also provide the volume, page, and line number where the passenger's name is registered.

Despite their convenience, indexes have distinct disadvantages. They lack much of the information found on the passenger lists. Variations in spelling and errors in alphabetization require researchers to search extensively when they use the indexes. Not all lists for every port have been indexed and there are gaps and illegible entries in the available indexes. The absence of an index for the port of New York from 1847 to 1896 has probably drawn the most concern. There are, however, three alternate ways to retrieve information from the New York passenger lists.

One approach involves the use of either National Archives Microfilm Publication M1066, *The Registers of Vessels Arriving at the Port of New York from Foreign Ports, 1789–1919* or the *Mortan-Allan Directory of Ship Arrivals*. Suppose, for instance, a researcher knows the names of a passenger and the name of the vessel and knows that the port of entry was New York; the purpose of this exercise, then, is to determine the date on which the vessel arrived in New York. To find this date, a researcher must first search through the records of ship arrivals and compile a list of the dates on which the vessel arrived at New York. After completing this compilation, the researcher should go to the passenger lists for the dates indicated, locate the passenger list for the designated vessel, and search through the list for the passenger in question. This procedure will have to be repeated for each date compiled until the desired name is found.

A second approach involves use of federal population censuses for 1900 and 1910, which indicate the year of arrival for alien and naturalized immigrants. Suppose, in this instance, a researcher knows the name of a passenger, and that the port of entry was New York, but does not know the name of the vessel or the date of entry. The researcher then will have to determine the date of entry and the name of the vessel. By going to the censuses, the researcher can narrow his or her search to the year of arrival. Armed with this knowledge, the researcher can go through the yearly accumulation of passenger lists until the desired passenger's name is found. By focusing on the year of arrival, the researcher can circumscribe the work somewhat. However, it is still necessary to review a considerable number of passenger lists since there are 12 to 15 rolls of microfilm per year for New York between 1847 and 1896.

The third approach enables a researcher to determine the name of the vessel by tracking it from the port of departure. The researcher begins by compiling a list of the names of vessels departing the foreign port. This compilation can be made by consulting National Archives Microfilm Publication M1066, *The Registers of Vessels Arriving at the Port of New York From Foreign Ports, 1789–1919*, which also indicates the port of departure for each vessel on the register. Suppose, for example, that the researcher knows the passenger's name, the port of departure, and again that New York was the port of entry. (The time and effort consumed on this task will be reduced if the date of departure is known or if the port of departure is small.) The researcher should begin, then, by compiling a list of ships departing the foreign port. Next, the researcher will have to search through the passenger list for each of these vessels until they find the name of the passenger in question.

There are, however, two constraints on this approach. First, the list of vessels may become too large, especially if the passenger embarked from a popular port or the date span is

too great. Second, the port recorded as the port of embarkation may not have been the port at which the passenger boarded. Suppose, for instance, that a passenger boarded at a Russian port. Suppose further, however, that the vessel made a brief stop in Hamburg, Germany. In this case, Hamburg would be recorded as the port of embarkation, and the vessel's identity as one likely to be carrying Russian immigrants would be obscured.

IMMIGRANT AND PASSENGER ARRIVAL RECORDS

Using ship passenger lists to locate specific information about family members can be a frustrating and arduous task. The passenger arrival records for the period 1891 to the present are part of the Records of the Immigration and Naturalization Service (INS). These records were transferred to the National Archives on microfilm. The original records were destroyed by the INS. Errors in arrangement and omission cannot be corrected. Some of the records may be difficult to read due to poor focus having been used during the filming process.

Sometimes the information is missing. Historians and genealogists may be further frustrated because precise places of birth were not recorded on passenger lists until 1906. In fact, ethnicity may be difficult to verify, because the "last permanent" or "legal" residence is not enough to determine ethnic background.

Occupation is also difficult to determine from ship passenger lists. For instance, a listing of "laborer" will distinguish a skilled from an unskilled worker, but it does not precisely define occupation. There is also the problem of explaining occupational changes. Immigrants may have changed jobs from time to time, but these changes are not indicated on the passenger lists. Certainly, if the passenger list indicates an immigrant is a laborer and the same immigrant is later found in census records to be a merchant, a significant degree of occupational mobility is suggested.

CONCLUSION

When asking questions about specific immigrants or immigration movements, researchers are advised to consult as wide a range of sources as possible before looking at the passenger lists. Oral histories from family members and friends may suggest the location of relevant material. Information about an immigrant ancestor may be found in family Bibles or other family records.

Local historical or genealogical societies may have helpful reference sources to regional activities. A check with local churches, schools, and fraternal associations may reveal indications of immigrant participation. Within the last twenty years many colleges and universities have developed archives that include materials related to the ethnic growth of an area.

State archives, historical societies, and/or libraries may hold useful sources. Along this line, a check of local tax records, census schedules, and vital statistics may be helpful.

Before visiting the National Archives or a state or local repository, researchers should inquire about the availability of records and research policies. Such advance inquiries can save time and frustration and increase research efficiency.

Research is enriched by a broadened base of resources. By coordinating the informational value of resources, researchers can enhance their work. Thus, material gathered from family, friends, and local repositories can add meaning to the information found on the passenger lists. Access through indexes is not always possible, and sometimes researchers must devise routes to access without the aid of indexes. Use of passenger lists is part of the process of coordinating sources of information, and the key to successful use of passenger lists is how well the researcher establishes his or her relationship with other sources.

BARRY A. CROUCH • LARRY MADARAS

Reconstructing Black Families: Perspectives from the Texas Freedmen's Bureau Records

Emancipation provided many former slaves with the opportunity to reassemble their families, many of which had been separated during the period of bondage. The National Archives houses excellent sources that enable the researcher to document these efforts. This essay examines some of the information available in the records of the Bureau of Refugees, Freedmen, and Abandoned Lands, Record Group 105, in the National Archives, which the researcher may find of value in documenting the lives of Afro-American families during the Reconstruction era, 1865–72.

In March 1865, a month before the Civil War ended, Congress created the Bureau of Refugees, Freedmen, and Abandoned Lands, commonly known as the Freedmen's Bureau. Established under the War Department for 1 year, the bureau had as its original goal the care and well-being of white and black Southerners who had been uprooted by the war. With branches located in every ex-Confederate state, the bureau provided a variety of services, some to schools and hospitals, but most to former slaves. The bureau distributed rations, provided legal aid, and offered information and assistance to clients in relocating to other counties or states and negotiating contracts with employers.

Most Southern whites avoided the agency for two reasons. First, whites would have to concede that the blacks were their social equals if both groups used the bureau, and this was something the white community was unwilling to admit. Second, in late 1865 President Andrew Johnson began to pardon former rebels and allow them to reoccupy their lands, which meant the bureau had few acres to redistribute to whites or blacks.

Until the late 1950s historians generally portrayed the Freedmen's Bureau as a political instrument of Radical Republicans. As a result, history books were sympathetic to the white southerners who hated the bureau. Since it was directed by the military and primarily aided the former slaves, the bureau served as a constant reminder that the Confederacy had lost the war. Critics of the bureau were quick to point out any corruption that occurred in the agency. Northern and Democratic newspapers magnified its problems through countless editorials. Many 19th-century Americans who believed in a minimal role for government were more hostile than 20th-century Americans to the notion of public assistance. Finally, the bureau was seen as one of the tools with which the Radicals persecuted the South after February 1866, when Congress overrode President Johnson's veto and extended the life of the agency.[1]

Revisionist writers, who reject the racial biases of traditional historians, also view the Freedmen's Bureau in an unfavorable light. Instead of portraying the bureau as the political arm of the corrupt Radicals, the revisionists believe the bureau did not go far enough to aid the newly freed blacks. The bureau failed to reach its potential because it was underfinanced by Congress, unsupported by the white American public, and undermined by the agency's own high-level officials, who believed the complaints of white southerners that the bureau was doing too much to help the ex-slaves. In the words of Forrest Wood, "it appears that the white South could have lived with a corrupt Bureau, but it could not live with a humanitarian one."[2]

The authors of this essay reject the negative views of the Freedmen's Bureau presented in the works of both the traditional and revisionist historians. Most of the histories of the bureau take an administrative approach and discuss policies set in motion by the national commissioner in Washington, DC, and his assistant commissioners, who were assigned to each of the former Confederate states. If one studies the bureau from a "bottom up" perspective, as the authors of this essay have done, a more favorable impression is formed concerning the work that the bureau performed.

Record Group 105 in the National Archives contains many letters and reports written by state bureau commissioners and local agents in Texas. This material demonstrates not only how national, state, and local agents worked with the black community but also how former slaves worked with the bureau in order to solve their immediate problems. Supplemental information can be found in the national administrative offices and divisions of the bureau in the same record group. Army materials in Record Group 393 complement

records of the Freedmen's Bureau since the two groups often worked together and many bureau officers came from the army.[3]

The bureau records vary in quantity and quality for every ex-Confederate state, largely depending upon the numbers of ex-slaves and the longevity of military occupation. The Texas records are only of medium size (174 volumes and 44 boxes), in contrast to the large collections of bureau records for South Carolina, Louisiana, and Mississippi.

The records of the bureau contain thousands of cases apropos to the inner workings of the black community across the South in the first 5 years following the Civil War. Combined with other manuscript source materials, the Freedmen's Bureau records provide a composite picture of how former slaves began their adjustment to freedom, what some of their conceptions were about the society in which they lived, and how they responded to the social values of the white community. These are exceptional papers, for they include both writings by whites about blacks adjusting to emancipation and materials written by the freedmen themselves. The records demonstrate, among other things, that the burdens of freedom were never easy and that many times the issues were bewildering for a largely illiterate people. How the freedmen began this long struggle of adjustment and how the controlling white majority reacted to their actions are clearly delineated in this invaluable collection.

For Texas, the records constitute a major source of information about race relations and the concerns of the state's black community during the early postwar years. Texas bureau agents were sympathetic in aiding Texas blacks in the reunification of families divided by slavery, in assuring fair treatment for children apprenticed to the former slaveholders, and in attempting to protect women and children from abuse by both the white and black communities.

The Civil War had ended in April 1865, but the first bureau agents did not arrive in Texas until early September. A large part of

WAR DEPARTMENT,

<small>BUREAU REFUGEES, FREEDMEN, AND ABANDONED LANDS,</small>

Washington, Feb. 5, 1867.

CIRCULAR }

No. 4. }

The attention of Assistant Commissioners is called to the imperative necessity for a prompt compliance with the Regulations of this Bureau calling for stated periodical reports and returns.

The following *Monthly* Reports are required :

Return of Refugees and Freedmen.

Land Reports.

School Reports.

Report of changes of Officers.

Report of operations of the Bureau and Freedmen's affairs.

Consolidated report of persons employed and articles hired.

Returns, *in triplicate*, accompanied with one set of Abstracts, Vouchers, &c., to wit:—Return of Quartermaster's Stores, and Return of Clothing, Camp and Garrison Equipage, when the property, clothing, &c., pertain to the Quartermaster's Department, to the Quartermaster-General *through the Commissioner.*

Return, *in duplicate*, of " Stores, *including Clothing*, pertaining to the Bureau of Refugees, Freedmen, and Abandoned Lands," with one set of Abstracts, Vouchers, &c., to the Commissioner.

Personal Report of Officers.

Report of sick Refugees and Freedmen (by Chief Medical Officer).

In addition to the above, *Quarterly* " statements of stores received, issued, &c.," and " *Weekly* statements of deposits," are required.

Chief Disbursing Officers will render their accounts *monthly* in the manner prescribed by the Regulations, and will be careful to observe the distinction to be made in accounting for receipts and expenditures under the different funds, *i. e.*, the appropriation of Congress, the Refugees and Freedmen fund, and the School fund.

Assistant Commissioners are required to forward to this Bureau copies of all their circulars and orders, *at the time of their issue.*

Whenever an officer or agent is assigned to. or relieved from duty by an Assistant Commissioner, a copy of the order will be forwarded immediately to this Bureau.

O. O. HOWARD,

Major-General, Commissioner.

OFFICIAL:

Directive from General O. O. Howard, who had overall responsibility for managing the Freedmen's Bureau.

the bureau's records for Texas cover the early Reconstruction process in large towns such as Houston and Galveston. Less information is available about the eastern part of Texas, which is equal in size to Mississippi and Alabama combined, since few bureau agents were immediately available to cover the entire state. The Texas bureau completed its operations in 1868.

Texas slaves were officially declared free on June 19, 1865. When the newly established bureau sent its agents into Texas, many middle-aged and young blacks asked for help to reunite their families. The records indicate that Texas blacks used whatever resources were at hand to gain information about absent family members. Often the hopes of the former slaves were dashed. Julia Shephard, for example, wanted to gain custody of her children and sister from their former owner, who was also their father. He was detaining them in West Point, MS. As is often the case, the final outcome is not part of the record.[4]

In another case, Julia Washington, a Houston black woman, had been brought to Texas by a slave trader when the war came. Her husband had last been heard of in Springfield, WV, and her two children, John and Ida, who had also been sold, were allegedly in the same vicinity. Mrs. Washington was well situated in Houston, had a good position paying fine wages, and desired that her family join her. She wrote to West Virginia several times but never received a reply. As a last resort, she turned to the Freedmen's Bureau, which was equally unsuccessful in locating them.[5]

Older and aged black citizens also sought reunion with their families. "Aunt Rachel," a 93-year-old Houstonian in good health, enlisted the aid of a Houston white teacher, Julia B. Nelson, hopeful that she could get back to Charleston, where her only daughter lived. Both women were attempting to raise money for the trip. Nelson wrote that if Aunt Rachel could "only get started first, she would be okay." The records do not reveal whether Aunt Rachel returned to Charleston. More successful was a "very feeble" octogenarian, Isaac

Thompson, who wanted to return to Linden, AL, where he had four children. The bureau first sent Thompson to a hospital and then paid his transportation to Alabama.[6]

The Freedmen's Bureau received numerous inquiries from black parents outside of Texas who wanted to know where their children had been taken in Texas. James Kelley, a black man from Chicot County, AR, made a painstaking search for his three offspring. His efforts were rewarded when he found them living with a Baptist preacher on the Horne plantation 6 miles south of Waco. From Madison, AR, came the plea of Coleman—a black man over 50, a porter at McCarty's Hotel, and a "worthy old man"—who reported that four of his five children were abducted from a plantation near Jefferson City, MO, by bushwhackers in August 1864. They were supposedly removed to Arkansas or possibly northern Texas. However, since it was virtually impossible to find children who had been forcibly removed in similar circumstances, Coleman's search was not successful.[7]

From mid-1865 until the 1870s, black parents attempted to locate or reclaim children who had been left on plantations, forcibly separated from them by sale, or detained unlawfully by a former master. Harry Pope and Sarah Timsy of Cherokee County requested that a provost marshall issue an order to the sheriff of the county and deliver to them their five children: Chaley Jane, 2; Henry, 17; Eddy, 14; and the twins, Chuff and Lucy, 12. The children had been abducted, and force was used to retain them. "Our children does not want to stay with ther former owner," the parents pleaded, and prayed that their "petition be granted" for their return. In another case, John E. Chisholm, a former slave-owner, spirited away the four children of Washington Ake shortly after federal troops invaded Texas. The children, according to the parents, had no desire to go with Chisholm, and neither Ake nor his wife gave consent.[8] As often happens, the records do not indicate the outcomes of these cases.

From all over Texas, black heads of families sought information, aid, or any type of help the Freedmen's Bureau could provide. According to the records, most of the requests came from black women, but black men were concerned with locating their offspring as well. Blacks, of course, did not rely solely on the bureau; they also searched individually. In certain cases the bureau agreed to pay transportation expenses, as in the example of Charity Watley, who lived in Galveston and sought reunion with her three children, who were 7 miles outside of Marlin, TX, approximately 400 miles away.[9]

Distances in Texas were immense, and black parents rarely had the money or the means to make the required journeys. Consequently, they turned to the black community or to the bureau for assistance. Betsey Webster attempted to locate two sons who last resided in Georgia—Hubbard Leonard, 30 or 40 years old, and William Leonard, 22. The Freedmen's Bureau was willing to pay the Leonard sons' transportation to Texas, but there is no indication they were ever found.[10]

A number of young black adults, according to bureau records, attempted to locate their parents. Sometimes they were successful, like 20-year-old Eliza Finnick, originally sold in Maryland as a young teenager in 1860 before being taken to Louisiana and Texas. Her parents lived in Charles County, MD, and she was able to trace them. Eliza Finnick was encouraged by the fact that her grandfather, a free black, had left some valuable property and Finnick's mother, Henny Adams, held some money for her that she had promised to keep until Finnick came of age.[11]

Both Flora Hewes and Adeline Strouder, Galveston black women, were anxious to find their parents and other blood relatives in Wainsborough (Burke County) GA, and Louisville, KY, respectively. In Austin, Mary Riggs resorted to the Freedmen's Bureau to learn if her mother, Matilda Riggs, still resided in Lexington, KY. In these series of cases none of the women succeeded in finding the whereabouts of their families.[12] As long as there was

an institution or an individual to aid them, many blacks continued to search.

Just how many orphan children there were in Texas in 1865 will never be known with certainty, but the number was undoubtedly large. Often either young children were not found by their parents or the parents were dead. In the closing months of 1865, former slaveowners and county courts were beginning to wonder what to do in these types of cases. In San Marcos a white planter had nine "orphans" among his ex-slaves. Some of the mothers had remarried and "others were not able to support and take care of [their children]." The blacks were getting ready to disperse, making the farmer "shudder at the thought of the suffering that must initially follow." He was willing to care for them "through sympathy," if he had the "power to retain them from their mothers who have no home or means of support for them." In Washington County the chief justice's office had been apprenticing or binding out children so they would have "good comfortable homes" and "receive some education." The office was satisfied that it was only acting properly under Texas law and that it could "select homes that will do justice to these children."[13]

The vast correspondence between the agents and the ex-slaves in the bureau's local Texas files reveals the concern of the black community that children apprenticed to the former slaveholders be treated fairly. Throughout Texas, county officials and military personnel began to apprentice children as soon as Union forces took control of the state. If the children's parents could not immediately be found or it was ascertained that the youngsters were orphans, they were usually apprenticed to a planter, who saw them as a cheap source of labor, or to the white person with whom they had formerly lived. The standard procedure was for the county court to give at least 10 days public notice of impending apprenticeship. Then, if no one came forward to challenge the action the child was "legally" apprenticed. Blacks correctly perceived that the apprenticeship system established throughout the South after the war was another form of slavery. Freedmen were at an enormous handicap simply because most of them were illiterate. Unless some sympathetic individual apprised them of the workings of the apprenticeship system, some blacks believed that they were at the mercy of not only the law but also of white society in general.[14] Blacks constantly urged the Freedmen's Bureau to void the apprenticeship agreements and restore the children to adoptive and fictitious kin.

Almost every volume or box in the Freedmen's Bureau papers on Texas contains material on apprenticing. These records substantiate the existence of clashes between blacks and whites over the issue of binding out children that would continue throughout the early years

of Reconstruction in Texas. In many instances the freedpeople were anxious to care for these orphans and were "clamorous" in their desire to see that the children were not left at the mercy of whites. But many white officials disagreed, believing the freedpeople wanted to "carry them over the country where they have nothing to support and maintain" them.[15]

In 1866 the Texas legislature enacted an apprenticing statute without regard to race. But it was quite clear to both black and white observers that the new law was to be used almost solely in regard to the freedpeople's children. One disgusted Freedmen's Bureau agent wrote that its aim was to "enslave the rising generation [in particular] of the freedmen in a worse condition of slavery than they have ever been."

The Freedmen's Bureau often found itself caught between angry whites and blacks.

And another argued that parents "[when able] are the most natural guardians of their own children."[16]

Blacks often succeeded in overturning what they considered to be illegal apprenticeship agreements. Sandy Mingoe, a Boston black, learned that his grandchild Julia had been bound without his consent to Edward Runnels after Runnels had forcibly taken the child from him. Mingoe made application to revoke the apprenticeship. As a result, the child was returned to her grandfather and an order was given to the chief justice of the county to cancel the bond that Runnels had given to fulfill the contract. Far to the South, in Galveston, Solomon Riley obtained his daughter, Louisa, who was being held by a widow outside Seguin. In Austin, Toby, the son of Nellie Thompson, was returned to his mother through the intervention of the Freedmen's Bureau. On occasion blacks used community information and support from relatives to negate an apprenticing arrangement. With the assistance of kin, Clara Rives of Austin reclaimed her son, and James Buck and Nancy Moss retrieved Lucinda and Kinchey, who had been indentured to a white woman.[17]

Some blacks, however, did themselves apprentice their children so as to gain income, and those who did so usually sought assurance that the child[ren] would be fairly treated. In the case of Lew Lewis of Columbia, who worked out an agreement for his son Gabriel with E. Burchard, Lewis' terms were specific and demanding, quite sufficient to protect his son. Burchard could employ Gabriel if he paid $12 currency a month and accepted the responsibility for boarding and schooling him. Lewis wished a guarantee to this effect and he also retained the right to take his son away whenever he saw fit. Lewis' objective was quite clear: to bind Burchard within the details outlined or he would exact double wages for the work performed by his son. The contract, moreover, was approved by a provost marshall. Although the terms were quite detailed, Burchard agreed to them and Lewis rested some-

what easier in the knowledge he had done all that was humanly possible to guarantee the maximum amount of protection for Gabriel. Although most blacks probably were not so careful in legally guarding their children, they seem to have taken measures to guard against their being badly treated.[18]

However, there is evidence of mistreatment. Lee Russell declared that he had seen Mr. and Mrs. Sam Ellington of Williamson County "shamefully beat" a black girl and that the "neighbors all talk about the way she is used." Josiah Coleman reported that two children, a boy and a girl, bound to William D. Patten of Austin, a white man, were abused and the girl had come to him "for protection." In other cases the evidence of child abuse was indisputable. Two black women, Ellen Jones and Mary Lewis, stated that a Mrs. Roberts mistreated a black girl named Mary, who was around 12. Mary was summoned to the office and "showed [the bureau agent] her marks and wished to be taken away."[19]

The local Texas bureau records indicate that the black community demonstrated a new sense of their rights as freedmen by their willingness to use the bureau's courts to deal with problems between members of their own community. Blacks insisted upon prosecuting and bringing to light child abuse not only by whites but also by other blacks. Howard, a black man, charged Ham Serell, also black, before the bureau court, with "unmercifully" beating Howard's daughter and refusing to pay for her hire. Serell, however, was found not guilty. In Ryan, Martha Gee complained that Berry Hodges cruelly whipped her 6-month-old granddaughter. Hodges pled guilty and was sentenced to 3 days hard labor in the guardhouse. In Galveston, Isiah Lemmons declared that Mahalia A. Morris abused and beat her adopted child. Morris was warned and gave the bureau assurances that the child would be well treated in the future. When it appeared that the disciplining of children might turn into child abuse, many blacks carefully watched the individuals involved.[20]

Transgressions committed by blacks were also reported to the bureau. These often concerned sexual indictments of one form or another. Wesley Henderson complained that Newton Collins, who was married, seduced his daughter Celeste. Henderson could not confirm her pregnancy when he made the charge, so the bureau was of little help. The agent advised the irate father to "wait and see the result." In another case, George Watrous stated that Stephen slept with his daughter, Georgianna, and wished to live with her. Stephen, who was already married, denied the charge. Nothing came of the allegation.[21]

The Texas black community also had their own internecine quarrels on behalf of children. Many women from Austin to Houston brought suits against their husbands and lovers for nonsupport of themselves and their children. Sara Tinsley, in Gonzales, stated that Elias Brown was the father of her 15-month-old child. After hearing the case the bureau decided that Brown was the father, and when Brown refused to take the baby and support it, the bureau ordered him to pay Tinsley a $10 settlement, $2 a month, and clothe the infant until "he saw proper to take the child and support it." Martha Pelham brought charges against Stewart Hamilton, who was the father of her daughter Mary's child. Hamilton had promised to support Mary and the child but had not done anything. There was also a $10 doctor's bill due because the infant had been ill. In bureau court, Hamilton agreed to pay the medical bill and take the child and raise it in a "proper manner," but Mary Pelham refused to surrender her daughter. Similar cases were settled in bureau courts. Women also reported men to the bureau for lack of financial support.[22]

Nonsupport of children was but one of several internal crises that racked the Texas black community. The bureau records contain cases too numerous to describe in detail in this essay. There were clashes over a sister who had been willed to a certain individual, both parents claiming a child, or blacks who took children and promised to return them but did not. There were runaways, stolen children, debts for delivering children, unlawfully keeping adopted children, and two young men claiming the same boy as a brother.[23]

A persistent problem involved enslaved black men who, after having fathered children, were sold away. The mother reared and supported them. After being freed, some fathers reappeared, desiring to take the children away so that they could be exploited and put to labor. In most cases of this nature the bureau and civil courts held the father had no right to the children, but they were also governed by the character of the parents and the wishes of the children. In Meridian, Lucie Williams had to take Mark Walker to court to retain her offspring. They had lived together during slavery, but afterwards she cared for the children. When the children became old enough to pick cotton, however, Walker wanted them. He was unsuccessful in his efforts.[24]

Some Texas blacks are known to have cared for orphaned children when circumstances either warranted or required it. When Jack Talbot's wife died in June 1867, she had charge of two orphan children. Talbot admitted that he was not able to keep them, but Jacob Fountain, a leader of the Austin black community, agreed to care for them. Jackson McKinney did the same thing for Abraham, an orphan freedboy from Huntsville. The following case clearly demonstrates the close ties, feelings of affection, and independent spirit of Texas blacks in taking care of their own. Cesar Kennedy and Mary McGee of Bastrop County had lived together as husband and wife for a year during slavery. A child was born to the union, but Kennedy was later sold. Both eventually remarried, and Kennedy admitted that he had no right to the child and did not claim him. But when Kennedy learned that Mary was having a very hard time supporting the boy and her other family, Kennedy assumed the responsibility to support, educate, and rear the young man. In another case, two children in Liberty were orphaned when their mother died during a smallpox epidemic, and Liberty blacks came forward to care for them.[25] Both incidents are strong reminders that blacks had deep attachments to their children, no matter to whom they belonged, and this general characteristic was perhaps a carry-over from practices made necessary under the institution of slavery.

Among other things, bureau records confirm that Texas blacks frequently turned to the bureau for assistance. They did so largely for two reasons. First, the bureau had a communications network throughout the South that made it possible to gain information from isolated areas that simply was not available to the vast majority of ex-slaves. Second, the bureau, because of its ties with the federal government, was supported by national law and served as a buffer for the black community against the often hostile legal and judicial decisions of local and state officials. This is not to argue that bureau agents were consistently sympathetic or always made the right decision when the interests of the former slaves were at stake. It merely suggests that blacks used the bureau in a myriad of ways. The tremendous number of cases involving the freedmen in the Texas records, and other Southern states, attests to that fact.

These cases indicate the Freedmen's Bureau records are a valuable source for historians interested in writing about the Afro-American family during Reconstruction. Most Reconstruction scholars are aware that microfilm copies of some of the Freedmen's Bureau records have been deposited in the 11 National Archives field branches across the nation so that these vital documents will be more accessible to historians. While these microfilmed records of national and state bureau offices are immensely valuable, they often focus on administrative problems with little direct relevance to blacks. The most penetrating insights into the Afro-American community are found in the records of local agents. Many of these records, such as correspondence between local citizens, black and white, and the agents, have

not been microfilmed, and therefore are available only at the National Archives.[26]

Fortunately, scholars who do not have immediate access to the bureau's files at the National Archives will be able to sample its rich holdings on black history in a multivolume work entitled *Freedom and Southern Society: A Documentary Record, 1861–1867*. Funded by the National Historical Publications and Records Commission and by the University of Maryland, this documentary publication is being edited with lengthy introductions by a team of scholars led by Ira Berlin. The first volume to appear, which is the second in the planned series, deals with the black military experience during the Civil War. Other volumes will follow. "Reflecting editorial interest in a *social* history of emancipation," the editors assert, "*Freedom* is organized thematically, following the process of emancipation." The records are "central to the transition from slavery to freedom." In future volumes the "transformation of black life that followed the conclusion of armed conflict" will be the central focus.[27] Even after this project is completed, however, it will still be necessary for scholars of Afro-American history to consult the local files of the Bureau of Refugees, Freedmen, and Abandoned Lands in Record Group 105 at the National Archives.

The Freedmen's Bureau records are unique. Through the use of local materials in the bureau's records for Texas, this essay has demonstrated the concerns of the black community for civil rights, a stable family life, security for their children, justice and independence. Although many of the conceptions are filtered through white perspectives, the beliefs and behavior of the ex-slaves is apparent at every stage of the Reconstruction era. Used cautiously, with other supporting evidence, these bureau records point to the fact that Southern blacks actively participated in Reconstruction. Just as important, these records reach across generations to researchers interested in learning more about black family and local history.

NOTES

1. The best and most complete explication of these ideas is George R. Bentley, *A History of the Freedmen's Bureau* (Philadelphia, 1955). This is the only major overview, based upon manuscript material, of the Bureau. See also Claude A. Elliot, "The Freedmen's Bureau in Texas," *Southwestern Historical Quarterly* 56 (1952): 1–24.

2. Forrest G. Wood, *The Era of Reconstruction, 1863–1877* (New York, 1975), p. 27. See also William S. McFeely, *Yankee Stepfather: General O. O. Howard and the Freedmen* (New Haven and London, 1968), and Herman Belz, *Emancipation and Equal Rights: Politics and Constitutionalism in the Civil War Era* (New York and London, 1978).

3. Barry A. Crouch, "Hidden Sources of Black History: The Texas Freedmen's Bureau Records as a Case Study," *Southwestern Historical Quarterly* 83 (Jan. 1980): 211–26; Crouch, "Freedmen's Bureau Records: Texas, a Case Study," *Afro-American History: Sources for Research*, ed. Robert L. Clarke (1981), pp. 74–94; James E. Sefton, *The United States Army and Reconstruction, 1865–1877* (1967); Joseph G. Dawson, III, *Army Generals and Reconstruction: Louisiana, 1862–1877* (1982); Robert W. Shook, "Federal Occupation and Administration of Texas, 1865–1877" (Ph.D. diss., North Texas State University, 1970); William Lee Richter, "The Army in Texas During Reconstruction, 1865–1870" (Ph.D. diss., Louisiana University, 1970).

4. Samuel Canby to Agent, Bryan, August 8, 1867, p. 101, vol. 57, Texas Records of the Bureau of Freedmen, Refugees, and Abandoned Lands, Record Group (RG) 105, National Archives (NA). Unless otherwise noted, all references are to these Texas bureau records in RG 105. See also Crouch, "Hidden Sources of Black History," p. 214. See also Elaine Everly and Willna Pacheli, comps., "Preliminary Inventory of the Records of the Field Offices of the Bureau of Refugees, Freedmen, and Abandoned Lands," 3 parts (mimeographed, 1973–74), part 3. Examples of work based on local agents' records are in Crouch, "The Freedmen's Bureau and the 30th Sub-District in Texas: Smith County and its Environs During Reconstruction," *Chronicles of Smith County, Texas* 11 (Spring 1972): 15–30; Crouch, "View From Within: Letters of Gregory Barrett, Freedmen's Bureau Agent," *Chronicles of Smith County, Texas* 12 (Winter 1973): 13–26; James Smallwood, "The Freedmen's Bureau Reconsidered: Local Agents and the Black Community," *Texana* 11 (Spring 1973): 309–20; Smallwood, *Time of Hope, Time of Despair: Black Texans During Reconstruction* (1981).

5. Statement of Julia Washington, April 10, 1867, n.p., vol. 96; Abner Doubleday to Agent, Springfield, WV, April 11, 1867, D-14, Box 42.

6. Julia B. Nelson to Louis W. Stevenson, October 30, 1869, Box 42; Statement of Isaac Thompson, February 14, 1867, n.p., vol. 96.

7. G. W. S. Benson to Agent, Waco, November 7, 1867, p. 62, vol. 165; endorsement, Charles Haughn, April 11, 1868, p. 63, vol. 165; Benson to Haughn, November 7, 1867, p. 26, vol. 166; endorsement, Haughn, April 11, 1868, p. 27, vol. 116; John Tyler to Agent, Napoleon, AR, April 22, 1867, Box 5, Arkansas; endorsement, J. C. Predmore, May 14, 1867, Box 5, Arkansas.

8. Harry Pope and Sarah Timsy to A. J. Hamilton, 1865, Governor's Correspon-

dence, A. J. Hamilton Papers, Texas State Library; C. E. Culver to J. T. Kirman, August 31, 1867, p. 35, vol. 86.

9. W. H. Sinclair to A. P. Delano, April 17, 1866, p. 191, vol. 4.

10. Edgar M. Gregory to Rufus Saxton, September 19, 1865, p. 5, vol. 4.

11. W. H. Sinclair to E. M. Gregory, May 20, 1867, Box 42.

12. Statement of Flora Hewes, April 15, 1867, n.p., vol. 96; statement of Adeline Strouder, April 13, 1867, n.p., vol. 96; James Oakes to Agent, Lexington, KY, April 6, 1868, p. 157, vol. 49.

13. L. Dixon to A. J. Hamilton, November 27, 1865, Hamilton Papers; O. H. P. Garrett to Hamilton, December 11, 1865, Hamilton Papers.

14. A. G. Haskins to W. G. Kirkman, July 9, 1867, pp. 6–7, vol. 66.

15. For an example of this see Garrett to Hamilton, December 11, 1865, Hamilton Papers. Additional material on apprenticing is in John P. Carrier, "The Era of Reconstruction, 1865–1875," in *Tyler and Smith County, Texas: An Historical Survey*, ed. Robert W. Glover (1976), pp. 65–66; "Book of Indentures to Bonds of Apprenticing, 1867–1870," University Archives, East Texas State University.

16. A. H. Mayer to Henry A. Ellis, November 24, 1866, pp. 43–44, vol. 212; W. G. Kirkman to Charles Garretson, October 31, 1867, p. 96, vol. 67; Theodore Brantner Wilson, *The Black Codes of the South* (1965), pp. 110–111; Smallwood, *Time of Hope, Time of Despair*, pp. 54–58. For a comparison with other states see Donald G. Nieman, *To Set the Law in Motion: The Freedmen's Bureau and the Legal Rights of Blacks, 1865–1868* (1979), pp. 76–82, 137–38, 199; Richard Paul Fuke, "A Reform Mentality: Federal Policy Toward Black Marylanders, 1864–1868," *Civil War History* 22 (September 1976): 222–26; Rebecca Scott, "The Battle Over the Child: Child Apprenticeship and the Freedmen's Bureau in North Carolina," *Prologue* 10 (Summer 1978): 101–113.

17. W. G. Kirkman to Edward Runnels, November 5, 1867, p. 4, vol. 69; *Sandy Mingoe v. Edward Runnels*, November 11, 1867, p. 12, vol. 70; statement of Solomon Riley, March 26, 1867, n.p., vol. 96; Byron Porter to George Glasscock, January 21, 1867, n.p., vol. 46.

18. Complaints and memo of business, June 20, 1867, p. 11, vol. 52; W. G. Kirkman, Circular No.?, January 6, 1868, p. 26, vol. 69; Kirkman to Mrs. L. Reid, January 6, 1868, p. 26, vol. 69; Kirkman to Mrs. S. Hull, November 20, 1867, p. 8, vol. 69; Kirkman to Charles Rochelle, November 5, 1867, p. 4, vol. 69; Kirkman, Order No. 55, December 23, 1867, p. 16, vol. 69; W. G. Hill to E. Burchard, January 24, 1867, H-4, Box 42.

19. Complaints and memo of business, August 9, 1867, pp. 32, 29, 34, vol. 52; *Thomas Glascow vs. Busley*, May 9, 1868, p. 49, vol. 75; J. A. A. Robinson to Agent, Huntsville, November 12, 1867, p. 29, vol. 110.

20. *Howard vs. Hamp Serell*, August 15, 1866, p. 1, vol. 131; *Martha Gee vs. Berry Hodges*, August 27, 1866, pp. 10–11, vol. 58; *Isiah Lemmons vs. Mahalia A. Morris*, March 1867, n.p., vol. 96; *Mary Jane Chapman vs. Ann Saunders*, April 22, 1867, n.p., vol. 96.

21. *Parry Lee vs. Patrick Gibben*, March 27, 1868, p. 42, vol. 75; complaints and memo of business, June 8, 1867, p. 7, vol. 52; *George Watrous vs. Stephen*, May 3, 1867, pp. 77–78, vol. 51.

22. *Sara Tinsley vs. Elias Brown*, August 18, 1866, p. 3, vol. 131; complaints and

memo of business, June 4, 1867, p. 4, June 7, 1867, p. 7, June 11, 1867, p. 9, and October 31, 1867, p. 59, vol. 52; *Juliann Stevens* vs. *Durke Woodall*, September 15, 1868, pp. 194–95, vol. 108.

23. These types of difficulties appear in almost every agent's records in Texas, RG 105.

24. *Minnie Qualls* vs. *Samuel Handy*, June 23, 1867, n.p., vol. 96; *George Brown* vs. *Former Wife*, October 16, 1867, n.p., vol. 96; Byron Porter to Agent, San Antonio, October 20, 1866, pp. 106–107, vol. 48; Chauncey C. Moore to Assistant Commissioner, Louisiana, September 15, 1865, p. 3, vol. 4; *William Smith* vs. *Eliza Smith*, May 15, 1867, n.p., vol. 131; *Doney Hamilton* vs. *Caroline Flash*, August 25, 1868, pp. 176–177, vol. 108; *Mary Ann Holmes* vs. *J. Tooke*, March 30, 1868, p. 40, vol. 75; *Clara Parker* vs. *Louisa Hutt*, August 19, 1868, pp. 170–171, vol. 108; *Jim McSween* vs. *Alfred Reddick*, December 25, 1867, pp. 28–29, vol. 54; J. P. Richardson to S. C. Plummer, May 29, 1867, p. 17, vol. 49; *Lucie William* vs. *Mark Walker*, n.d., pp. 88–89, vol. 138.

25. Complaints and memo of business, June 28, 1867, p. 14, vol. 52; James C. Devine, Order No. ?, October 12, 1866, p. 12, vol. 110; J. P. Richardson to Byron Porter, June 10, 1867, p. 30, vol. 49; complaints and memo of business, June 10, 1867, p. 8, vol. 52; A. H. Mayer to W. H. Sinclair, August 28, 1868, pp. 2–3, vol. 121; Mayer to J. B. Kiddoo, August 31, 1868, p. 6, vol. 121.

26. National Archives and Records Service, *Black Studies: A Select Catalog of National Archives Microfilm Publications* (1984), pp. 19–81; *Records of the Assistant Commissioner for the State of Texas, Bureau of Refugees, Freedmen, and Abandoned Lands, 1865–1869*, National Archives Microfilm Publication M821; *Records of the Superintendent of Education for the State of Texas, Bureau of Refugees, Freedmen, and Abandoned Lands, 1865–1870*, National Archives Microfilm Publication M822.

27. Ira Berlin, Joseph P. Reidy, and Leslie S. Rowland, eds., *Freedom: A Documentary History of Emancipation, 1861–1867*, Series 2, *The Black Military Experience* (1982), p. xxi; Berlin, Barbara J. Fields, Reidy, and Rowland, "Writing *Freedom's* History," *Prologue* 14 (1982): 129–39; LaWanda Cox, "From Great White Men to Blacks Emerging From Bondage, with Innovations in Documentary Editing," *Reviews in American History* 12 (1984): 31–39.

CYNTHIA G. FOX

American Indian Families: Selected Sources on the Eastern Cherokee

American Indian history is replete with monumental events that make Indian genealogical research difficult. Intertribal warfare and numerous migrations blur the history before the Indians' first encounters with Europeans. Interaction with whites further complicated matters, culminating in massive relocations of tribes westward as the white population expanded into Indian lands. All of this makes Indian genealogical research seem formidable at first glance.

Because of the unique history of the American Indian, however, there exists a number of very important sources of Indian genealogical information. Only recently have family historians discovered the rich genealogical information to be found in the records that document the longstanding relationship between the federal government and the American Indian. National Archives microfilm publications relating to American Indians are listed in a recently revised catalog.[1] These publications and other often overlooked information available at the National Archives can be of great assistance to anyone tracing his American Indian ancestry.

Excellent examples of sources of genealogical information are records documenting the history of the Cherokee. Of particular note are two series of Cherokee records available on microfilm from the National Archives: *Records Relating to the Enrollment of Eastern Cherokee by Guion Miller, 1908–1910*, M685 (12 rolls) and *Eastern Cherokee Applications of the U.S. Court of Claims, 1906–1909*, M1104 (349 rolls). These records are invaluable to both genealogists and historians of the Cherokee.

The Cherokee, one of the Five Civilized Tribes, were the largest southeastern tribe at the time of initial contact with whites in 1540. They numbered around 29,000 and controlled about 40,000 square miles of land in the southern Appalachian region. Beginning in 1794, small groups of Cherokee moved to Arkansas, where they became known as the Western Cherokee. Those remaining in the east, and known as the Eastern Cherokee, began to prosper in the early 19th century. A highly advanced, agriculturally oriented people with extensive fields and livestock holdings, they also established schools, a government with a constitution patterned after that of the United States, and newspapers in the Cherokee language.

During this period, gold was discovered on Eastern Cherokee lands, and pressure to remove the Eastern Cherokee westward resulted in the Treaty of New Echota in 1835. The treaty ceded the Eastern Cherokee lands to the U.S. government, required the removal of the tribe to Indian Territory to join the Western Cherokee, and provided for compensation to the tribe for its lands. In the winter of 1838–39, more than 15,000 Eastern Cherokee made the trek west, with one-fourth perishing along the way, in a journey that came to be known as the Trail of Tears. About 1,400 Eastern Cherokee avoided removal by hiding in the mountains. Later a reservation was established in the Smoky Mountains of North Carolina for this group, who became known as the Eastern Band or North Carolina Cherokee.[2]

This long history of Cherokee interaction with white men, represented by the federal government, has resulted in extensive records on the tribe that are useful for genealogical research. More so than for most other tribes, individual family backgrounds, as well as tribal history, can be traced in federal records. Of particular interest are the records of the U.S. Court of Claims relating to claims to financial compensation for their lands as provided to the Eastern Cherokee by the Treaty of New Echota. It is these records that are reproduced on the two microfilm publications highlighted in this article.

Before the U.S. Court of Claims was established in 1855, there was no formal procedure by which claims of any kind arising against the U.S. government could be enforced by suit. Congress assigned the responsibility for consideration of claims to the Treasury Department when the department was established in 1789; later acts of Congress authorized the department to settle all claims by or against the government. If a claim was rejected by the Treasury Department, the claimant's only course of action was to appeal directly to Congress. By the middle of the 19th century, Congress was beginning to find it impossible to make the proper and necessary investigations for actions on the claims.

Th U.S. Court of Claims was established in 1855 to hear claims against the United States, including those referred to the court by Congress or those based on any law of Congress, any regulation of an executive department, or any contract with the government, whether explicit or implied. The court served only as a fact-finding agency, and its conclusions were submitted to Congress for approval and for the granting of awards. In 1863, however, Congress enlarged the court's jurisdiction and gave it authority to render judgments against the government, with the right of appeal to the Supreme Court. An act of 1925 abolished appeals from the Court of Claims to the Supreme Court and substituted writs of certiorari.

In 1902, Congress gave the Court of Claims jurisdiction over any claim arising under treaty stipulations that the Cherokee Tribe, or any band thereof, might have against the United States, and over any claims that the United States might have against the Cherokee Tribe or any band thereof. Suit for such a claim was to be instituted within 2 years after the act was approved. As a result, three suits were brought before the court concerning grievances arising out of the treaties: *The Cherokee Nation* v. *The United States, The Eastern and Emigrant Cherokees* v. *The United States,* and *The Eastern Cherokees* v. *The United States.*

On May 18, 1905, the court decided in favor of the Eastern Cherokee and instructed the Secretary of the Interior to identify the persons entitled to participate in the distribution of funds for payment of the claims. On June 30, 1906, Congress appropriated more than $1 million for this purpose. The task of compiling a roll of eligible persons was begun by Guion Miller, special agent of the Interior Department. In a decree of April 29, 1907, the court vacated that part of its earlier decision that had given the Secretary of the Interior responsibility for determining the eligibility of claimants and appointed Miller as a special commissioner of the Court of Claims.

The same decree also provided that the fund was to be distributed to all Eastern and Western Cherokee who (a) were alive on May 28, 1906, (b) were members of the Eastern Cherokee Tribe at the time of the treaty of 1835 (or descendants of such persons), and (c) had not been affiliated with any tribe of Indians other than the Eastern Cherokee or the Cherokee Nation. The decree further provided that claimants should have applications already on file with the Commissioner of Indian Affairs or should file such applications with the special commissioner of the Court of Claims on or before August 31, 1907. Applications for

Louis Rogers Bean,
Pryor Creek, Okla

June 10, 1909.

Sir:

You are hereby notified that in my report to the Court of Claims of May 28, 1909, I have enrolled you ~~and your~~ ~~minor children~~ as entitled to participate in the fund arising from the judgment of the Court of Claims of May 28, 1906.

Your number on this roll is *4510*

A copy of all the names enrolled by me as entitled to participate in said fund has been forwarded to the following places, where said roll may be examined:

Commissioner to the Five Civilized Tribes, Muskogee, Okla.
Dana H. Kelsey, U. S. Indian Agent, Muskogee, Oklahoma.
Secretary of Cherokee Nation, Tahlequah, Oklahoma.
U. S. District Indian Agents at:--Vinita, Nowata, Sapulpa, Okmulgee, Checotah and Westville, Okla.
The Clerk of District Courts at:--Bartlesville, Miami, Claremore, Pryor Creek, Tulsa, Wagoner, Tahlequah, Sallisaw, Stigler and Grove, Oklahoma.
The City Clerks at:--Coffeyville and Chetopa, Kansas, and Porum, Oklahoma.
The Cherokee Indian School, Cherokee, North Carolina.
The Clerk of U. S. District Courts at:--Rome, Savannah and Atlanta, Georgia; Knoxville and Chattanooga, Tenn., and Birmingham, Alabama.
The Clerk of Courts at:--
North Carolina:--Murphy, Robbinsville, Franklin and Bryson City.
Tennessee:--Maryville, Cleveland, Ooltewah, Jasper, Decatur, Madisonville and Benton.
Alabama:--Center, Fort Payne, Gadsden and Guntersville.
Georgia:--Cartersville, Canton, Marietta, Dawsonville, Blue Ridge, Rome, Cumming, Ellijay, Calhoun, Dahlonega, Alpharetta, Spring Place, Jasper, Hiawassee, Blairsville, Lafayette, Dalton, Clayton and Gainesville.

A limited number of copies of this roll, with the order of the Court, have been printed and will be sold at $2.50 each, and the proceeds applied to the cost of printing.

A total of 45,857 applications, including about 90,000 individual claimants, have been considered and of these a total of 30,254 individuals have been enrolled; 3,203 of which were Eastern Cherokees residing east of the Mississippi, and 27,051 residing west of the Mississippi.

The Court of Claims in its order of June 10, 1909, has directed that all exceptions to my report shall be forwarded to the Clerk of the Court of Claims, Washington, D. C., to be filed in the Court on or before the 30th day of August, 1909.

The Court has further ordered that all exceptions to my report shall be set down for hearing before the Court on the third Monday of October, 1909.

Until these exceptions have been acted upon by the Court no money will be distributed.

Please retain this circular and present it at the time of payment.

Very respectfully,

GUION MILLER,

Special Commissioner.

On June 10, 1909, Guion Miller notified applicants of the disposition of their claims. For some, such as Louis Bean of Pryor Creek, OK, it was good news.

minors and persons of unsound mind were to be filed by their parents or by persons having their care and custody; applications for persons who had died after May 28, 1906, were to be filed by their children or legal representatives of their children.

In a report of May 28, 1909, Miller submitted to the court his enrollment of Eastern Cherokee who were entitled to a share of the fund.[3] On June 10, 1909, the court confirmed and approved the enrollment, except: "so much as shall be expected [excepted] to on or before August 30, 1909." The Court of Claims allowed rejected applicants to file objections in the form of exceptions, and Miller reported to the court on all of the exceptions filed. After the exceptions had been filed and investigated, Miller submitted a supplemental report and enrollment of the court on January 5, 1910.[4] On March 15, 1910, the court finally decreed that the enrollments be approved and that, after certain deductions for expenditures, payments were to be made equally among the enrolled Eastern Cherokee. The court also authorized the Secretary of the Treasury to issue a warrant in favor of each person. Each Cherokee entitled to participate in the payment received an equal share, $133.19, of the settlement.

The records compiled by Miller during this time, as well as older records that he used as sources of information in evaluating Cherokee applications, are reproduced on microfilm publications M685 and M1104, which hereafter will be referred to as the Miller Records and the Cherokee Applications, respectively. The Miller Records contain a name index; Miller's original report; a printed, condensed version of his report; exceptions filed; and previous Bureau of Indian Affairs (BIA) enrollments used by Miller as sources of information. The Cherokee Applications contain the applications by each claimant, together with other information relating to the claims, such as sworn testimony, as well as a series of name indexes to the applications. All of these documents contain considerable information of importance to genealogists.

Roll 1 of the Miller Records (M685) contains a name index to the Eastern Cherokee claims applications. The index provides an alphabetical list of persons claiming a share of the Cherokee payment, but not the names of all the individuals mentioned in the applications. The references in the index may be either the applicant's English or Indian name. The index also provides the application numbers needed to locate specific application files; these files are arranged by application number rather than enrollment number.

Rolls 2–5 contain Miller's original report filed May 28, 1909, listing all the claimants by application number. Each entry in the report gives the name of the applicant, the number (but not the names) of any children included in the claim, address (including street addresses for residents of cities), and whether the claimant was admitted to the enrollment or rejected. These entries usually include notes about the application, such as whether the applicant or applicant's parents were previously enrolled, names of previous enrollments, previous enrollment numbers, and cross-references to relatives. Miller's report also contains cross-references to testimony given before the commissioners.

Miller's report was condensed and published as *The Roll of Eastern Cherokees*. This printed version of the enrollment as well as Miller's report to the Court of Claims on exceptions filed by rejected claimants and supplemental applications accepted by the Court in 1910 are reproduced on roll 6 of the Miller Records. Together these records provide the complete list of all applicants qualified to receive payment under the 1907 Eastern Cherokee settlement. The Miller report, however, does not contain the names of *all* Cherokee tribal members. Descendants of the "Old Settlers," or Cherokee Indians who had moved west before 1835, were not entitled to a share in the settlement and their names do not appear in the report. Names of only Cherokee Indians who had remained in the east after 1835, and their descendants, appear on the Miller enrollment.

Entries in the printed *Roll of Eastern Cherokees* give names, addresses, position in the family, age in 1906, and enrollment and application numbers. The enrollment is divided into two sections—Eastern Cherokee living east of the Mississippi River and Eastern Cherokee living west of that river. Within each section the entries are arranged alphabetically by family name. The names of enrollees are numbered in order. The enrollment also includes the individual's FCT (Five Civilized Tribes) number if the number is known.[5]

Also reproduced on roll 6 of the Miller Records is Miller's report on exceptions. This report contains personal data on those who filed exceptions, the action taken on each exception, any additional appropriate information, and references to sworn testimony. Each entry in the exception report contains the name of the applicant, address of the applicant, and the name of the individual who filed the exception or the number of exceptions filed on applications claiming entitlement through the same ancestor. The action taken on each exception is noted. Any additional information and references to testimony are included in the report.

As a result of Miller's report on the exceptions, a supplemental enrollment dated January 5, 1910, was filed with the Court of Claims. This supplemental enrollment is also reproduced on roll 6. The supplement added names to the list of Eastern Cherokee, struck several names from the original enrollment, and corrected clerical errors in the spelling of names or in numbers cited. On December 12, 1910, the Court of Claims admitted an additional 109 names to the enrollment of Eastern Cherokee. The printed enrollment and the supplement available on this single roll of microfilm (roll 6), constitute the final listing of the Guion Miller enrollment.

The records reproduced on the remaining six rolls of the Miller Records consist of material Miller used to certify the eligibility of applicants. Rolls 7–11 contain transcripts of testimony taken before special commissioners

between February 1908 and March 1909. These transcripts are arranged chronologically by the date of the statement. Each signed statement relating to a specific application bears that application number. Applicants made statements relating to their heritage and often had relatives and friends testify in their behalf. These transcripts, which are predominantly typescript copies of the original depositions, are cross-referenced in Miller's original report and in the individual application files.

Also included with the Miller Records are transcripts of the compiled testimony relating to selected groups of rejected claims. The Sizemore claims, for example, were filed by applicants claiming Cherokee heritage through a single ancestor, Ned Sizemore. Another group, the Poindexter applications, were filed by applicants who claimed Cherokee blood from a Chief Donnahoo through Betty Pledge Poindexter. The "Sizemore" and "Poindexter" claims, and a similar group of "Creek Indian Claims," were rejected because their Indian ancestor was not listed in early Cherokee enrollments, but the transcripts of testimony contain much information of interest to genealogists.

The last roll (roll 12) of the Miller Records contains various earlier enrollments provided by the BIA, which were used by Miller in his work. In certifying the eligibility of the Cherokee, he used copies of earlier census lists and enrollments that had been made between 1835 and 1884 by Interior Department agents Joseph Hester, Alfred Chapman, John Drennen, and others. These earlier enrollments of Cherokee were originally made to determine eligibility for payments due under various provisions of treaties between the federal government and the Cherokee Tribe. If an applicant was listed on these previous enrollments, or was descended from an individual who appeared on these enrollments, his application was generally approved.

One of the BIA enrollments, however, was used to exclude applications. The 1907 settlement was due only to Eastern Cherokee and their descendants—those who remained east of the Mississippi River at least until the time of the Cherokee treaty of 1835. The descendants of the Texas or Old Settler Cherokee (those who had moved west before the Treaty of New Echota in 1835) were not entitled to participate in the settlement. Miller used the Old Settler payment enrollment, compiled in 1851, to determine the *ineligibility* of these applicants. The court settlement, however, did allow payments to members of the Eastern Band of North Carolina Cherokee, those Indians still residing east of the Mississippi in 1909.

Like the 1851 Old Settler enrollment, most of the earlier enrollments of Cherokee were made to determine eligibility for payments due under various provisions of treaties between the federal government and the Cherokee Tribe. Miller used copies of the Drennen enrollment, the Chapman enrollment, and the Hester enrollment, as well as the Old Settler enrollment. Each of these enrollments had its own system of numbering entries, so that an individual's name may appear with a different enrollment number on several different payment enrollments. Therefore, it is necessary to know the name of the enrollment as well as an enrollment number to locate the entry for an individual. For this reason Commissioner Miller created and used marking copies of name indexes to previous enrollments as well as the rolls themselves. The copies of the enrollments and indexes that Miller used may be cross-referenced to the applications he was verifying. The application number usually appears in parentheses after the name. If the application number is followed by a question mark, a researcher may wish to check for a cross-reference to testimony given to support an application.

The Chapman enrollment used by Miller was a copy of an 1851 payment enrollment originally compiled by Alfred Chapman, an agent of the Interior Department. Chapman had been responsible for dispensing per capita payments to Eastern Cherokees in the fall and early winter of 1851. Chapman's payment enrollment was based on an earlier census, the Siler enrollment, and included only the names of Cherokee Indians residing east of the Mississippi River. The Chapman enrollment provides a listing by county and thereunder by town of the Cherokee Indians who received payments. The head of the household is listed first, followed by the members of the family, their relationship to the head of household, and their ages. Families are grouped together but each individual on the list has a separate number.

Miller also used the enrollment compiled by John Drennen in 1851. At that time government payments were also made to that part of the Cherokee Nation (approximately three-fourths of the tribal population) who had been required to transport themselves in 1838–39. This Drennen roll lists the recipients of the distribution of funds in 1851 to the Emigrant or Eastern Cherokees who had come to the Indian Territory before that date. The Drennen enrollment is organized by tribal electoral district (Flint District, Going Snake District, etc.), with a separate section for persons whose status had been disputed by tribal authorities. Each person who was paid a share of the per capita payment is listed, and families are grouped together. However, the Drennen roll does not include information about the family relationships, age, or sex of the persons enrolled.

The Hester roll of 1884 is not a payment record but a census of the Eastern Band of Cherokees. Hester enumerated 2,956 Indians residing in 12 states. The census included several Indians actually residing west of the Mississippi River. Hester justified their inclusion on the grounds that they were descended from the Eastern Band and had not severed ties with the group. The census prepared by Hester includes previous enrollment references, spelling of name on previous enrollments, names of persons born since the last census, relationship to the head of the household, sex, age, names of ancestors on previous enrollments, relationship to ancestors cited, address, and often remarks on family relationships, dates of birth, and in some cases professions.

In addition to copies of previous enrollments, Miller used copies of a consolidated index to the Drennen and Chapman enrollments and a separate index to the Old Settler roll. Because these were copies of the earlier rolls, all of the information contained in the original may not be present on the records that Miller used. However, since they are copies, they are often typed and easier to read than the manuscript originals. All of the copies of the rolls described are available on roll 12 of the Miller Records.

The publication *Eastern Cherokee Applications of the U.S. Court of Claims, 1906–1909* (M1104) begins with a copy of Miller's enrollment of the Eastern Cherokee entitled to participate in the settlement and a set of name indexes to the application files. The indexes provide an alphabetical list of persons claiming a share of the Cherokee payment, but contain only the names of the claimants, not the names of all the individuals mentioned in the applications. The reference in the index may be either the applicant's English or Indian name. The index also provides the application numbers needed to locate specific application files. The application files are arranged by application number rather than enrollment number.

The remaining 348 rolls of microfilm in this publication are the applications reproduced in numerical order. There are some gaps in the application numbers; these gaps are explained on insert sheets at the appropriate places on the film. A descriptive pamphlet prepared by the staff of the National Archives includes a table of contents for each roll of microfilm.

The applications were filed with the Interior Department's Office of Indian Affairs until April 29, 1907, after which the applications were filed directly with the court. The application required each claimant to state fully his or her English and Indian names, residence, age, place of birth, name of husband or wife, name of tribe, and names of children. It further

required the following information on the claimant's parents and grandparents: English and Indian names, places of birth, places of residence in 1851, dates of death, and a statement as to whether any of them had ever before been enrolled as Indians for annuities or other benefits and, if so, with what tribe. Each claimant was also to furnish the names of all brothers and sisters, with their ages and residences, and the names and residences of all uncles and aunts. Applications were required to be made under oath and to be supported by affidavits of two witnesses who were well acquainted with the applicant. With each application is a card showing final action taken and the reasons therefore.

Filed with many of the applications are inquiries concerning the status of the cases, requests for further evidence, protests about unfavorable actions, form letters that had been sent as notices of rejection by the special commissioner to the applicants but returned by the Post Office Department as unclaimed, affidavits and statements of witnesses, powers of attorney, and last wills and testaments. The applications are arranged by the number assigned at the time the application was received.

These two microfilm publications relating to the Guion Miller enrollment of the Eastern Cherokee Indians from 1906 to 1909 can provide a wealth of genealogical information. They represent, however, a small part of the records that contain data valuable to Indian family historians. Other records available at the National Archives, including those identified in the catalog of microfilm publications described in note 1, constitute a source of priceless information available to those attempting to trace Indian ancestry or to study the history of the American Indian.

This essay is based on descriptive work prepared by the following National Archives and Records Service staff members: Carol Blanchard, Kent Carter, Jerry Clark, William Grover, Edward Hill, Robert Kvasnicka, Kathleen Riley, and Carmelita S. Ryan. It was compiled by Cynthia Fox, with assistance from Robert Fowler.

NOTES

1. National Archives Trust Fund Board, *American Indians: A Select Catalog of National Archives Microfilm Publications* (1984). This catalog describes records available as National Archives microfilm publications that relate to individual Indians, Indian tribes, and federal policy toward the Indians. The catalog is available from the Publications Services Branch (NEPS), National Archives and Records Administration, Washington, DC 20408. All microfilm publications are available for sale from the Publications Services Branch. Single rolls or entire publications may be purchased. To order, indicate the full publication (the "M" or "T") number and the specific numbers of the rolls desired. Checks or money orders should be made payable to the National Archives Trust Fund (NEPS). Many of the "M" publications have descriptive pamphlets to aid the researcher in locating the correct roll or rolls of a publication. Copies of the descriptive pamphlets are available at no charge from the Publications Services Branch. Please specify the full publication number when requesting a descriptive pamphlet.

2. Henry T. Malone, *Cherokees of the Old South* (1956); Irvin M. Peithmann, *Red Men of Fire* (1964).

3. In his report of May 28, 1909, Miller stated that 45,847 separate applications had been filed, representing a total of about 90,000 individual claimants, 30,254 of whom were enrolled as entitled to share in the fund—3,203 residing east and 27,051 residing west of the Mississippi River.

4. In this report, he stated that about 11,750 exceptions had been made, that the names of 611 persons (238 east and 373 west of the Mississippi) had been added to the enrollment, and that the names of 44 persons (5 east and 39 west of the Mississippi) had been stricken from the enrollment to correct clerical errors. Thus, the final figure on the total number of persons entitled to share in the fund was 30,820—3,436 east and 27,384 west of the Mississippi River.

5. The designation "Five Civilized Tribes" was the result of negotiated agreements between the U.S. government and the Cherokee, Choctaw, Chickasaw, Creek, and Seminole tribes providing for the dissolution of tribal governments and the allotment of land to each tribal member. An act of Congress authorized the establishment of a commission to negotiate these agreements and to prepare citizenship (tribal membership) rolls for each civilized tribe. These rolls were the basis for the allotment of land.

PART VII

REDRESSING GRIEVANCES

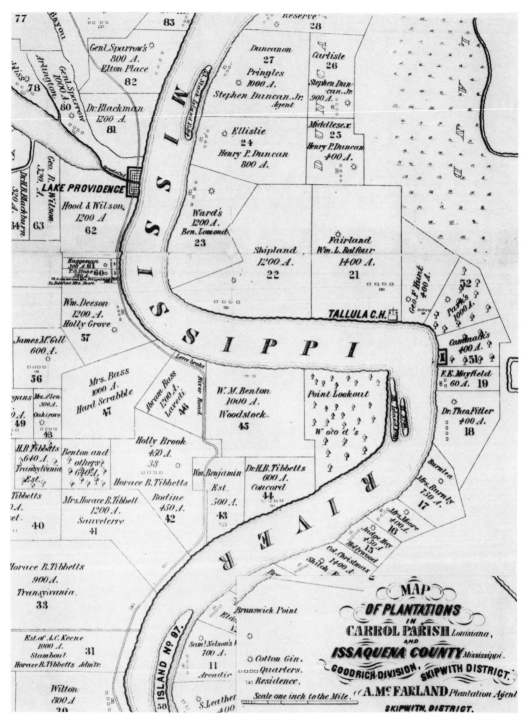

Map used by special agents investigating claims made to the Southern Claims Commission.

The United States of America is a litigious nation. Whenever conflict arises in America, one can expect to see the opponents and their attorneys involved in protracted legal proceedings. All of this activity has kept American lawyers quite busy. In fact, the United States has more attorneys per person than any other country in the world. It has become something of an American tradition for citizens to "have their day in court."

The records created as a result of these legal or quasi-legal proceedings have often ended up in the National Archives. Literally hundreds of thousands of cubic feet of such records are stored in the National Archives in Washington or in one of the 11 National Archives field branches across the country.

The records are used for a wide variety of purposes, not the least of which is historical research. Yet the value of these records specifically for family and local history research lends to be overlooked. Case files created through petitions to Congress or through legal proceedings in federal courts or before federal regulatory commissions provide insight into family and community conflicts. Such records often provide pieces of information unavailable in other sources.

The three essays that follow focus on the value of three series of legal records for family and local history research. Sarah Larson writes on the Southern Claims Commission, a body set up by Congress to review and authorize monetary compensation to southerners who provided goods or services to Union troops during the Civil War. Thomas Wiltsey shows how territorial court records are a vital source for the history of families and communities in the American West. Leonard Rapport details the rich documentation to be found in the case files of the Interstate Commerce Commission, the first federal regulatory agency. These are but three of the many series of legal records that should be consulted by family and local history researchers.

The authors are all former employees of the National Archives and Records Administration. Sarah Larson is currently a family and local history consultant in Washington, DC. Thomas Wiltsey is a historian with the U.S. Air Force at Shaw Air Force Base, SC. Leonard Rapport retired from the Archives in 1985 to work on a Library of Congress project to update Max Farrand's *Records of the Constitutional Convention of 1787* (1907).

SARAH LARSON

The Records of the Southern Claims Commission

Senator Waitman T. Willey, his square-cut beard sweeping his shirt front with every declamation, took to the floor of Congress in 1870 to defend the rights of Southerners who had remained loyal to the Union during the Civil War. Addressing his colleagues, the senator from West Virginia insisted, "Wherever the heart beat loyally, whether in rebel dungeons or in the hiding places of mountain or morass, there the Constitution promised the faithful citizen rescue and redress."[1]

At issue was whether the government was obligated to pay for supplies and stores appropriated from Southern unionists by federal forces. Union troops were instructed to differentiate between rebels and unionists, yet were given no guidelines for doing so. Enemy supplies were seized without compunction to support an army living off the land, but policy toward allies was hazy.

And so, the contributions of Southern unionists, offered up with varying degrees of willingness, were handled on an ad hoc basis. Some officers paid outright for supplies, making their own decisions as to loyalty. Others made partial payment and issued vouchers to be redeemed after the war, while others were willing only to sign vouchers, abandoning to the politicians the problem of payment.

In 1865, unionists clutching vouchers that ranged from printed forms to the backs of dirty envelopes turned to a federal government suddenly reluctant to recognize them as true and faithful allies. Excuses were given that, in the confusion of Reconstruction, it would be impossible to sort out fraudulent claims; that the government, saddled with an enormous war debt, couldn't afford to pay; and that all residents of Confederate states were rebels by association.

But by 1870 men like Senator Samuel C. Pomeroy of Kansas were arguing that patriotism was not a matter of region. He asked, "Did we not have as bad a fire in the rear as we had in the front; and were there not disloyal persons living in New York, and Kansas, and Illinois?"[2] Senator Daniel D. Pratt of Indiana suggested that "the records of patriotism during the world's history do not show sublimer examples of fortitude than we were furnished by Southern loyalists during this devastating war."[3]

After 6 years of petitioning and 2 years of congressional debate, Southern unionists finally prevailed in Washington: a three-member Southern Claims Commission was established in 1871 to shuffle through those much-handled vouchers. Staffed by Radical Republicans, the commission was an uneasy compromise, satisfying no one. But at least the claims would be heard.

THE COMMISSION RECORDS

The temptation would be to assume that no Southern ancestor, that no member of a Southern community, could possibly have made his case before the Southern Claims Commission. After all, why would there be this family tradition of Southern pride, how could this person have remained a well-respected member of his town, if all along he'd been a Yankee sympathizer?

However, loyalty to the federal government and to the South as a region were not mutually exclusive at the time of the Civil War. Consider that many Southern adults were only one or two generations removed from the American Revolution. They'd been brought up not only on stories of the war itself but on the struggle to weld the new nation together and justify it to Europeans who didn't take this democratic experiment too seriously. For many of these Southerners, while they might vehemently disagree with Yankee policies, dissolving the Union was too drastic a remedy.

Then, too, many a Confederate sympathizer might have found himself destitute at the end of the war and not unwilling to angle for money from a government that had involved the South in a ruinous war. Yankee cash used to stave off starvation was not likely to shatter a man's local reputation. For these reasons, any genealogist would do well to check the records of the Southern Claims Commission.

Covering roughly the period from 1871 to 1880, the records of the Commissioners of Claims, known as the Southern Claims Commission, are among General Records of the Department of the Treasury, Record Group 56, and have been filmed on the 14 rolls of National Archives Microfilm Publication M87. The three-member commission was chartered March 3, 1871, to investigate and review the claims of Southern unionists for supplies and stores yielded up to the Union army. On May 11, 1872, Congress voted to include property used by the navy. Enabling legislation deliberately did not include real property used or damaged by occupation troops.[4]

The commission was to certify the Union loyalty of the claimant, determine the appropriate value of the claim, and make a recommendation to the House of Representatives. The House then would vote to allow or disallow the claim and appropriate money for payment. Usually, the House followed the recommendation of the commission.

The three commissioners were backed by a staff of special commissioners appointed on the local level to hear small claims and by special agents who served as roving investigators for all claims. A petition would be presented to the commission by the claimant or, more often, by his or her attorney. Depositions of witnesses were then taken, usually by the special agent, who sent a written report to the commission. After reviewing the report, the petition, depositions, and letters of affidavit, the commissioners would send a summary report to the House with their evaluation. Of $60,258,150.44 in claims, only $4,636,920.69 was approved and paid. Ultimately, only 7,092 of 22,298 claims were approved.

The microfilmed collection includes the daily journals of the commissioners; miscellaneous letters received by the commissioners; other miscellaneous papers, such as bills and receipts; 57 summary reports sent to the House; letters from and about the special agents; a list of claimants by geographical distribution (incomplete); and a consolidated index of claims by name of claimant.

Because the case files on individual claims are neither consolidated nor microfilmed, using the claims commission records becomes a true exercise in sleuthing. Summary information on claims is found in the commission records, but testimony and other documents on individual cases are found in the series of case files. Most of the pertinent information on each case is there to be found among the filmed records; it is, however, somewhat elusive.

The first step is to check the consolidated

index on roll 14, which is organized by name of individual. Bear in mind the possibility of creative spelling. This index lists the nature of the claim, such as "wood, sugar, molassas [sic], and rent of steamer"; amounts claimed, allowed, and disallowed; state and identifying numbers; and, most crucially, year.

The year in which a claim was granted leads to the microfilmed daily journals of the commissioners on roll 1, which briefly make note of letters received and sent. Most of the

letters themselves, those received by the commission, are arranged chronologically on the next eight rolls of microfilm, rolls 2 through 9. Thus the journal entries serve as a rough index to the letters received. Likewise, the journals indicate which special agent handled each claim, directing the researcher to those microfilmed letters grouped by agent and shown on rolls 10 through 12.

The geographical index of claims on roll 13, organized by state, county, and name of

LOUISIANA.

No.		Amount.
	ASCENSION PARISH.	
6,937.	François Bedat............	$1,088
12,359.	Estate of John M Brown	70,580
2,733.	Victorin Keller............	3,528
9,013.	Jean C Mathieu............	1,449
1,826.	Ernest Pedesclaux........	16,430
9,015.	Michael Rubi............	7,039
	ASSUMPTION PARISH.	
16,882.	George Dejean............	1,000
1,220.	Elisha Eastwood............	8,850
3,401.	François Gaudin............	1,762
1,057.	E E Mallot............	11,315
13,016.	Frank Webb............	102,300
	AVOYELLES PARISH.	
19,980.	James Callaham............	43.005
6,583.	Lucien Dominique Coco.	4,914
15,695.	Valery Coco............	2,125
15,696.	Fielding Edwards............	400
1.238.	Rosella Hays............	15,040
5,534.	Ann Moreau............	9,130
	CADDO PARISH.	
15,787.	Mary S & Wm J Bruner..	4,570
8,308.	Milton S Shirk............	126,602
9,202.	Leon Strauss............	657
	CALDWELL PARISH.	
14,605.	George G Williams............	765
	CARROLL PARISH.	
9,201.	Estate of William Benja-min............	990
3,179.	Warren M Benton............	45,267
18,385.	Estate of David F Black-burn............	19,710
17,368.	Owen H Brewer............	450
12,107.	William C Currie............	17,700
7,729.	Laura L DeFrance............	2,275
8,065.	Jeremiah F Dorris............	11,357
13,737.	Charles H Goffe............	4,579
12,108.	William H Harris............	8,100
11,774.	Louisa Henderson............	32,040
729.	Ellen Kehoe............	2,154
1,251.	Ida B Lonsdale and An-nie B Thompson............	65,020
14,601.	Julia H Morgan and heirs of A C Keene............	139,927

No.		Amount.
7,124.	Estate of Dr Andrew Owen............	2,490
10,441.	Estate of James Railey...	30,958
17,838.	Matthew Bacon Sellers...	1,487
5,250.	Nancy Short............	1,125
3,086.	Hiram B Tebbetts........	4,443
703.	Horace B and John C Tebbetts............	65,660
1,251.	Annie B Thompson and Ida B Lonsdale............	65,020
16,762.	Thomas L Van Fossen....	59,471
22,190.	Narcissa P Williams......	37,400
17,022.	Hattie E Winn............	3,025
235.	Julius Witkowski.........	16,900
10,443.	Simon Witkowski........	12,650
	CATAHOULA PARISH.	
7,621.	William Bradford..........	1,970
	CONCORDIA PARISH.	
18,567.	Evins Brooks............	251
7,125.	Stephania M Chotard....	51,172
1,362.	William C Ferriday.......	7,005
18,717.	Jacob Kelley............	175
16,224.	Julia Ann Shelton........	420
14,911.	Anthony Weakley........	245
	DE SOTO PARISH.	
14,682.	A I Brown............	9,945
862.	Paul Gregory............	27,049
19,022.	Thomas L Terry............	9,998
	EAST BATON ROUGE PARISH.	
20,746.	Henry Avery............	15,271
15,362.	Henry Badley............	7,637
19,077.	H B Benjamin............	1,953
21,944.	Foster Bradford, Sr......	4,283
20,109.	Mary K Brown............	3,000
20,745.	John Carmena............	5,290
21,359.	Mary C Daigre............	19,558
20,740.	Alfred Duplantier......	55,675
5,019.	Robert J Elliot............	15,250
3,549.	James H Gibbens.........	32,772
3,550.		
3,592.	George Kleinpeter, Jr...	1,800
3,593.	Sarah A Kleinpeter......	2,030
1,264.	Thomas Lilley............	7,900
20,741.	Hiram Mansur............	24,440
16,884.	William Markham........	1,173
21,945.	Daniel Morgan............	4,900
21,336.	Estate of Stephen Roberts	18,525
20,747.	Clark Shelvin............	8,557
22,993.	George Smizer............	5,184

[handwritten annotations in margins: "Allowed 130." beside Fielding Edwards; "Disallowed" beside Warren M Benton; "Disallowed" beside Matthew Bacon Sellers; "Disallowed" beside James H Gibbens]

"Geographical List of Claims," Records of the Commissioners of Claims, M87, roll 13.

claimant, can lead to Southerners who didn't file claims but testified on behalf of their neighbors. Depositions included background information on the witness as well as details of his relationship to the claimant. Descriptions of the physical arrangement of the community as well as the habits of its citizens are woven through the testimony.

These documents can do more than locate and identify individuals and their communities. Settled into context, the commission records give a sense of what it meant to live in a particular community, beleaguered by conscience and by war.

HOW THE CLAIMS PROCESS WORKED

Just two pages of scraggly handwriting, the summary report on the claim of Theresa Mahon is as convoluted as any plot by Charles Dickens, combining personal intrigue and tragedy with social commentary—and all somewhat inadvertently.[5]

Beginning "This is a very peculiar case," the report hangs on the testimony of Theresa herself and "an acquaintance who is usually employed as a Steamboat Stoker but loafs a great deal in Memphis."[6] It seems that Theresa's two mules were spirited away by Union soldiers. The mules had been purchased by Theresa's husband immediately after their wedding and left in Memphis, TN, to hire out when the couple moved to Chicago. The report notes, "Down to this point there is not a witness to corroborate any matrial [sic] fact in her statement."[7]

However, when the mules were taken from Theresa, who was at this time back in Memphis, the stoker was "providentially round the corner."[8] He recognized one of the absconding soldiers who invited him for a drink, which the stoker declined, "so he says, with emphasis. . . . And, what seems a singular circumstance, this witness didn't know that Claimant saw the soldiers take her mules, and yet, as intimate as

he was with her, and seeing her as he did, very frequently, never mentioned it till five years afterward."[9]

Despite this dubious evidence, the claim was allowed. The report concluded that, after all, it was not Theresa's fault that all her more reliable witnesses, including her adopted parents, had died. Moreover, if somewhat obscurely, "Claimant is not a myth, and her claim to loyalty is plausible."[10]

From a genealogical standpoint, Theresa's testimony is invaluable. She explained that she was born in New York and moved to St. Louis with her parents, who died shortly thereafter. She was adopted by another family "and was known as their daughter by the neighbors."[11] In 1854 the family moved to Memphis, where Theresa married "Mahon" in 1861, at age 14. Mahon was a sailmaker, and, after purchasing the mules, he took his bride to Chicago in October 1862. There he died in April 1863, leaving Theresa to give birth to a child who lived but 3 weeks. By August of that summer, Theresa was back in Memphis, in time to see her mules dragged off by Union soldiers.

The commission rejected many a better documented claim summarily. Yet, it was willing to give Theresa Mahon, whose only witness was a riverboat stoker, $300 on the strength of her own testimony. Perhaps the commissioners felt sympathetic to an orphaned widow who had lost her only child. Whatever the reason, this claim indicates how arbitrarily decisions could be made. Essentially, claims were approved or disapproved on the basis of whether the special agent or commissioners felt the evidence was satisfactory. "Satisfactory" varied from case to case.

To appreciate fully Theresa's loss, or any other, it is necessary to think of the larger context. What was it like to be a 16- or 17-year-old woman suddenly stranded in Chicago in 1863? How important were the two mules to Theresa's survival? More generally, how many bales of cotton could be taken or burned before a farmer became destitute? Studying the local economy of the time would help place the claims in context. In town, the loss of a horse might just translate into a lot of walking. Conversely, without a horse or a mule on a farm, who would pull the plow? Local histories, newspapers covering the community, even state-wide surveys on the effects of the war, all would serve to place the claims commission records in historical context.

Though it is a useful guide, the consolidated index of Southern Claims Commission records should not be taken as a complete roster of all Southern unionists and the nature of their losses. The commission itself was highly political. Three Radical Republican attorneys served on the commission throughout its existence: Asa Owen Aldis of Vermont; James B. Howell of Iowa; and Orange Ferris of New York. This party affiliation reflects a begrudging congressional compromise. Radical Republicans, losing control of Congress as more Southern states were readmitted and more of their moderate colleagues were being elected from the North, decided to recognize the legitimacy of unionist claims while the party could still orchestrate all appointments to the commission. Likewise, unionists who had clamored for recognition for 6 years agreed to what they considered the limited scope of the claims under consideration and to the one-party composition of the board, just so that hearings could finally begin.[12]

This compromise is significant to the researcher. Owing to rigorous limitations established by the commissioners, many Southern unionists had their claims disallowed. And, because claims relating to real property were barred, a whole category of unionist losses was not even considered by the commission.

Likewise, because claims were a matter of public record, reaction of the community to the commission and the special agents is important. Notices were printed in local papers encouraging unionists to put forth their claims. If these announcements were accompanied by editorials denouncing carpetbaggers and Yankee traitors, people might think twice before ferreting out forgotten vouchers. Just as these unionists would have remained invisible, so, too, would those who never came in contact

with federal troops and had no lost property to report.

In evaluating the legitimacy of commission reports, the researcher should remember that politics also figured heavily in the appointment of special agents. For example, E. Stafford, of Greenville, Mississippi, wrote to President Grant in 1876, urging that R. B. Avery be hired as an agent. The letter noted that Avery "is an honest capable man; has been a hard working faithful Republican . . . has spent his time and money for our cause in the South; & above all, he has a helpless family to support."[13] Stafford pointed out that special consideration must be paid to "those of us with families, who are ostracised & the ordinary avenues of business closed to us, because we *are* Republicans."[14] Modestly reminding the President of outstanding political debts, Stafford suggested that Grant "give Avery his appointment, & send him home to his wife & babies rejoicing."[15] Avery got the job.

The perspective and opinions of each special agent had a great impact on how the claims were evaluated. For instance, there were numerous claims pressed by former slaves and free blacks. Few were granted, but the tone of the reports indicates no deliberate hostility toward the claimants. Rather, there was an assumption that the claimant probably did not own the property in question. Discounting, or perhaps not knowing, that many slaves earned money or credit for overtime work and had personal property, special agents suspected that slaveowners signed over their goods to trusted slaves just before Union troops arrived. Most free blacks rented land, and special agents assumed they also rented their livestock and farm equipment, although no such out-of-hand assumptions were made about white renters, be they ever so poor.

In their judgments, the special agents reflected the mores of their society, North and South. There is little evidence in the records of the commission to suggest that agents deliberately set out to nourish or thwart the claims of any particular group or class. In fact, agents were frequently hauled before the commission by irate claimants, always to be vindicated after exhaustive hearings. The commission had doubts about the special commissioners appointed on the local level to hear small claims. The "Fifth Annual Report" to the House of Representatives noted that "Some [special commissioners] do their work admirably; others, from indifference to duty, from haste, negligence, or kindly good nature toward their neighbors [accept suspect testimony]."[16] In that same report, special agents were singled out for praise. In considering the accuracy of special agents' reports, however, the researcher would do well to remember the commission's own reservations:

> These reports show, too, that these agents, besides having to endure many physical discomforts in the ruder districts wherein their duties take them, are harrassed, clogged, and fettered in numerous directions by the efforts and combinations of claimants, witnesses, attorneys, and other interested parties to defeat their inquiries after the truth, as well as by the general indifference of private persons to the interests of the Government, and the reluctance, and sometimes fear, of persons acquainted with the facts of a case to testify, when those facts are against the interests of their friends and neighbors.[17]

Propped against the backdrop of local history and viewed with an understanding of how the claims process worked, the records of the Southern Claims Commission can be illuminating. What emerges is some sense of how people lived and how they constructed their communities and shored themselves up after the war. Above all, there is a sense of the diversity of the South. Sprinkled throughout the records are references to claims by foreigners domiciled in the South during the Civil War. In the "First General Report" to the House, the commissioners explained at length that all of these petitions were barred from consideration; citizenship at the time of the war was a prerequisite to loyalty.[18] Although many Americans tend to think of all immigrants as being crowded into Northern cities, they neglect to consider that there were many newcomers to America with their own traditions and perspectives in the South.

In the "First General Report," the commissioners singled out the mountain people of Virginia, Tennessee, Georgia, and Alabama for special commendation as staunch allies.[19] Just the fact that there were sufficient Southern unionists to warrant the creation of the commission should give pause to those who think of the South in broad-brush stereotypes.

In places, the records tell the story of unique communities, detailing lifestyles and livelihoods long gone. The claim of unionist "Rose Hayes, Administratrix," of New Orleans, is one such, requesting compensation for the use and damage of the steamboat *Starlight*.[20] According to the claim, the *Starlight* was built in Louisville, KY, and "brought out" in December 1858 to ply the Red River trade between New Orleans and Shreveport, carrying 1,800 bales of cotton and 100 passengers.[21] The *Starlight* was pressed into service by Union troops from May 1863 to October 1865, only to be returned damaged and stripped of her property and stores.

In order to make this claim, attorneys had to establish what the per diem hire for the steamboat would have been, as well as what she was worth in mint condition. Thus they pulled together river captains from the New Orleans area and up the Mississippi who gave expert testimony on the basis of their own experience. Each riverman detailed his own work history, describing the various boats he had shipped on or owned. The per diem value of these vessels was recorded and compared to that of the *Starlight*. Eventually, what emerges is a full portrait of the steamboat business at the time of the Civil War, with discussions as to what had happened to it since.

Included in the claim is a list of all the furnishings of the *Starlight*, down to chandelier globes, gold-fringe tablecloths, mosquito bars, celery glasses, ivory-handled knives, cam hooks, wheel stirrups, kedge anchors, and oak deck buckets.[22] Reading through the list of furnishings and equipment, one can almost see the steamboat from deck to deck and make out the containers of coffee and sugar, molasses and paint, crammed into dim corners of the hold.

This claim is unusually detailed and an incredible find for any researcher interested either in particular captains and rivermen or in the steamboat trade itself. The measurements and tonnage of numerous vessels are given, often specifying where the boat was built and who commissioned her. And, for those interested in the Hayes family, the claim begins with a delineation of the surviving heirs of Capt. Barry Hayes, father of Rose and purported owner of the *Starlight*. The report also mentions the names of the men married by Hayes's daughters and the fact that most of the children were born in Ireland.

Ironically, all this documentation was for naught. The commission determined that the steamboat belonged not to Barry Hayes, Sr., a man too old to have chosen sides in the Civil War, but to his rebel sons who tried to transfer title to him just before impressment.[23] Only claims that passed from unionist claimants to unionist heirs were honored by the commission. There could be no transfer of claim from a rebel claimant to unionist heirs. Thus, the *Starlight* claim was disallowed.

Patterns of ordinary communities can be picked out by tracing back a claim. Often individuals who filed no petitions themselves will figure as witnesses for those of neighbors. Thus, it is important to check the geographical index among the commission records, which is organized by state and then county. Frequently, people testified for their relatives, especially because many a Southerner might have been unwilling to admit to unionist sympathies except before trusted kin. Always, witnesses had to identify themselves and outline their relationship to the claimant. From this genealogical base, it is possible to discover how the neighborhood was laid out and what social patterns existed.

The claim of Jeptha J. Booth, of Jackson, AL, is particularly interesting because many of his neighbors neither liked nor trusted him, though they had socialized with him for, in some cases, almost 25 years. In the terse testimony of these Southern farmers, there emerges an image of the local nuisance. Booth was a renter, not worth more than $300 or $400, who neglected to pay his rent, proved difficult to evict, and showed an alarming tendency to side with whichever army was in the area, telling troops where the livestock and produce of his neighbors were hidden. Booth frequently stayed overnight with Henry Gluck, but the elderly unionist testified that he was afraid to express his political sentiments for fear Booth would betray him to the Confederates. More prejudicial in the eyes of the special agent, Booth circulated the area telling his neighbors how they could "fix up" their appeals to the claims commission.[24]

One wonders whether Booth was really the opportunist portrayed by his "friends" of 25 years. Perhaps he was merely a dirt-poor farmer who sent his two sons off to the Confederate army and then didn't have enough help to work his land. Someone so marginal might have found large political issues and invading armies irrelevant.

Booth's claim includes the testimony of both unionist and Confederate neighbors. For instance, there was Alexander Alley, a 53-year-old farmer who had lived in Jackson County 23 years at the time of the inquiry. Alley was a former justice of the peace who, during the first year of the war, enlisted in the Alabama Regiment. In 1862, he returned home to his farm three-quarters of a mile from Booth's.[25] Alley would have been unlikely to press a claim himself. He was a Confederate, yet he is included in the commission records by virtue of living in Jackson County, AL, near Jeptha Booth.

Letters of affidavit sent in support of a claim can spotlight a web of community friendships and power networks and identify the intimate associates of a particular individual. A claimant would naturally ask his most influential acquaintances to speak on his behalf; these letters could indicate who the community leaders were. Moreover, the testimony would detail the relationship of witness to

Little Rock, Ark, Jan. 3d 1878

Dear Sir:

The other day P. C. Dooley Esq., an attorney of this city, spoke to me about the appointment of a Special Commissioner at this place, it seems that Mr. Eakin the ~~present~~ ^present^ incumbent has been married and has gone to live on a plantation in Clarke Co. or Hempstead Co. and Mr. Dooley says they can't get him to attend to work up here, and as the time for taking evidence is now limited, he requests me to write to Washington and recommend some one for the position.

In accordance with his desire I have made inquiries, and would state that Mr Geo H. Benton, an attorney here seems to me to be well qualified for the position, he is a Canadian of about 25 years old, and has been here about two years, is a young man of liberal education, and is said to possess integrity of character, the U.S. District Atty. C. C. Waters, and others to whom I have spoken, give favorable reports of him, he is already a U.S. Commissioner

Respectfully
John D Edwards
Spec. Agt.

C. F. Benjamin Esq,
Clerk Comm's of Claims,
Wash. D. C.

Just one letter, snatched out of context, presents numerous research leads. Who did Mr. Eakin marry, which plantation did he move to, and what did he do there? Why was George Benton, a U.S. commissioner, still referred to as a Canadian? Where, specifically did he come from, and why did he move to Little Rock, AR?

claimant, indicating ties of business, religion, politics, or close friendship.

However, these letters cannot be accepted too blithely. Obviously, no claimant would deliberately set out to antagonize the Radical Republican commissioners. Therefore, local pro-Confederacy politicians might not be solicited for support, although they still wielded great power within the community. Of more importance at this time might be letters from clergymen or politically inactive businessmen.

A unionist might have seen his circle of acquaintances melt away in reaction to his highly unpopular decision. Senator Pratt said of the unionist position, "Ties of kindred, social, domestic, religious ties, were snapped asunder."[26] Thus, patterns of personal loyalty and friendship as revealed by the affidavit letters might not be a totally accurate reflection of the normal social structure of the community.

Unraveling a claim gives insight into a Civil War at once more mundane and less glorious than military myth. An extensive letter, with transcripts of affidavits, is tucked among the claims commission records regarding the grain shipments of A. M. White of Baltimore, MD.[27] Three loads of grain were sent by White to Capt. Mark D. DeMarke in October and November of 1863. Two shipments being of similar size, White encountered great difficulty proving that he held three original vouchers rather than two and a copy. No one could figure out whether DeMarke had actually received the third shipment; the quartermaster records were silent on the issue.

Sure that he had received the entire consignment, DeMarke checked with the railroads and found payment for three carloads of grain. His prosaic explanation of the mixup conveys a real sense of the effects of the war. He apologized for the "great confusion" in the quartermaster's department, "attendent [sic] upon the battle of Gettysburg."[28] It seems that "the Cumberland Valley railroad, over which a large part of the troops were supplied, had been injured by the rebels, and shipments were necessarily delayed, until there was a large accumulation of cars."[29] This, then, was one of the

aftereffects of the Battle of Gettysburg, a large accumulation of railway cars.

An irony of the war was that the border states, most torn over the issue of secession, served largely as the battleground for most of the war; yet, unionists there were compensated less fully than those in the Deep South.[30] As explained in the "Fifth General Report" to the House, the concept of "stores and supplies provided to the army" was more liberally interpreted when the army was on a long march, subsisting off the land.[31] So long as the Union army sat in the border states haggling with Confederate troops, unauthorized appropriations by Union soldiers were not honored by the commission.

Troop activity, by either army, cannot be overestimated in analyzing claims. While Southern unionists who lived in an area untouched by federal troops would not appear on the records, the unionist under constant siege might have found it difficult to hold onto political principles of any sort. Likewise, it would have been foolhardy for a unionist to proclaim his opinions in an area dominated for most of the war by the Confederate army. But he might then have found it difficult to convince the commissioners of his loyalty to the Union. Loyalty had to be proven. Disloyalty, which was assumed of every resident of a Confederate state, had to be disproven. Neutrality was not tantamount to loyalty in the eyes of the commissioners.

Troop activity, coupled with the details given in the claims, gives a fair indication of the extent to which particular areas were depleted during the war. This depletion could suggest why a family migrated after the war or sent children to be raised by relatives. The specific reasons for family activities may even be detailed in the claims commission records. By county, the records would explain the fate of specific towns or communities, hinting at why certain areas were quick to grasp the New South ideal of industrialization and commercialization, while others seemed reluctant to take the financial risk.

What does it mean if a Southerner turns out to have been a unionist? Was he a traitor to his region? An opportunist? A scalawag? Probably not. Ask, instead, What kind of a Southerner was he? What part of the South did he live in? What was his ethnic group, religion, and political party before the Civil War? What kind of work did he do? What was his educational background; his economic class? How many people was he responsible for? How isolated was his home? How long had he lived in the South? What was his town like?

Just as many Southerners in 1860 were only one or two generations removed from the Revolution, many contemporary researchers are but three generations from the Civil War. Yet, over those three generations, the focus of American life has been reversed and it takes an effort to recapture the perspective of a Southern unionist. Today, life is nationally directed. Television has made national news as accessible as back-fence gossip and advertising has, to a certain extent, homogenized tastes and expectations. By contrast, in the mid-19th century, life centered around the local community, with sporadic dealings with the state government and virtually no direct contact with the federal government.[32] For many Americans, in both the North and South, loyalty to the community was synonymous with loyalty to state and nation.

With the Mason-Dixon Line taking on new significance, people were forced to redefine their notion of patriotism. They were asked to distinguish between state and nation and commit themselves to one to the exclusion of the other. Many chose not to make the change until the Civil War forced it upon them. And then they had to determine, in the crisis of the moment, what it meant to be a good Southerner or a good Northerner. Small wonder if definitions differed.

RELATED RECORDS

Many of the individual case files on claims placed before the Southern Claims Commission are available for examination, either at the National Archives Building in Washington or through written inquiry to the National Archives Reference Services Branch. However, before seeking out specific files, the researcher must consult the consolidated index to claims commission records (on roll 14 of Microfilm Publication M87), listed by name of claimant. Files on allowed claims are organized by state, then county, then alphabetically by name of claimant. Disallowed claims are arranged by report number and then office number as assigned by the commission and indicated in the index.

Files on allowed claims (176 cubic feet) are in Records of the U.S. General Accounting Office (Record Group 217) among the records of the third auditor, held by the National Archives.[33] Armed with state, county, and name, a researcher can either come to the National Archives and see the original documents or write for photocopies. This grouping of records by locality is particularly useful for the local historian. Contents vary from file to file, but most include the petitions for payment, depositions of witnesses, summary report of the claim sent to the House of Representatives, and the receipt of payment. Some files include extensive documentary evidence: letters of affidavit, reports by special agents, and, in a few cases, marriage and death certificates.

Files on disallowed claims and claims barred from consideration for lack of sufficient evidence or ineligibility (190 cubic feet) are in Records of the U.S. House of Representatives (Record Group 233), held by the National Archives.[34] While disallowed claims are filed by report and office number, barred claims are arranged alphabetically by name of claimant. The *Consolidated Index of Claims*, referred to above, must be used to find the report and the office number. In order to examine or receive copies of these documents, prior consent from the clerk of the House of Representatives is required.[35] Only after approval has been granted should the Legislative Records Division be approached.

Reference might also be made to a four-volume summation: U.S., *Commissioners of Claims, Summary Reports in All Cases Reported to Congress as Disallowed Under the Act of March*

3, 1871 (1876–81). While not a transcription of the documents within each file, these reports contain most of the facts collected on each case. The volumes can be located through *The National Union Catalog of Pre-1956 Imprints*, vol. 613, and studied at the Washington National Records Center at Suitland, MD.

The collections of Southern Claims Commission case files are incomplete. Some claims were submitted to Congress before the commission was chartered; some were filed after the deadline set for the commission. Other claims were appealed to Congress by Southerners unhappy with the findings of the claims commission. These case files, although indexed in the claims commission records, would have been refiled after review among the records of a congressional committee.

As a matter of course, any disallowed claim should be checked for a later appeal and possible grant. Likewise, some files were lost and evidence of these claims remains only in the official records of Congress. Even within existing files, individual documents may have been lost or misfiled before accessioning by the National Archives.

References to all of these claims may be found in the lists of private claims submitted to the Senate and House, organized chronologically and then alphabetically by name of claimant. Contained in the Congressional Serial Set, the volumes to consult are: U.S., Congress, Senate, *List of Private Land Claims, 14th-46th Congresses*, 46th Cong., 3d sess., 1880–81, Sen. Misc. Doc. 14, Serials 1945 and 1946; U.S., Congress, House, *Index of Private Land Claims, 32d-41st Congresses*, 42d Cong., 3d sess., 1872–73, H. Misc. Doc. 109, Serial 1574; U.S., Congress, House, *Alphabetical List of Private Land Claims, 42d-46th Congresses*, 47th Cong., 1st sess., 1881–82, H. Misc. Doc. 53, Serial 2036; U.S., Congress, House, *Index to Private Claims, 47th-51st Congresses*, 53d Cong., 2d sess., 1893–94, H. Misc. Doc. 213, Serial 3268. The Congressional Serial Set may be found at the National Archives and in major libraries.

For general background information on the Southern Claims Commission, see Klingberg.[36] His study places the commission in historical perspective by examining both the notion of Southern unionism and the workings of the claims commission.

NOTES

1. U.S., Senate, *Congressional Globe*, 41st Cong., 2d sess., 1870, p. 1691.

2. Ibid., p. 1686.

3. Ibid., p. 3019.

4. Frank W. Klingberg, *The Southern Claims Commission*, University of California Publications in History, vol. 50 (1955), p. 117.

5. "Claim of Theresa Mahon of Memphis Tenn., no. 586," *Records of the Commissioners of Claims (Southern Claims Commission), 1871–80*, National Archives Microfilm Publication M87, (hereafter cited as M87), roll 9, Summary Reports on Claims.

6. Ibid.

7. Ibid.

8. Ibid.

9. Ibid.

10. Ibid.

11. Ibid.

12. Klingberg, *Southern Claims Commission*, p. 56.

13. E. Stafford to U.S. Grant, Dec. 4, 1876, M87, roll 10, Letters From and About Special Agents, R. B. Avery, Mar. 21, 1877–Nov. 8, 1879.

14. Ibid.

15. Ibid.

16. "Journal of the Commissioners, vol. 1; Mar. 16, 1871–Dec. 31, 1877," M87, roll 1, frame 564.

17. Ibid.

18. Ibid., frame 67.

19. Ibid., frame 69.

20. "Rose Hayes, Administratrix, vs. The United States, no. 8,383," M87, roll 9, Miscellaneous Papers, Mar. 29, 1864–Apr. 17, 1900, pp. 1–39.

21. Ibid., pp. 8–9.

22. Ibid., pp. 30–34.

23. "Journal of the Commissioners, vol. 1," M87, roll 1, frames 791–793.

24. "Claim of Jeptha J. Booth, Jackson County, Alabama, no. 4907," M87, roll 9, Summary Reports on Claims.

25. "Claim of Jeptha J. Booth," Testimony of Alexander C. Alley, M87, roll 9, Summary Reports on Claims.

26. U.S., Senate, *Congressional Globe*, 41st Cong., 2d sess., 1870, p. 3019.

27. Bvt. Brig. Gen. James A. Ekin to Bvt. Maj. Gen. M. C. Meigs, May 14, 1869, M87, roll 9, Miscellaneous Papers, Mar. 29, 1864–ca. Apr. 17, 1900.

28. Ibid.

29. Ibid.

30. Klingberg, *Southern Claims Commission*, p. 5.

31. "Journal of the Commissioners, vol. 1," M87, roll 1, frame 565.

32. Robert H. Wiebe, *The Search for Order, 1877–1920* (1967), p. 1.

33. Judicial, Fiscal, and Social Branch (NNFJ), National Archives and Records Administration, Washington, DC 20408.

34. Legislative Records Division (NNL), National Archives and Records Administration, Washington, DC 20408.

35. Clerk of the House, Room H105, U.S. House of Representatives, Washington, DC 20515.

36. Klingberg, *Southern Claims Commission*.

THOMAS E. WILTSEY

Court Records and Local History: A Case Study

The popular image of law and order in the Old West is that of a town sheriff gunning down a bank robber or of a local vigilante committee hanging a cattle rustler. Popular novels, movies, and television shows of the past few decades have reinforced this image in the minds of millions of Americans. There is, to be sure, some truth to this image; quite a number of 19th-century desperadoes were shot down at the scene of the crime, and more than a few rustlers swung from trees for stealing longhorns. Nevertheless, this image of swift justice is distorted. Most legal disputes in the western states and territories during the 19th and early 20th centuries were settled in the courts, not in the streets. The records of these legal disputes reveal a picture of the American West that is in conflict with the popular image.

One major reason that the popular image of western law and order continues to the present is that historians have largely ignored the court records that document life in local communities in the western territories in the late 19th and early 20th centuries. The territorial court records for states such as New Mexico are rich in information about the lives of citizens as well as the resolutions of their legal disputes. As one major historian of the western territories noted, the work of the territorial courts "provides a useful yardstick with which to measure the practices and functions of local county government in a territory."[1] In short, territorial court records are rich sources for writing the social, legal, and economic history of the American West.

A brief examination of three types of cases among the territorial court records for one state will provide useful illustrations of the kinds of information to be found by local historians. The case files among the territorial court records of New Mexico relating to bankruptcy, naturalization, and the public domain provide new insights into almost every facet of local history in New Mexico at the turn of the century. The files include affidavits that chronicle life histories, personal letters that detail success and failure, and photographs that give poignancy to otherwise dry case files. Most importantly, these underutilized documents provide the details of everyday life in turn-of-the-century New Mexico.

BANKRUPTCY CASE FILES

Bankruptcy case files are an important source of information on the economic life of local communities. Such records provide specialized data on particular business firms and also provide glimpses of the impact of national economic trends. Researchers will find in the records, for example, complete inventories of the stock and fixtures of local business firms, the tools and property of assorted craftsmen, and the personal belongings of typical families. Other case files document some of the hardship that resulted from national events such as the panic of 1893, the repeal of the Sherman Silver Purchase Act, and the depression of 1907. The files detail all classes and segments of local communities because no business firm or profession was immune to financial failure and resultant court action. A brief examination of three bankruptcy cases will illustrate the kind of information that can be extracted from these records.

Gutierrez and Sons of Tularosa, NM, filed

Tularosa, N. M.

Bought Of **HAYMON KRUPP**

WHOLESALE

SHOES, HATS, CLOTHING, FURNISHINGS, NOTIONS, ETC.

BOTH TELEPHONES
P. O. BOX 566
NEW YORK OFFICE
50 LEONARD ST.

314 SOUTH EL PASO ST.

TERMS:_____ Salesman_____ Checked_____ Packed_____

Item	Qty	Description	Price	Total
0589	2 Doz.	Mens hose	.80	1.60
0924	2 "	" "	.80	1.60
0102	2 "	" "	.80	1.60
200	4 "	" "	.80	3.20
A F	6 "	" "	.85	5.10
416	3 "	Ladies hose	1.00	3.00
111	4 "	" "	1.20	4.80
101	4 "	Misses hose	1.20	4.80
600	3 "	Inf "	.85	2.55
650	1 cabinet	Pearl Buttons	4.50	4.50
535	1 Doz.	Hair Brush		2.00
	1 "	Pencil Boxes		.45
3	1 "	Crochet needles		.35
43	1 "	" "		.25
4470	1 "	Combs		.90
1220	12	Hair pins	.7½	.90
6256	1	Barett		1.25
808	5	Hand	.70	3.50
826	1 "	Barett		.85
556	5 "	Fancy hand	.85	4.25
	5 "	Mens shirts	4.50	22.50
1501	½ "	Cord pants	.15	7.50
511	1 "	Overalls		8.50
T619	1 "	Youths overalls		4.50
	6 pr	Blankets Elsmere	1.00	6.00
	6 "	Hixon	.80	4.80
	3 "	Vicuna	3.25	9.75
	1 "	President susp		4.25
7230	1 "	Boys "		2.00
1326	1 "	Fancy susp		4.50
	2 "	Child ass'd	2.25	4.50
				126.15

When Gutierrez and Sons of Tularosa declared bankruptcy, creditors such as Hayman Krupp filed "proofs of debt." Invoices such as the one above give researchers a detailed view of store inventories at the turn of the century. Courtesy Denver Federal Archives and Records Center.

a petition for bankruptcy in August 1911, and among the court documents are "proofs of debt"—petitions that document claims for payment by local, state, and national creditors. The proofs of debt indicate that Gutierrez and Sons catered to a sophisticated clientele that suffered no deprivation because of Tularosa's remote location. To satisfy the desires of its customers, Gutierrez and Sons contracted with suppliers in every part of the country, with only partial reliance on middlemen. Gutierrez and Sons went right to the source for the products their customers so desired.

The court records document the diversity of the products stocked by the Tularosa firm. In 1911, in a frontier community of the Territory of New Mexico, Gutierrez and Sons ordered crackers directly from the National Biscuit Company (Nabisco) in Kansas City, calendars from Cincinnati, coffee from Gatling Manufacturing in Kansas City, duck canvas from the Denver Tent and Awning Company, Red Top Oil from Gulf Refining in Houston, and a surprisingly wide assortment of whips from Westfield, MA. Shoes and free storefront advertising signs from Noyes-Normal Shoes in St. Joseph, MO, and from the El Paso office of New York's Boston Store. The Boston Store also sent flannels, ladies' hats and hose, perfume, muslin, men's clothing of all types, and one wreath (funeral or Christmas not specified). Similar items plus needles, pins, barrettes, combs and hairbrushes, buttons, and elastic came from Haymon-Krupp of New York via its El Paso branch. From the same Texas town came brooms, rope, Brass King washboards, Bob White bags and soap, envelopes, ladders, shoe nails, Western Wooden Ware's galvanized hardware, and an outrageously expensive (two dollars) Merry-go-Round Pencil Assortment. The St. Louis firm of Butler Brothers contributed children's treasures such as balloons, fireworks, marshmallows, cream cakes, suckers, licorice, ice cream cones, and party decorations. Last, but not least, from the Chattanooga Medicine Company came the ubiquitous patent medicines—of commanding potency if their exorbitant cost is any guide.[2]

These inventories show that this firm not only stocked a wide range of items, but also tried to provide its customers with a fair choice of styles and with luxury goods. Each item is carefully priced, individually and by total amount. Advertisements in newspapers of that era would permit some comparison of transportation costs and markups, especially over a period of years, by comparing the market price asked by Gutierrez and Sons and similar firms with the price that the bankruptcy files indicate they paid for their stock.

The Gutierrez file also reveals that Tularosa did not develop its trade ties through El Paso to eastern Texas, New Orleans, and the Gulf Coast ports, as its southern rail link would seem to indicate. As the city had done for decades before the coming of the railroad, Tularosa continued to use a commercial network that followed the Santa Fe Trail northeastward to the traditional business centers of the Midwest and the East.

Personal bankruptcy files also provide local historians with a glimpse of family life and possessions. A surveyor listed his transit, surveying chains, and a bicycle. A teacher had books, typewriters, and desks. A stone mason claimed his tools. All give graphic, often poignant, descriptions of their personal belongings—children's toys, clothing, a kitchen table, chairs, one or two nice pieces of furniture, some treasured item from a woman's premarital days, a man's pocketwatch, or a rifle. Often, a bankrupt family was turned out of its home, and a large wall tent was claimed for its relief. More so than for businesses, these personal bankruptcies are the real testimonies of heartbreak and struggle on the raw western lands. Many of the families moved again and again, starting over, trying, and failing. Here, coupled with usable statistics, are illustrations by the hundreds of that restless American nature, upon which writers such as de Tocqueville and Frederick Jackson Turner have long commented.

One example of a personal bankruptcy was that of W. S. Millikin and his wife, Daisy. Millikin was a teacher who tried to start a business school in Anthony, KS, and failed. He tried and failed twice again, in Albuquerque and in Amarillo, before declaring bankruptcy in 1909.[3] In his attempts to teach, Millikin contracted debts with merchants of all three towns. Through local agents, he received goods from typewriter companies and book publishers all over the country, including New York's Isaac Putnam Sons, Shaw Advertising in Kansas City, Smith Premier Typewriters in Denver, Musselmen Publishing of Quincy, Chatier Publishing in New Orleans, Remington Typewriter of Dallas, Goodyear Marshall of Cedar Rapids, the Phonographic Institute Company of Cincinnati, and others.

These activities brought Millikin personal property relating to his profession in the form of a rolltop desk; a teacher's desk; 14 shorthand and 12 mission tables; 7 Remington, 2 Smith Premier, and 1 each Oliver and Underwood typewriters; and 3 stoves. As personal property exempt by law, Millikin claimed a White sewing machine, rugs, dishes, a dresser and washstand, a gasoline stove, 2 clocks, a refrigerator, books and a bookcase, a Kimberly piano (property of Daisy), a desk, and 12 chairs.

The Millikins were geographically mobile and perfectly willing to try again in a new locale—traits common in the history of American settlement and exemplified time and again in the bankruptcies. These cases give insights into the lives of average people—not the bonanza kings, the gunmen, the army officers, or the Indians who have been so exhaustively written about.

Another bankruptcy case illustrates a different form of business, reflecting a different trading pattern than the far-flung connections of Gutierrez and Sons. The case occurred when Joseph D. Morris, operator of two bars, went bankrupt in 1900.[4] Morris was what was called a "retail liquor dealer," with an outlet in Taos and another one at Copper Hill. Part of the business was incorporated as Russell and Morris, although Russell does not enter into this case. Morris's bars were not elaborate establishments or boom town saloons, but rather unassuming places that stocked whiskey and beer—no wines or champagne—and had, other than bar fixtures, only two card tables and a pool table. Unlike the mercantile companies that stocked goods from all over the nation and even some imports to satisfy consumer demands, Morris sold a limited range of items whose manufacture was the next closest thing to local industry. Only his expensive Chancellor Havana cigars at $60 per 1,000 could really be considered luxury goods or imports. Thirty-four barrels of bottled beer came from Neef Brothers in Denver, and another 65 barrels came from Crystal Springs Brewing and Ice in Boulder, CO. From Essinger and Judell of New York, Cincinnati, and East Las Vegas came three barrels of comparatively expensive whiskey. Simon Sanders of Trinidad, CO, provided cigars. The balance of Morris's debts were local in nature. The Taos firms of P. M. Dolan, Juan Santisteven, Alexander Gusdorf, and M. M. Miller provided unidentified goods on open accounts. A. Staab in Santa Fe sent two barrels of expensive Mellwood whiskey and a barrel of very inexpensive liquor. Lastly, Morris owed to one R. C. Pooler bartender wages of $112, at $60 per month.

There are some interpretations about the Morris case that are different from the others. Obviously, he relied heavily on middlemen for distribution. On occasion, as with Neef Brothers or Crystal Brewing, goods came from the brewery directly to him, but, more commonly, his connections were with the local dealers. Reflecting the type of business it was, Morris's help was well-paid, but a long list of small accounts owed to him suggests that the business was not and could not be a cash-and-carry operation.

Claimed exempt as personal property, Morris listed the family's clothing and bedding, cook stove and utensils, heating stove, dining table and chairs, bureau, washstand and chamber set, lounge, small writing desk, carpets, and sewing machine, as well as a .22 caliber rifle and a large tent to house the family. As head of a household and not having a homestead, Morris was allowed by New Mexican law to protect a portion of his personal property from liquidation. Unfortunately, his claim to the stock of the Copper Hill establishment caused extensive litigation with Neef Brothers that tied up the estate settlement for a long time. Correspondence in the file shows that a destitute Morris ended up laboring in the Copper Hill mines to support his family.

The bankruptcies of Gutierrez and Sons, the Millikins, and Joseph Morris represent different aspects of New Mexican life at the turn of the century. These people operated contemporaneously, but on different planes, each contributing to the growth and progress of their local community. However, even though they failed, many of their colleagues succeeded and contributed to the essential economic development of New Mexico. The cases are, however, generally illustrative of the thousands of bankruptcies in the records of the U.S. district courts, not just of the territory of New Mexico, or the state after 1912, but of the entire frontier West.

NATURALIZATION CASE FILES

Naturalization case files are another example of court records that have useful information on local communities and their families. America is a nation of immigrants, and these files provide graphic evidence of the ordeal of immigration and Americanization. Through naturalization case files, scholars and genealogists can document the histories of individual immigrant families and give life to the bland statistics listing the number of packet ships, embarkations, and arrivals. More importantly, genealogists and family historians will find in naturalization records unique information on the critical years of immigration from 1880 to 1900—information that can not be found in any other source. The accidental destruction of the 1890 census makes naturalization case files a source of unparalleled value.

The naturalization process began with the declaration of intention and, upon completion of all legal requirements, concluded with the petition for citizenship and the naturalization certificate. If favorably judged, a court order admitting the petitioner to citizenship was entered in the record book. In this essay, only the declarations are discussed; however, the other records are potentially of equal importance. Most of the declarations filed in New Mexico are the short forms printed two to a page in a leather-bound docket. These give the date of arrival, date and place of petition, and, through the renouncement of allegiance, the national origin. A longer form contains, in addition to this information, a brief physical description, occupation, age, birthplace, current residence, previous foreign residence, point of departure, date and port of arrival, manner of arrival, and the name of the transporting ship or railroad. Obviously, there is a wealth of both genealogical and historical information on these forms.

Using as an example the declarations of intention filed for the First Judicial District, 1882–1911, Territory of New Mexico, researchers can find data on the background of people who were in the territory when they decided to initiate the naturalization process. A random sample of 447 naturalization cases revealed a high percentage of literate male applicants, and from this sample one might conclude that the territory's foreign-born population was dominated by unmarried males seeking employment or adventure. Comparison of these records with other sources, such as the 1900 and 1910 census schedules, would show whether this was the case, or whether many of the naturalized males were heads-of-households.

The immigrants in the sample came from 20 different countries, but the use of empire or sovereign for country sometimes blurred the distinction. For example, names that are obviously Scottish, Irish, or Welsh are listed under "Great Britain and Ireland" because, on the short form, national origin is indicated only by the sovereign of renounced allegiance. In this manner, entries of "Queen Victoria" and "Edward VII" covered a lot of people who might not have considered themselves English, given

UNITED STATES OF AMERICA

Department of Commerce and Labor

BUREAU OF IMMIGRATION AND NATURALIZATION

DIVISION OF NATURALIZATION

DECLARATION OF INTENTION

(Invalid for all purposes seven years after the date hereof)

Territory of New Mexico
County of Rio Arriba   ss.:

In the   D I S T R I C T   Court

of   the 1st Judicial District

I,   Barne Carranta , aged 36 years, occupation   Miner , do declare on oath that my personal description is: Color white, complexion light, height 5 feet 4 inches, weight 150 pounds, color of hair brown, color of eyes blue, other visible distinctive marks   none : I was born in   Valdieri, Italy, on the 20th day of August, anno Domini 1871 ; I now reside at Monero,County of Rio Arriba, New Mexico. I emigrated to the United States of America from   Valdieri,Italy on the vessel* Bretanne, French Line : my last foreign residence was   Valdieri, Italy It is my bona fide intention to renounce forever all allegiance and fidelity to any foreign prince, potentate, state, or sovereignty, and particularly to King Humbert 111 of Italy, of which I am now a subject ; I arrived at the port of   New York, in the State of   New York on or about the 25th day of October, anno Domini 1894 ; I am not an anarchist; I am not a polygamist nor a believer in the practice of polygamy; and it is my intention in good faith to become a citizen of the United States of America and to permanently reside therein: SO HELP ME GOD.

Barne Carranta

(Original signature of declarant)

Subscribed and sworn to before me this 11th

[SEAL.]   day of June, anno Domini 19 07.

Clerk of the District Court.

By   Clerk.

*If the alien arrived otherwise than by vessel, the character of conveyance or name of transportation company should be given.

Declarations such as the one above have useful information for genealogists as well as social historians. Such forms reveal occupation, U.S. residence at the time of declaration, birthplace, and last foreign residence. Courtesy Denver Federal Archives and Records Center.

a choice. Likewise, many Germanic names are entered for Russian allegiance.

Given such a caveat, however, these records can indicate roughly the origins of the people who settled in New Mexico. The widespread British Empire, as might be expected, tops the list with 153, of whom perhaps half were non-English. Germany (70), Italy (62), and France (40) are also heavily represented, although their immigration tends to be more evenly distributed than the British, who came in a rush during the 1880s. The Austro-Hungarian Empire (29), Mexico (24), and Russia (21), are significant areas of origin. Spain (10), Sweden-Norway (7), Portugal (6), Turkey (6), Belgium (4), China (3), Switzerland (3), and Chile (2), as well as Bavaria, Egypt, Luxembourg, Denmark, and Waldeck (1 each) are the other regions of origin.[5]

A researcher working with these records would find comparisons with the census returns useful for determining the number of people such statistics actually represented. State and local records, the petitions for naturalization, and the certificates of naturalization would enrich much of this data.

From 1903 until 1912, the district court used a long form that more completely defined national origin and included occupation at the time of filing. Since the entrants for this period had, in general, been in the country for less than 3 years, the listed occupations were probably the ones many of them held before immigration. A random sample of 50 long forms for those years revealed 19 different occupations. There were nine farmers; seven priests; five miners; four merchants; three shepherds; three stockraisers; two each for locomotive engineers, teachers, salesmen (both from Turkey), musicians, and housekeepers; and one each for cook, fruitgrower, shoemaker, mason, clerk, housepainter, saloonkeeper, and bank clerk. The breadth of job distribution is a little surprising, as is the heavy immigration of French Catholic priests.[6]

Certain information about internal migrations can also be drawn from the naturalization records, particularly the long forms, which show port and date of entry. The greatest number of people arrived in the first few years after the Atchison, Topeka, and Santa Fe Railroad penetrated the territory. A little more curious is that a majority of the immigrants had come to the United States a minimum of 2 and a maximum of 8 years before beginning the naturalization process. Naturalization begun in one court did not have to be finalized there, thus allowing unrestricted alien mobility; it would seem that a majority of immigrants, if this small sample is valid indication, waited awhile, and perhaps traveled around, before committing themselves to the new nation.

PUBLIC DOMAIN CASE FILES

Case files relating to the public domain are a particularly rich source for the study of local history in the western states. Cases involving trespassing, illegal cutting of timber, false and perjured homestead filings, enclosures and illegal fencing, intimidation of homesteaders, and preventing surveys were routine concerns of the courts in every western judicial district. The core of the problem was that the provisions of the Homestead Act and similar land acts were designed to solicit family-sized agricultural units for development of western land. Although legislation such as the Timber Culture Act of 1873, the Desert Land Act of 1877, and the Reservoir Sites Act of 1897 gradually increased the amount of land a homesteader could potentially acquire, the philosophy of the land laws remained linked to the Jeffersonian concept of the sturdy yeoman farmer.[7]

Except for some highlands and river valleys, New Mexico was ill-suited for farming but well suited for grazing. Sheep and cattle flourished when they had access to a source of water and lots of room to graze—a fact of New Mexican life that encouraged cattle companies to acquire large tracts of land with water rights at any price.[8] In cases involving controversial

Spanish-Mexican land grants, land acquisition was often attempted by inflating the boundaries of the grant to massive proportions.[9] In other cases, such as those involving great cattle companies like the Red River, Prairie, Dubuque, or Palo-Blanco, the cattlemen fenced millions of acres of the public domain. Examples of these cases are found in all districts but especially in the First Judicial District, which had at least 50 illegal fencing cases in the years between 1886 and 1888. These cases ranged from the vast amounts of land just noted to such modest proportions that they could have enclosed little more than the 640 acres of a typical desert land entry. The court records reflect violations by all classes of New Mexican society, indicating a widespread contempt for a law that was uniquely unsuited for prevailing conditions in most of the territory. All told, as a result of grant inflation, fraud, illegal fencing and enclosures, railroad grants, and other pillagings of the public domain, considerably more land was claimed than existed.

Another very common answer to the desire for land in New Mexico was to falsify records in the homestead process with the collusion of a land office agent. This was usually done by filing entries for fictitious or ineligible people or having one's employees file claims. Patents on these fraudulent entries were rushed through and finalized with the cooperation of the corrupt official. Classic examples of this are found in the separate but similar series of indictments against Pedro Sanchez and Max Frost in the First Judicial District, 1884–85.[10] Frost so flagrantly abused his position as register of the land office, even by the lax standards of the era, that he was indicted for official misconduct as well as for his land frauds. The Sanchez and Frost case files, with their supporting documentation, provide excellent but hardly unique examples of a pattern of widespread fraud and corruption concerning the public domain.

The courts also became involved in questions of the public domain in numerous other ways besides enclosures and land frauds. As the Governor of Colorado recently observed, the

history of the West is written in water, and irrigation and reclamation projects were recognized as vital concerns early in the territory's history. In 1855–56, the explorations of John Pope raised the possibility of artesian wells for irrigation and led to instructions for the first surveyor general of New Mexico, Richard Pelham, to run an early survey of the dread Jornada del Muerto region.[11] Land entries would often be filed to enclose as much water as possible because control of the water gave practical control of vast amounts of waterless public domain adjacent to the claim. In 1902, Congress passed the Newlands Act to fund large-scale reclamation projects all over the Southwest. Paradoxically, the building of such projects often involved the destruction of the scarce naturally fertile areas, as dams were built and reservoirs inundated river valley land. Because these areas were usually the earliest settlement sites, the courts often were called upon to enforce government condemnation proceedings against owners reluctant to part with their homes.

One way these actions could develop is illustrated by the 1909 Seventh Judicial District case of *The United States* vs. *Victorio Land and Cattle Company and Gregario Gonzales*.[12] The Victorio Company occupied a large tract of land on the Rio Grande that had been selected by reclamation surveyors for a dam and reservoir. Gonzales had a prior dispute with the company over ownership of a small portion of the land and was thus involved in the larger case. The government not only wanted land for what became the Elephant Butte Dam and Engle Reservoir but also claimed a right-of-way for a railroad spur to the project—which was especially irritating to the company. In addition to records typically found in large civil case files, papers relating to this case contain a wealth of information about the operations of a cattle company. The limits of the land condemned by the government are precisely given, as is some legislative history of the reclamation process. The projected acreage to be irrigated in New Mexico, Texas, and Mexico by this part of the Rio Grande project is listed. Tax returns for the 13th school district, 13th precinct, show a complete breakdown of the ranch assets, including a $1,500 valuation on barbed fencing, a 14-foot tall windmill with a 225-foot well, 8 horses, 4 mules, a thousand head of cattle, and hundreds of thousands of acres belonging to the Armendaris grant and the Coon, Vaughn, and Lohman ranches.

The Victorio Company fought the condemnation and the railroad right-of-way without success. The negative court judgment was, however, assuaged by an award of $199,097.25 damages and, perhaps of more value, the right to water stock along the edge of the new reservoir. In a separate settlement, the court also granted an award to Gonzales, but did not try to settle his claim of ownership of the disputed tract because, with the ruling for the government, the question had become irrelevant.

This case and others like it vividly point out the fact that water was all important in the Southwest. Researchers have a unique opportunity to correlate other sources with such court records because the reclamation projects are still in existence. Also, in the National Archives Denver Branch are the Rio Grande project records created by the Bureau of Reclamation, which give a wealth of information about the acquisition of the land and the construction and operation of the project.[13]

Another aspect of the court's involvement with reclamation projects is typified by *The United States* vs. *Samuel V. Rhodes*, June 1910.[14] This and other similar cases dealt with the problem of ejecting homesteaders who had moved onto land once opened for settlement but later withdrawn for reclamation projects. In the Rhodes case, land had been selected for the Leasburg Diversion Dam and Canal of the Rio Grande project and closed to homesteaders in 1903. In April 1910, the defendant allegedly took unlawful possession of a tract of withdrawn land and filed a homestead entry, serial number 04427, in the land office at Las Cruces. The files contain the usual documents of a civil proceeding plus correspondence and records relating to the 1903 withdrawal.

There are a great many cases in the court files relating to violations of the public domain. In fact, their aggregate total constitutes an enormous block of records in the criminal files of all the judicial districts. For example, Criminal Docket No. 1, 1882 to 1896, for the First Judicial District, indexes over 800 cases, of which 344 are violations of the public domain. Perjury in the homestead process predominated, although enclosures were also common.

Territorial court records are an underused, invaluable source of information about categories of people, communities, and regions in 19th-century America. Bankruptcy records reveal how businesses operated, who their customers were, what their commercial practices and procedures were, and why these companies so often failed. The records tell us about the objects that people valued and the objects they chose to leave behind. Naturalization case files reveal the national origin of immigrant populations in regional America and useful information about educational levels, family structure, and occupations. These records provide particular insight into personal ethnic identity—insight that is not available in the census schedules. Finally, case files involving the public domain provide evidence of specific crimes and illegalities and of the tense relations between entrepreneurs, farmers, cattlemen, and the government. Territorial court records demythologize much of our view of the American West and help us to separate reality from nostalgia. It was through the courts that many ordinary Americans told their stories of success and failure, pledged their allegiance to the United States, and contested the ownership of the land.

These court records are available to genealogists, family and local historians, and other users who want to "people" the pages of history. They are located in the 11 National Archives field branches across the nation. They are readily accessible to all citizens. Using these records will add life and feeling to any recounting of the stories of American communities.

NOTES

1. Howard Lamar, *The Far Southwest: A Territorial History* (1966), p. 20.

2. The company's order of medicines, mostly codeine-based and in small vials, totaled $78.24. Proof of Debt, Bankruptcy Case No. 81, Bankruptcy and Civil Case Files, Bankruptcy Case Files, 1910–11, Sixth Judicial District, U.S. District Court New Mexico, Records of District Courts of the United States, Record Group 21, National Archives—Denver Branch (hereafter cited as USDC NM, RG 21, NA Denver Branch).

3. Bankruptcy Case No. 30, Bankruptcy Case Files, 1908–10, Second Judicial District, USDC NM, RG 21, NA Denver Branch.

4. Bankruptcy Case No. 2, Mixed Bankruptcy, Civil, and Miscellaneous Case Files, 1899–1905, First Judicial District, USDC NM, RG 21, NA Denver Branch.

5. Declaration of Intention Record Books, 1882–1917, 4 vols., First Judicial District, USDC NM, RG 21, NA Denver Branch.

6. Naturalization Record Books, vols. 3 and 4, contain the long form, USDC NM, RG 21, NA Denver Branch.

7. Victor Westphall, *The Public Domain* (1965), pp. 76–84; Roy M. Robbins, *Our Landed Heritage: The Public Domain, 1776–1936* (1962), pp. 217–235.

8. Westphall, *The Public Domain*, pp. 100–114; Westphall, "Fraud and Implications of Fraud in the Land Grants of New Mexico," *New Mexico Historical Review* 49 (1974): 189–218; Robbins, *Our Landed Heritage*, pp. 236–254. See also Everett Dick, *The Lure of the Land* (1970), pp. 199–241.

9. Ibid., esp. Westphall, "Fraud."

10. Civil and Criminal Case Files, First Judicial District, USDC NM, RG 21, NA Denver Branch.

11. Westphall, *The Public Domain*, pp. 17–18. The Jornada del Muerto is a dry desert region between Socorro and Las Cruces where the Rio Grande makes a sharp westward curve. The name, Journey of the Dead, colorfully indicates the forbidding terrain that Pelham was directed to survey for homesteads.

12. Civil and Criminal Case Files, 1909–11, Seventh Judicial District, USDC NM, RG 21, NA Denver Branch.

13. Bureau of Reclamation, General Correspondence Files (Engineering), Rio Grande Project, Records of the Bureau of Reclamation, Record Group 115.

14. Civil Case No. 71; Civil Case Files, 1900–11, Third Judicial District, USDC NM, RG 21, NA Denver Branch.

Interstate Commerce Commission Case Files: A Source for Local History

When Alexis de Tocqueville visited the United States in 1831–32, the steam railroad was in its infancy. Persons and goods moved from place to place much as they had in the days of the first settlements—by foot, animal power, or water. Even by 1840, when de Tocqueville published the last two volumes of the first great commentary on the United States, *Democracy in America*, his only mention of this new form of transportation was, "The longest railroads which have been constructed up to the present time are in America."

Less than half a century later, however, when the next great commentator, James Bryce, published *The American Commonwealth*, long-distance travel and hauling were horse-drawn only from place of origin to a railhead. From the railhead, goods and people moved over 135,000 miles of track, which connected almost all sections of the country.

Bryce had traveled across the United States by rail in 1870, 1881, and 1883, so his chapter on railroads was based in part on first-hand experience. He recognized how much the railroads controlled the economic, political, and social life of the nation, a degree of control difficult to envision today. Describing the impact of the railroads, he wrote:

> Railroads and those who own and control them occupy a place in the political and social life of the country which requires some passing words,

for it is a place far more significant than similar enterprises have obtained in the Old World . . . . A city or a district of country might depend entirely upon them for progress. If they ran a line into it, emigrants followed, the value of fixed property rose, trade became brisk; if they passed it by, and bestowed transportation facilities on some other district, it saw itself outstripped and began to languish.[1]

By the time Bryce wrote *The American Commonwealth*, the U.S. Congress had enacted the February 4, 1887, Act to Regulate Commerce, which established the Interstate Commerce Commission (ICC). Bryce noted that the power and influence of the railroads was to some extent checked by the recent establishment of this new federal agency:

> As the Federal courts decided a few years ago that no State could legislate against a railway lying partly outside its own limits, because this would trench on Federal competence, the need for Federal legislation, long pressed upon Congress, became urgent; and after much debate an Act was passed in 1887 establishing an Interstate Commerce Commission, with power to regulate railroad transportation and charges in many material respects.[2]

Bryce realized how important the new commission would be to the individuals and communities fighting the railroads.

The ICC was the first major federal regulatory agency. When Bryce wrote *The American Commonwealth*, the commission's authority extended only to interstate railroads. Its duties were to see to it that: rail rates were reasonable and just; rates were not discriminatory; there were no rebates, drawbacks, or pooling operations; and railroads did not charge more for a short haul than for a long haul over the same line. In years to come, its authority was extended to cover motor carriers; intercoastal and inland water carriers; and express, sleeping car, and pipeline companies.

Following the practice of courts of record, the ICC could summon witnesses, hold hearings, record testimony, and receive and file exhibits. It docketed its cases much as courts did, and it thereby created thousands of case files.[3] A by-product of these case files is the information they contain that is of value for the study of local history. When communities, businesses, or individuals aired their grievances, they often put into the record considerable information about themselves and the interests they represented.

The contents of the formal case files, like those of courts of record, include testimony heard by the commission, depositions, affidavits (all usually recorded by shorthand reporters and transcribed), and exhibits submitted by one side or the other to illustrate its points or to bolster its arguments. The testimony is the speaker's own words either as recorded by the commission's shorthand reporter or in the form of depositions. In either case, what was said or written was under oath, and those testifying were subject to legal rules of evidence and to cross-examination by the opposing lawyers. These are the documents that hold the most interest for local history researchers. Also in the case files are briefs filed by the plaintiffs and defendants, exceptions, summonses issued to witnesses, correspondence with attorneys, notices, copies of the published decisions of the commissioners (but nothing of their deliberations), and other documents relating to the cases.

USING ICC FORMAL CASE FILES

Held by the National Archives and Records Administration are 16,000 formal case files of the Interstate Commerce Commission for the years 1887 to 1924. In volume, these case files amount to approximately 3,800 cubic feet of materials. Thus it is important for researchers to approach the case files with two important points in mind. First, these case files were not created for the use of historians, but rather to document a quasi-judicial function, the hearing of and deciding on complaints under the Act to Regulate Commerce. Whatever got into the case files that is of interest to the historian was incidental to the purposes for which the files were created. Second, there is no single index of localities. With some effort on the part of the researcher, however, there are sources that can produce leads to specific cases that provide information on the history of a particular locality.

The most valuable source is the Interstate Commerce Commission's published *Reports*, which can be found in many larger libraries, particularly law libraries. (During the early years the titles varied, beginning as *Reports and Decisions*. These *Reports* should not be confused with the published ICC annual reports submitted to the Congress.) With no body of statute law designed specifically for its guidance, the ICC and those who practiced before it depended on these published decisions to establish and record precedent. The ICC's second annual report described their format and content:

> [The Interstate Commerce Act] requires the Commission to set forth its findings in every case. It has been the procedure of the Commission, in executing the mandate of the statute, in every report to give a statement of the substantial arguments of the pleadings in order to show the nature of the issues, with the substance of the evidence, so far as material, followed by the findings of fact of the Commission, and lastly its conclusions or opinions.

It is the "substance of the evidence, so far as material" that usually furnishes clues to the case files that may be of interest to local history researchers.

There is little evidence that these published *Reports* have been used by historians or by persons other than lawyers and judges. Even if the case files did not exist, these *Reports* alone would constitute a useful, if abbreviated, source for local history. For example, the published *Reports* devotes to a case discussed later (Case No. 29, the refusal of the Northern Pacific to sell to W. V. Smith a "land explorers and settlers" ticket) the equivalent of about 20 printed pages.

For the first years of the ICC, two private companies, L. K. Strouse of New York City and Lawyers' Cooperative Publishing Company of Rochester, NY, each published its own version of the *Reports*. The ICC considered the Strouse volumes the official version. After five volumes each, the latter firm bought out the former. Thereafter, Lawyers' was considered the official version until November 1906, when, beginning with volume 12, the Government Printing Office took over publication of the *Reports*.

Also beginning with volume 12, the index to each volume lists place names under "localities"; so from November 1906 on finding a locality is a matter of looking under this heading in each volume. For the years 1908–13, this process can be shortened by using a volume by Herbert Lust and Ralph Merriam, *Digest of Decisions Under the Interstate Commerce Commission Act from 1908* (1913), which indexes by locality all ICC cases between those years. The ICC's annual reports to the Congress give brief summaries of the formal cases. These annual reports are found in many libraries that do not have the more voluminous *Reports*.

Researchers planning to come to the National Archives to use the ICC docketed case files for local history research would be well advised to identify from the *Reports* or the annual reports as many apparently pertinent cases as possible. This can be done in Washington, but usually it can be done more cheaply at a library closer to home.

One question remains unanswered. What kind of information will researchers find in the ICC records? Perhaps the best way to answer this question is to examine a sampling of cases from different regions of the country. Each case provides unexpected and often unique information that will be of interest and value to state and local historians.

DAKOTA FARMERS AND IMMIGRANTS

In April 1887, a petition arrived at the ICC and was docketed as ICC Docket No. 1, *Holbrook, Wm. M. et al* vs. *St. Paul, Minneapolis and Manitoba R.R. Co.* The ICC's published *Reports and Decisions* devoted two pages to the case. It reported that the complaint accused the railroad of refusing to furnish cars and of making itself a preferred shipper; but there was no further identification of the complainants, in what state or section of the country they lived, or why they needed the cars. The *Reports and Decisions* did note that the defendants had supplied affidavits but that these affidavits were not legal evidence. For almost a century these affidavits have rested in Docket No. 1 (despite the railroad's petition to strike them from the files), and they furnish the information missing from the printed decision. What this file—and many other ICC case files—tells about a place and its people might be difficult to reconstruct from other sources.

The locale was the town of St. Thomas, in Pembina County in the northeast corner of Dakota Territory, bordering Minnesota and Manitoba. St. Thomas had then, as now, about 500 inhabitants.

This first docketed case begins with a handwritten petition (all the documents filed by the Dakotans are handwritten; those of the railroad and of the commission are mostly typewritten) signed by Holbrook and seven others and notarized on April 12, 1887. Describing themselves as wheat producers, they complained that during the past year the railroad had denied them the cars they needed to get their wheat to market. The reason, they said, was that the railroad was using the cars to haul material and men to a new extension it was building westward into Montana. This petition was followed on April 18 by another and longer petition, signed by seven residents and sworn to before the same notary. It stated in part that:

> It is necessary to call your attention to the fact that a ring or conspiracy is in existence, with its headquarters at Minneapolis and St. Paul, which has for its object the handling, shipment, storage, and price of wheat. . . . By your aid the pioneer in this country will soon take a different position from that to which the railroads would consign him, that of a laborer working upon starvation wages solely as their vassal, and to swell the dividends upon their watered stock.

On July 2, less than 2 weeks before their scheduled hearing, the original complainants sent another petition, explaining that they could not afford the trip to Washington and expressing the hope that in the future the commission could take evidence in their locality. They then went on to detail, in 13 legal-length pages, the present and past complaints that they would have presented if they could have appeared before the commission. They closed:

> Trusting that our ignorance of legal forms and methods of procedure, together with our inability to be present at Washington with witnesses will not utterly prejudice our case, nor that the Government will stand quietly by and see an industrious community skinned and guffed, and its good gifts brought to naught, or diverted to other hands, than those in which they were first placed, we subscribe ourselves
> . . . .

Five days later, on July 7, one of the signers wrote to the commission that the petitioners had received a number of communications relating to methods of procedure, but that the commission had to understand that these methods were not always possible. "You should understand more thoroughly the position of this community—we are in a remote section of the country" and at the mercy of railroad developer James J. Hill and miller Charles A. Pillsbury. It was to one of Pillsbury's grain elevators that the complainant, 3 years before, had been ordered to deliver his wheat. "And it was intimated to him that if he did not wish to ship through this elevator he could stop raising wheat—At that time cars were seized by the farmers and loaded with wheat by force . . . ."

Two days later, the complainant, still having things on his mind, addressed seven more pages to the ICC, ending:

> If individuals are to be set above us—I refer now to the heads of corporations—who are to set a price upon our products . . . under a free government those individuals should be such as we ourselves may select. . . . Where colossal fortunes, counting up into twenties and thirties of millions, have been accumulated by individuals who came to this country penniless fifteen years ago, and a whole community is held just above the verge of want, working year to year apparently simply to still further dilate the bulging pockets of these millionaires; the explanation of our position by the assertion there is an over production of the crop by which we subsist, and these men grow rich, is untenable—

The final entry on the summary document in Docket No. 1 said:

> There being no evidence of any violation of the act to regulate commerce since the date when it took effect, and the answer avowing a purpose to comply with the law: *Held,* That nothing was presented calling for an order by the Commission, and the complaint was dismissed.

The American Emigrant Company published and distributed this Swedish
language almanac as an advertisement of its services.

In a different kind of case, on September 5, 1887, the American Emigrant Company, which had been representing Scandinavian immigrants since the Civil War, swore out a complaint against the seven railroads that carried immigrants from New York to Chicago. This was docketed as case No. 77. After hearing some days of testimony, the commissioners decided to initiate their own investigation; and so on January 17, 1888, the ICC docketed as case No. 114, "In the Matter of the Inland Transportation of Immigrants from the Port of New York." In the files of these two cases are considerable testimony and some exhibits, such as a Swedish-language almanac published by the American Emigrant Company and four Finnish-language newspapers published in Ohio and Minnesota in which the company advertised. These newspapers would have been familiar to Pembina County settlers, many of whom were Scandinavian immigrants whom the American Emigrant Company had conducted westward.[5] Included in the testimony is that of one of the commissioners of emigration of the state of New York, who, conducting his own investigation, rode an immigrant train to a station within 20 miles of St. Thomas and described the detraining there.

Even before the American Emigrant Company complained, the ICC had docketed a case (No. 29) that had to do with immigrants to Dakota Territory. On June 1, 1887, W. V. Smith, a resident of St. Paul, MN, swore out a complaint against the Northern Pacific Railroad, charging that the company was selling tickets at reduced prices to "land explorers and settlers." If the purchaser, often an immigrant, later bought some of the millions of land-grant acres owned by the Northern Pacific, part of the price of the ticket was applied against the land purchase.

Smith, who did not claim to be a land explorer or settler, had applied to buy such a ticket from St. Paul to Jamestown in what is now North Dakota and had been refused. He complained to the ICC and won his case. The ICC ordered the Northern Pacific to "cease and desist from selling either of said special classes

of tickets at lower rates than those established by it for the sale of tickets to the public generally."

In this case filed are exhibits of particular interest for North Dakota local historians. There are samples of regular first-class, second-class, and excursion tickets; explorers' and settlers' tickets, with attached certificates appli-

The Northern Pacific Railroad supplied prospective settlers of its western lands with maps and high expectations.

cable to the purchase of 160 acres or more of the railroad's land; and maps issued by the Northern Pacific, measuring 2 feet by 4 feet, showing for each quarter-section of railroad land which parcels were sold, unsold, settled, unoccupied, or reserved for schools. On the reverse was considerable information, with illustrations, about the area. Also included were other maps of the area and promotional publications illustrated with engravings of homes, farms, churches, stores, and the like.

Other complaints filed with the ICC about minor matters furnish glimpses, sometimes intriguing, of a time, place, or person. For example, in August 1887, the editor of the Mandan, Dakota Territory, *Daily Pioneer* and *Weekly Pioneer*, charged that the Northern Pacific Railroad had furnished free passes to Judge William H. Francis of the Sixth Judicial District of Dakota. "Such practices as this by this corporation has a most corrupting and demoralizing tendency." This was docketed as case No. 72. In November he withdrew his complaint: "Francis about being removed & it was this I was after."[6]

Another Dakota citizen also took on the Northern Pacific, complaining he had been charged $1.72 for freight on a 25-pound keg of black powder from Minneapolis to Buffalo, Dakota Territory. In January 1888, he spelled out his complaint on an early typewriter which, having only well-spaced capital letters, lent emphasis to his anger. The railroad admitted the charge should have been 73 cents. On May 3, 1888, the secretary of the ICC, in longhand, asked whether the complaint had been satisfied. Four days later (attesting to the mail service of the time) the complainant, abandoning his typewriter, returned the secretary's letter with the following note handwritten across the bottom:

Yes-sir; I thought I had notified you, if not it was neglect on my part.

Buffalo, D. T. 5/7-88   Yours Truly
                                        W. J. Hawk

MID-ATLANTIC MILK AND PRODUCE

In Dakota Territory, neither the exact hour the grain trains started nor the exact time they arrived at their destinations needed to be precise, but in other parts of the country, departure and arrival times were critical. In 1887, both a group of New York State milk producers and the Delaware Grange of the Patrons of Husbandry, representing fruit growers and businessmen of the Delaware-Maryland-Virginia eastern shore, filed complaints against the railroads that hauled their produce to market. Their common complaint was the uncertainty of the railroads in getting their perishable products to Jersey City in time for early morning delivery in New York City.

The testimony and exhibits in the New York State milk producers case (ICC case No. 4) provide a picture of what happened to milk from the time it left the Hudson River Valley farms until its delivery on the doorsteps of Manhattan. It is a picture of boxcars specially designed for high speeds, with crews of 26 men for the round trip; of train runs of 200 miles, with stops at scores of stations along the way; of the problems involved in keeping the milk cool in summer and preventing it from freezing in winter; and of the details of ferrying it to Manhattan. A late arrival in summer could mean worthless sour milk. There is testimony of farmers, milk train conductors, a railroad milk freight agent, and an agent at the Jersey City terminal. Among the exhibits are included: lists of milk train stops; a drawing on linen of the receiving area in Jersey City; statistics on meat, butter, cheese, berries, fruit, eggs, and passengers that sometimes traveled on the milk trains; published tariffs; issues of *The Milk Reporter*; and a set of three-by-five rate cards, one of which read:

New York, April 29th 1885
At a meeting of the "Milk Exchange, Limited," held this day it was resolved that on the first day May next and UNTIL OTHERWISE OR-

DERED, the market price of Milk produced from Meadow Hay and Sound Cereals be 2½ cents per quart, and that produced from Brewers Grains, Glucose, and the Corn Starch refuse be 2 cents per quart.

Like the milk trains, the Delaware-Maryland-Virginia peninsula fruit trains seasonally ran special cars at relatively high speeds to Jersey City and other markets, such as Philadelphia and Boston.[7] Several dozen witnesses, mostly farmers, told in their own words, which were transcribed in more than 500 typed pages, how they grew, financed, harvested, packed, and shipped their fruit—mainly berries and peaches. The buyers' demand for freshness was almost as great as that for milk. "From 8 to 11 we pick for Philadelphia; from 1 to 4 we pick for Boston; and then from 4 until the morning we pick for Jersey City." A New York fruit dealer testified that peaches should be there at 2 a.m., berries no later than 3 a.m. He described a busy Manhattan nighttime scene with buyers from as far away as Rhode Island. Several Jersey City truckmen submitted logs they had kept of late-arriving trains.

One of the witnesses was the Governor of Delaware, who had grown peaches since before the Civil War. He was also president of a small railroad, from which he had never received any dividends; but "we live in hopes."

Q. What became of the original stock in that company?
A. It went where the woodbine twineth.

He was one of the few whose testimony favored the carriers.

I think the railroads are the making of the country. You can always find people everywhere who complain who are properly termed old foggies.

Q. Then we should class you as a special friend of the railroad.
A. Where justice and merit belongs always class me there.

The case dragged on until 1891, when the ICC issued an order in favor of the growers. The railroads refused to obey the order, and the ICC began proceedings against them in the U.S. Circuit Court for the Eastern District of Virginia. These proceedings produced 125 pages of depositions from 15 persons, almost all farmers, from the southernmost, or Virginia, part of the tri-state peninsula, where the fruit trains began their runs north. Most of their testimony, however, concerned potatoes, which traveled to the same markets and by the same routes as the fruit. Again, every aspect of the crop and its relation to the community was discussed. Sometimes what the witnesses had to say touched on prerail history. An elderly farmer, when asked why, if he disliked the rail service, he didn't transport his crops as he did before the coming of the railroad, answered:

One reason is the fact that I have before alluded to that the seaside creeks and inlets to a considerable extent have filled up and are not now as accessible as they were heretofore. That is one reason why vessels do not come here and why more of our produce is not transported by vessels.

Even before hearing the eastern shore farmers tell of their problems, the ICC commissioners had learned about peach-growing. In July 1888, 2 months before the Delaware Grange case, the commissioners had listened to testimony about peaches grown in the Flemington area of New Jersey and, like the eastern shore peaches, delivered by rail to Jersey City.[8] One of the witnesses was the president of the New Jersey Fruit Exchange. He was asked, "Will you tell us something about the working of this Exchange, and also something about the peach-growing business of your county?" He obliged at some length. The commissioners also heard the secretary of the Exchange and four peach growers. Six railroad employees concerned with the handling of the peach crop testified. Among them were the freight agent in Jersey City, who described what happened when the peaches arrived there, and the master car builder of one of the railroads, who described the special cars used for hauling peaches. Their testimony, excluding the exhibits submitted, totaled 164 pages.

SOUTHEASTERN COMMERCE

The cases examined thus far have been illustrative of late 19th-century American agriculture, agricultural communities, and farmers. There were also other kinds of cases. In May 1887, in Virginia, the Danville Chamber of Commerce filed a complaint against the Richmond and Danville Railroad Company, charging the railroad with discriminating against the people of Danville and vicinity.[9] The town's commerce, it was charged, was at the mercy of the railroad.

There was testimony that Danville's considerable trade in provisions and hay with the region north of the Ohio River, and in meat, meal, flour, lard, and grain southward as far as Augusta, GA, had been cut off because of discriminatory freight rates. Several manufacturers of tobacco products told of losing customers in cities as distant as San Francisco and Los Angeles. Entered as an exhibit was a letter received from a customer in Muldon, MS, complaining that the freight rate on his smoking tobacco "is a *little* too much." That summer in Danville may have been a hot one. A wholesale produce dealer, protesting the rates, entered invoices for 60 tons of melons received during a single week in July.

Just a week after Danville filed its complaint against the Richmond and Danville Railroad, another group of citizens in a small community, Hot Springs,[10] in the North Carolina mountains also turned to the newly created ICC for relief from oppression by the same railroad.[11]

The mayor of the community testified that after a number of prosperous years, business in the past year had fallen off 25 percent, and, after a building boom, not a single new house

had been built. A merchant said currency in circulation had decreased by 25 percent; another merchant testified that his business had fallen off nearly 50 percent, "That previous to July 1886, this was a lively little town in a financial standpoint; but at present, and for the past 8 or ten months, there has been a great financial depression."

The cause of the town's economic depression was established by the next witness.

> I was put off the train because I refused to pay fifty five cents fare from Hot Springs to Unaka—I tendered the Conductor thirty cents but he refused to let me go for that and stoped [sic] the train and I got off.

He was able to establish with some exactness the distance the Richmond and Danville Railroad was willing to transport him for 55 cents.

> I have measured the distance by counting the rails on one side of the track from Hot Springs to Unaka. There was 1203 rails 24 ft long each.

On June 10, 1887, the Richmond and Danville Railroad revoked its 1886 rate of 55 cents, reducing it to 30 cents. This presumably put an end to the Hot Springs depression of 1886–87.

OKLAHOMA COMMUNITIES

Between September 1906 and April 1907, the ICC docketed three complaints from the Muskogee area of Indian Territory. One of these cases was the *Muskogee Commercial Club and Muskogee Traffic Bureau* vs. *Missouri, Kansas & Texas Railway Company*, docketed on December 21, 1906 as case No. 954.

Muskogee was in the cotton-growing section of Indian Territory. The railroad had designated points to which cotton was hauled and compressed so that it could be shipped more efficiently. Muskogee was such a point, as was McAlester, 60 miles distant. Muskogee charged that the railroad was discriminating in favor of McAlester. Fourteen witnesses, including cotton buyers, the president of the Muskogee cotton compress company, bankers, merchants, and representatives of the railroad, gave 450 typed pages of testimony. They discussed almost every aspect of cotton culture in the territory, from planting to the final shipment in compressed bales. There are descriptions of hauling cotton by wagon, the road conditions, and the compressing equipment, as well as a map of the 13 surrounding counties, showing for each the amount of cotton ginned in 1906. There is enough detailed discussion of the rivalry with McAlester to constitute a source of local history for that town also. Furthermore, the first-hand information about cotton culture makes the case applicable to the cotton-growing areas beyond Muskogee and Indian Territory.

The last two cases are remarkably similar. Within the span of 6 months, two communities in northeastern Indian Territory filed with the ICC almost identical complaints. In November 1906, three residents of an ambitious settlement called Chase complained that the St. Louis and San Francisco Railroad had moved its station 3½ miles away.[12] In April 1907, four residents of Fanshawe charged that the Chicago, Rock Island & Pacific Railway Company had closed the station there and had opened another station 4½ miles away.[13] In the first case, the residents of Chase claimed that the town (which did not appear in the 1900 federal census) had four families, a post office, two churches, and two schoolhouses, and that is served three or four hundred people within a 4-mile radius. The Fanshawe complainants contended that the town had a population of 150, three stores, a saw mill, a grist mill, a cotton gin, two blacksmith shops, and "a good school building." The Chase witnesses included what must have been a large percentage of that town's founders, promoters, and residents. Among the Chase exhibits is a six-page brochure extolling the virtues of the townsite, with "the Frisco system of railways making six passenger stops at CHASE each day." The bro-

chure included a plat showing the town, its streets, and scores of lots available at $37.50 each. It predicted that "Muskogee in its rapid strides toward a great metropolis city will soon claim Chase as one of its suburbs"—which it eventually did.

The Fanshawe complaint noted that "the defendant now passes its trains through the town of Fanshawe at full speed, against the will of the citizens thereof." The hearings began with a witness who testified:

> Well about fifteen years ago I came to a place called 'Fanshaw', and they had established a depot there and . . . I placed my money there and established by business there and the depot remained there until about 1901, when the Company took it away and placed it about four and one half miles from us to a place called 'Turkey Creek,' a coal mine. . . .

His testimony and that of others occupy 71 pages and provide a picture of the community; its lumbering, farming, and mining activities; and the effect of the loss of its station.

CONCLUSION

The variety of local history materials in the ICC formal case files is extraordinary. In fact, each case file is something of a portrait of local citizens, companies, and communities in conflict with each other and with the railroads. The files reveal the turmoil of everyday life in local communities.

The files contain all manner of documents. In addition to the correspondence, testimony, and affidavits that researchers expect to find in each case file, there also are important exhibits that document community history. Printed items such as the almanacs and newspapers in case No. 114, *In the Matter of the Inland Transportation of Immigrants from the Port of New York,* are extremely rare and often unique. Other case files contain handbills, advertisements, maps, and other items that document the hopes and aspirations of the thousands of local communities that emerged in the last quarter of the 19th century and the first quarter of the 20th century.

Using the ICC case files is not easy. Unfortunately, there is no index linking cases and

communities. But researchers who use the *Reports and Decisions* as a finding aid and come to the National Archives in Washington to use the files will find the effort worthwhile.

NOTES

1. James Bryce, *The American Commonwealth*, 3 vols. (1888), vol. 3, p. 400.

2. Ibid., p. 406; Bryce was a correspondent of Thomas M. Cooley, chairman of the Interstate Commerce Commission, who, during the first year of the ICC, was reading the drafts of chapters of *The American Commonwealth*. In the Thomas C. Cooley Papers in the Michigan Historical Collections, Bentley Historical Library, University of Michigan, Ann Arbor, are more than 50 pages of notes and criticisms that Cooley sent Bryce. However, there are none on Bryce's chapter on transportation. In his preface to *The American Commonwealth*, dated October 22, 1888, Bryce's first acknowledgement is to Cooley, "Now Chairman of the Inter-State Commerce Commission in Washington."

3. The dominant figure during the first 4 years of the ICC was its chairman, Thomas M. Cooley. Cooley had been for 7 years a reporter of the Michigan Supreme Court, then a justice of that court and a member of the University of Michigan Law School faculty. Cooley's papers in the Bentley Historical Library indicate that Cooley determined the ICC's method of keeping its case records and of reporting its hearings, decisions, and orders.

4. Records of the Interstate Commerce Commission, Record Group 134, National Archives, hereinafter referred to as RG 134, NA.

5. Inquiries indicate that the newspapers, published in Ashtabula, OH, and New York Mills, MN, are the only known extant copies of these particular issues.

6. Case No. 72, *Robert M. Tuttle* vs. *Northern Pacific Railroad Company*, RG 134, NA.

7. Case No. 102, *Delaware State Grange of the Patrons of Husbandry* vs. *New York, Philadelphia, & Norfolk Railroad*, RG 134, NA.

8. Case No. 138, *President and Directors of the New Jersey Fruit Exchange* vs. *Central Railroad of New Jersey*, RG 134, NA.

9. Case No. 24, *B. S. Crews et al* vs. *Richmond & Danville Railroad et al*, RG 134, NA.

10. The letterhead of the first letter from the petitioners' attorney was printed Warm Springs; thereafter his letterhead read Hot Springs. When a witness testified, "I reside at Hot Springs," the attorney asked, "How long have you resided at Hot or Warm Springs?" After that the petitioner settled on Hot Springs.

11. Case No. 26, *W. L. Ray et al* vs. *Richmond & Danville Railroad et al*, RG 134, NA.

12. Case No. 898, *Cornelius J. Jones et al* vs. *St. Louis & San Francisco Railroad*, RG 134, NA.

13. Case No. 1029, *John H. Lewis* vs. *Chicago, Rock Island, and Pacific Railroad*, RG 134, NA.

Index